Scenic Routes & Byways

YELLOWSTONE & GRAND TETON NATIONAL PARKS

SUSAN SPRINGER BUTLER

travel

Guilford, Connecticut

To buy books in quantity for corporate use or incentives, call **(800) 962-0973** or e-mail **premiums@GlobePequot.com**.

All photos by Susan Springer Butler.

Editor: Kevin Sirois
Project Editor: Heather Santiago
Layout: Joanna Beyer
Maps: Trailhead Graphics; updated by Alena Pearce © Morris Book Publishing, LLC

ISBN 978-0-7627-7957-4

CONTENTS

The Scenic Routes & Byways

For my late father, Kenneth Springer, who early on gave me an appreciation and love for the beauty of creation, and to my mother, Jean Springer, who ever encouraged my sense of adventure.

ABOUT THE AUTHOR

Susan Springer Butler has been an English teacher and education consultant. She began visiting Yellowstone and Grand Teton National Parks in the 1950s and has loved every minute of every visit, every camping disaster, every animal encounter, every moment of awe-inspiring wonder and breathtaking beauty. Her husband and four adult children and grandchildren indulge her passion for travel and adventure. They frequently are enticed to travel along.

ACKNOWLEDGMENTS

This had to be one of the best writing assignments in the country. What a privilege and experience to travel these two magnificent parks. I'm very grateful to the friends, strangers, and family who made it as easy, fun, and special as it was. I owe major thanks to those who kindly offered help, encouragement, and information while I drove around the West, writing and taking photos.

First, I really appreciate the good people at the Teton Village Hostel, my home away from home. Once I had a room on the second floor, rather than on the fourth, and didn't have to lug all my gear back and forth to the top, the accommodations were great. Big thank-yous to Greg Esdale, Justus Stearns, Evan Padua, and Kari Grigsby for their help, suggestions, and friendliness.

Jackie Skaggs, public affairs officer for Grand Teton National Park, was so generous with her time, tips, and information. How special to know that such good, caring people are promoting and protecting the parks.

Debbie and Gary Durham, and Beverly and Kenneth Baumer deserve thanks for so patiently showing me where a giant moose was lying, camouflaged, and I just couldn't see him. "You got him right in the sight. Take the picture!" Debbie instructed, so I did. When I reviewed the shot and zoomed in three times, there he was, making a face at me. Thanks, guys, for the good time.

Wonderful people staff the small museums scattered around the parks. Trent Redfield at the Grizzly and Wolf Discovery Center in West Yellowstone; Judy and Jack Swann, volunteers at the Rockefeller Preserve; Angie Thomas at the Museum of the Mountain Man in Pinedale; Jerelyn Hill at the Teton Valley Museum; and Sarah Auer, Ray Hammond, and Janette Jankauskas at Old Trail Town were so helpful, interesting, and giving of their time and expertise.

At Big Sky in Montana, Meg O'Leary and Chad Jones were great ambassadors for their resort and very generous with their resources. We had a great time.

Al Nash at the National Park Service in Yellowstone never seemed too busy to find answers to even my most arcane questions. Rangers and park employees are always great resources, but I especially want to thank rangers Andrew Langford in the Tetons, and Mike Hassall and Meagan Gamble in Yellowstone, who pointed me in the right direction for extra information. A special thanks, actually, to all rangers in the parks for the wonderful stewards they are of their mission to preserve and protect. Rangers, themselves, are national treasures.

To Kevin Sirois and Heather Santiago, my patient editors at Globe Pequot Press, your help has been so appreciated. Thank you, too, for the opportunity to

do this a third time. It never gets old. I'm especially grateful to Bill Schneider, author and friend, who gave me the first opportunity to play, officially, in the parks.

I have to mention personal friends who offered their support—among them, Joan Yenerich Evans for her helpful input and good companionship, and her husband, Dave. Those who talked me through computer traumas—Shawn Whyte, John Bacino, Chick Canterbury, Julia Demaree, Renee Boundy—have my gratitude, as does the faithful Rusty Rogers, who, by his own admission, knows not much about computers but solved my problem. Then there were the duck identifiers: Jason LaForest, Kice Brown, Andy Nemethy, and Steve Patterson all weighed in, but Kathy Wasik had the winning answer of Barrow's Goldeneye. What fun to have the Internet providing so many friends with so many answers.

Last, but first in my heart, thank you again, family, for companionship and support. Amy and Katie, Peter and Ken, thank you for your good humor and helpful perspectives, and for telling me when my photos were out of focus. To my husband, Chuck, who encouraged, motivated, and harassed me while I finished this project, I love you. Everyone, it's been fun. We'll have to do it again.

Alluring thermal pools dot the landscape of West Thumb Geyser Basin.

Interstate Highway/ Featured Interstate Highway		—— 90 —— / —— 90 ——
US Highway/ Featured US Highway		—— 89 —— / —— 89 ——
State Highway/ Featured State Highway		—— 22 —— / —— 22 ——
Local Road/ Featured Local Road		———————— / ————————
Unpaved Road/ Featured Unpaved Road		------------ / ------------
Trail		-------------------------

Airport	✈	Picnic Area	⛱
Boat Ramp	⟓	Point of Interest	▫
Bridge	⏝	Rapids	∥
Building or Structure	■	Ranger Station	🛈
Campground	⛺	Route Number	⑩
City	◉	Ski Area	⛷
Geyser/Spring	⚲	Small State Park, Wilderness or Natural Area	▲
Historic Site	♨	Town	○
Lodge	⊨	Waterfall	≋
Marina	⚓	Wildlife Management Area	⌁
Museum	🏛	Visitor, Interpretive Center	⑦
Pass	) (		

Mountain, Peak, or Butte	▲ *Deseret Peak* *11,031 ft.*
River, Creek, or Drainage	～～～
Body of Water	⬭
State Line	-----·-----·-----·-----
National Park	▭
National Forest	▭
Wilderness Area	▭

INTRODUCTION

Henry G. Merry was a trendsetter. On June 2, 1902, he stomped on his throttle, raced his automobile to a terrifying 25 miles an hour, and stormed Mammoth Hot Springs, headquarters of Yellowstone National Park, startling the horses of the two cavalrymen who had been posted to prevent just such an incident. But the floodgate, as they say, had been opened. Although Mr. Merry was arrested, fined, and escorted out of the park, there could be no turning back. The campaign was on to allow automobiles into Yellowstone. By the 1940s, driving had become the preferred way to view firsthand the area's wonders and wilderness preserves.

Yellowstone was declared a national park in March 1872. In its first 62 years the park welcomed three million visitors; by 1994, more than three million people were passing through the gates each year. Grand Teton National Park, established in 1929, annually welcomes close to that number. These two national parks attract attention because of their aura of wildness, their extraordinary geologic features, and their breathtaking beauty. Welcome to an unforgettable adventure—exploring Yellowstone and the Tetons.

The two areas, bound by proximity, are in almost every other way distinct. Yellowstone offers the opportunity to witness ongoing geologic creation, the earth itself as a work in progress, through nature's seemingly willful uncontrollable force. The Tetons, though still rising, provide a more serene view of nature. Where one park is rugged dynamics, the other is solace and a sense of solitude, even among crowds of people. Driving either or both of the parks is an exquisite touring experience.

Using This Guide

This guidebook contains 28 routes included in two sections: Yellowstone National Park and Grand Teton National Park. The Yellowstone section describes 20 routes—6 to the park, 5 pleasant drives from the park entrances to the Grand Loop (the park's main road, designed in the shape of a figure eight), and the Grand Loop itself, described in 9 segments. The section on Grand Teton National Park describes a total of 8 drives, including 5 routes to the Jackson, WY, area, and 3 park drives—Wilson to the Moose entrance; Moose to the Rockefeller Parkway leading to Yellowstone, known as the Inner Loop Road; and Jackson Lake Junction to Jackson along US 89/191/26, known as the Outer

Loop Road. With the exception of the routes to the parks, all drives are less than 40 miles long.

With the increasing number of visitors to these parks every year comes an immense amount of very slow traffic, especially in the peak months of July and August. Park highlights are plentiful; take time to savor them by giving in to the pleasure of leisurely travel. If your allotted vacation time is short, concentrate on one park and save the other for a return visit. If you have a week or more, you should be able to enjoy both.

Time estimates for each trip may seem exaggerated, but you must allow for the nature of the parks, where the flow of traffic is slow. Inevitably, the line of cars you follow will be led by a trailer going 25 miles an hour, and wildlife on the roads—called moose jams or buffalo jams or bear jams by park personnel—encourage gawkers and photographers. With stops for animals, picnics, or exploration, a trip of 15 miles can easily take an hour. Take your time and enjoy it all!

In fact, the most heartfelt advice I can give you is don't hurry. Whatever time you have allowed for your drive, slow down and give the tour your full attention. Many people enter Yellowstone, race to Old Faithful to watch it erupt, then exit, a little disappointed. Although wonderful, Old Faithful is but one of the marvels of this magnificent place. The more you understand about the formation of this region, the time frame of its creation, and the fundamental forces at work, the more you will value your experience.

Activities abound in both parks. Hiking, biking, camping, boating, horseback riding, fishing, and even swimming in Yellowstone and rock climbing in the Tetons are all available in summer. Seasonal sports such as whitewater rafting and downhill and cross-country skiing are possible in the Tetons, and cross-country skiing, snowshoeing, and snowmobiling are popular wintertime sports in Yellowstone. Whether you want a pleasant scenic drive or to engage in outdoor exploration, endless opportunities present themselves.

The following general information should give you an idea of what to expect while touring this special part of the West. In addition, appendices at the end of this book contain sources for more information, as well as suggestions for further reading. Once you arrive at either park, personnel will cheerfully answer questions and offer help with problems that may arise.

Park Entrances

There are five entrances to Yellowstone and three to Grand Teton National Park. At all park entrances you will find stations staffed by park rangers who collect

Kettles and erratics indicate the course of geologic time.

fees, answer questions, and provide free maps and newspapers with information about park activities and regulations, as well as practical suggestions. In the newspaper you'll find safety tips, emergency numbers, regulations, road construction schedules, important advice regarding hiking, biking, and camping in the park, as well as schedules for ranger talks and walks. If you are traveling with children between the ages of 5 and 12, be sure to ask about the junior ranger programs, the young scientist program in Yellowstone, and the young naturalist program in the Tetons. These active learning experiences allow your children to earn junior ranger patches. In addition, many great programs exist on the Internet, such as www.greateryellowstonescience.org or www.windowsintowonderland.org. Visit them in preparation for your visit, and get a head start. At the entrance gates to both parks, note the bulletin boards that post emergency messages, weather, closed roads, the status of campgrounds, and other useful information important for travelers.

Opening & Closing Dates

Neither park is completely open year-round, but both have accessible portions summer, fall, winter, and spring. Weather concerns—particularly snow levels— dictate the definite opening and closing dates, but as a rule, most parts of the parks are open from May through October, and some areas are open for snow-mobiling and cross-country skiing from December through March. Other factors, such as severe weather or animal migration, may necessitate the temporary closing of certain roads. Park personnel at the entrances and information stations advise you of road or trail closings. Approximate road opening and closing dates appear at the beginning of each description. Check with the National Park Service for specific dates each year. Phone numbers are provided in Appendix A.

Entrance Fees

You pay an entrance fee at the gated entrances to all national parks. Currently, a 7-day pass good for both Yellowstone and Grand Teton national parks costs $25 for private automobiles or $20 for snowmobiles or motorcycles. A permit that gives you entrance to both parks for a year is $50. For $80 you can purchase an America the Beautiful Pass, good for all national parks and federal fee areas for a year from date of purchase—a terrific option to consider if there are national parks or monuments in your part of the country, or if you just want to make a valuable contribution. When you compare the cost of a few movie tickets or a day at an amusement park, you may agree that these passes are a bargain. Also note that a Golden Age Passport, now called a Senior Pass, a lifetime permit for people age 62 and older, costs only $10, and an Access Pass is free to any blind or permanently disabled citizen of the United States. All fees, of course, are subject to change.

Thanks to recent legislation, national parks now keep 80 percent of the fees they collect to use for their own maintenance and park improvements. The remaining 20 percent goes into a fund to be shared collectively with other national parks. This revenue redistribution is a boon to the entire National Park System.

Campgrounds

The National Park Service and park concessionaires operate campgrounds within the parks' borders—the park service on a first-come, first-served basis, while Xanterra and the Grand Teton Lodge Company, which operate the lodging concessions in the parks, require reservations. In Yellowstone, National Park Service campgrounds are located at Mammoth, Indian Creek, Pebble Creek, Slough Creek, Tower Fall, Lewis Lake, and Norris. The earlier you arrive at these campgrounds, the better your chance of securing a site. Xanterra Parks and Resorts, the concessionaire for Yellowstone, runs five campgrounds: Bridge Bay, Canyon, Grant Village, Madison, and Fishing Bridge RV. Make your reservations as early as possible, since many people plan their travel a year in advance.

In Grand Teton National Park you may set up your tent or camper at Flagg Ranch, Colter Bay, Jenny Lake, or Gros Ventre campgrounds, all operated by Grand Teton Lodge Company, or Lizard Creek or Signal Mountain, both operated by Signal Mountain Forever Resorts. Campgrounds are on a first-come, first-served basis, but Jenny Lake and Signal Mountain generally fill up the earliest. The phone numbers for Xanterra Parks and Resorts, the Grand Teton Lodge Company, and Signal Mountain can be found in Appendix A. For those traveling in RVs, the Fishing Bridge RV Park in Yellowstone and the Colter Bay RV Park in the Tetons accept reservations. In addition, plentiful Forest Service and commercial campsites lie in the vicinities of Yellowstone and the Tetons. This book notes the location of many of these modestly priced campgrounds. If you enjoy the outdoors and have the equipment, camping is a great way to experience the parks at their best.

Lodging

In Yellowstone *rustic* is the word. The wonderful old hotels at Mammoth and Yellowstone Lake and the magnificent log Old Faithful Inn place patrons in a bygone time. Popular both for their architecture and location, the hotels' rooms, many without private showers or bathroom facilities, were constructed before the conveniences of televisions and computers. However, you probably won't be sorry for choosing ambience over luxury. All three hotels boast excellent full-service restaurants. Lodges and cabins located at Tower-Roosevelt, Canyon, Lake, Old Faithful, Grant Village, and Mammoth offer less expensive alternatives to the hotels, and again, there is always camping. If you require facilities with a television, a pool, and an Internet connection, plan to stay outside the park in one of its gateway communities. Even then, in Gardiner or Cooke City, finding accommodations with these amenities can be iffy.

Lodging in Grand Teton National Park is a little more upscale. The high room rate at terrific Jenny Lake Lodge includes biking, horseback riding, breakfast, and a 5-course gourmet dinner, but requires a minimum 3-night stay. Jenny Lake is a popular vacation spot, so reservations must be made well in advance of your visit. Jackson Lake Lodge is a full-service hotel in a beautiful setting. Stop here to view the mountains and lake from the picture windows. Like Jenny Lake Lodge, Jackson Lake Lodge has its own stables and a Western atmosphere that is quintessential Wyoming. Signal Mountain Lodge, the only in-park accommodations not operated by Grand Teton Lodge Company, rents cabins and bungalows. The lodge itself houses a restaurant and gift shop.

You'll find the least expensive lodging in the park at Colter Bay, where uninsulated but heated historic log cabins sleep from two to ten people and are priced accordingly. These cabins are on a par with the cabins found in Yellowstone. Colter Bay also boasts tent cabins, structures on a cement slab with two wooden and two canvas sides and a wood-burning stove. Other accommodations are found in the nearby town of Jackson, or surrounding vacation spots and dude ranches. Write or phone the local chamber of commerce (see Appendix A) for complete listings of available accommodations.

Weather

Yellowstone's personnel and park visitors celebrate Christmas on August 25 each year, commemorating an early snowfall on that date in the 1940s (or so the story goes). Although rain and snowfall have been recorded in all 12 months in the parks, so have warmth and sunshine. Recorded weather patterns lead to some safe generalities.

In spring, serious snowplowing gets under way in March, and the cold and snow gradually taper off through April and May. Daytime temperatures climb from about 40 degrees Fahrenheit to the 60s and even 70s by the end of May. At night, temperatures remain cold and can even drop below freezing.

Summer warms to the 70s and occasionally the 80s, but at high mountain altitudes that average 8,000 feet, the sun's rays may not seem as warm as they do at lower elevations. Nighttime temperatures remain cool, in the 30s or 40s. June generally brings more rain than July or August, although patterns vary from year to year, and thunderstorms disrupt the sky throughout the summer.

Early autumn may still be sunny, but temperatures drop rapidly during late September and October, when nighttime temperatures can fall to the teens and below. Snow may arrive at any time, making it difficult to predict road closures, which are generally slated for late October. Occasionally, early snowfall can dictate an unexpected closing of the Beartooth Highway leading to the Northeast Entrance to Yellowstone.

In winter, temperatures remain below freezing during the day and often drop below zero at night. Although annual snowfall varies, an average of 150 inches blankets much of Yellowstone in winter, and the higher elevations in the park can receive twice that amount; average snowfall at Moose in the Tetons is a staggering 191 inches. Whatever time of year you plan to visit, a variety of layered clothing should keep you comfortable and eager to explore.

Wildlife

One of the main thrills of the parks is the opportunity to observe animals at close range, literally in the wild. Consequently, one of the first things you will read in both your Yellowstone and Teton newspapers (distributed at the entrances) will be a warning. Wildlife, no matter what kind or size, can be dangerous. As tempted as you might be to think some animals harmless, please watch them from a distance.

Animals are easily observed in both parks. Bison walk alongside your car on many roads; elk graze only a few feet from the highway; moose, though shy, tolerate people who click away with their cameras; and bears have been known to wander through campgrounds, parking lots, and other populated areas. However, despite appearances, park animals are not tame. Each year people are seriously injured because they venture too near to animals that appear non-threatening. In spring, be particularly wary of protective and unpredictable females with their young. Park rangers recommend maintaining a distance of 100 yards from most animals. As a rule of thumb, if an animal is disturbed by your presence, you are too close.

If you are lucky enough to spot a bear, 100 yards between you and the animal is an absolute minimum. Report all observations to a park ranger. Bear sightings have become more common, which signifies a healthy population. Most sightings still occur in the backcountry, however, so don't be disappointed if your drive through the park doesn't produce an encounter.

A great difference exists between grizzly and black bears. A grizzly's coloring varies from a light, rather silver color to dark brown, while black bears,

Sniffing the air at the Grizzly and Wolf Discovery Center in West Yellowstone.

regardless of their name, range in color from cinnamon to black. A grizzly has a "dish face," rather scooped from the forehead to the tip of the nose, and a discernible hump above the shoulders. My favorite way to tell the difference from a distance is from photographs. Black bears have prominent ears, while grizzlies' ears tend to resemble those of a teddy bear, smaller and rounder. However, don't be fooled.

Black bears often retreat in the face of a loud noise or confrontation; grizzlies are likely to charge when they sense a threat. Larger, generally fearless, and more ferocious, grizzlies can bite through a half inch of steel and are able to run as fast as 35 miles an hour when threatened or provoked, far faster than a human can sprint. Running in front of a grizzly has been likened to throwing a ball of yarn in front of a kitten. The chase is irresistible. For further reading, pick up a copy of *Bear Aware* (Third Edition) by Bill Schneider (Globe Pequot, 2004), a small, informative volume about encountering bears in the wild.

Wolves have been successfully reintroduced to Yellowstone and are often spotted in the northeastern Lamar Valley and in the Hayden Valley, although they now range throughout the entire park. Currently, 11 wolf packs comprising about 97 wolves roam freely throughout the mountains and meadows. People frequently mistake coyotes for these wide-ranging animals, but the differences between the two are marked. Wolves can be twice as tall as coyotes, are often three times as heavy, and their coats vary widely in color. Their legs are proportionately much longer than those of the coyote; their ears and muzzles are rounded rather than pointed. A full-grown coyote is about the size of a medium-size dog (a border collie, for example), while a full-grown wolf might be more than 3 feet tall and have a massive build, almost the size of a Rottweiler or a very large husky. Should you spot a wolf, please report the sighting to a park ranger.

Other mammals you might see in the parks are bison, moose, bighorn sheep, pronghorn antelope, bobcats, beaver, river otters, red fox, mountain lions, lynx, martens, badgers, marmots, squirrels, and chipmunks. Rare or unusual birds that take refuge in the parks include bald eagles, sandhill cranes, ospreys, pelicans, and trumpeter swans. If you are armed with a good pair of binoculars, a strong telephoto lens, or a keen pair of eyes, you may enjoy some spectacular wildlife viewing.

Fishing

Fishing is allowed in both parks, and fish are plentiful, but different sets of regulations govern the sport in Yellowstone and Grand Teton. In Yellowstone most but not all fishing is of the catch-and-release variety, with a barbless hook. A notable exception is at Yellowstone Lake, where predatory lake trout have invaded waters formerly dominated by indigenous cutthroat trout. You can help the park rid its waters of these predators. As of this writing, you are allowed to catch and keep an unlimited number of lake trout, but upon catching, the fish must be killed. Anyone 16 or older who is planning to fish must purchase a permit at any ranger station, visitor center, Yellowstone General Store, or from a flyshop in a surrounding community. Children under the age of 15 may fish without a permit if they are supervised by an adult with a permit, or they may obtain a free permit, which should be signed by an adult who will ensure that the child complies with all regulations. No special state license is required. When you obtain a permit, you will receive a complete list of fishing regulations, or you can go online to www.nps.gov/yell/planyourvisit/fishing.htm to read them in advance of your visit. As they say in Yellowstone, animals have first priority for fishing. Regulations have been designed to protect the native species, while still allowing you to enjoy the sport.

In the Tetons whitefish and cutthroat, lake, and brown trout fill the rivers and lakes. Purchase a Wyoming fishing license in the park at Signal Mountain Lodge, Colter Bay Marina or Village Store, Dornan's, or Flagg Ranch Lodge. Fishing regulations dictated by the National Park Service and the state of Wyoming can be picked up at visitor centers in Moose, Jenny Lake, or Colter Bay.

Geothermal Areas

The unrivaled geologic features of Yellowstone Park and the numerous hydro-thermal areas have captured the human imagination since native tribes first frequented the region thousands of years ago. Hot springs, steam vents (fumaroles), mud pots, and geysers—all remnants of giant volcanic explosions over the last 600,000 years—have mystified and enticed both serious scientists and curious onlookers. Activity in the thermal zones offers a vivid reminder that earth's creation is unfinished. Nothing here is static; hot springs become geysers, geysers become dormant, and steam vents appear where once was dry land. The earth's conformation changes season by season, year by year. Any visit to Yellowstone encourages close scrutiny of these phenomena.

Again, a warning: These irreplaceable geothermal splendors of Yellowstone National Park are fragile treasures that can easily be damaged or destroyed by careless actions. Yellowstone is one of the few places in the world with substantial visible geothermal activity. Please respect and protect it. When exploring a geyser basin or other geothermal area, stay on the boardwalks and designated trails. Not only will this help to preserve the area, it may preserve you! The earth's crust, normally 25 to 30 miles deep, is approximately 3 to 5 miles thick in this region, and hot water bubbles through the very thin crust in unexpected places. You could be badly burned if you step off the paths.

Interpretive Trails & Ranger Talks

In specific locations in the parks, self-guided interpretive trails lead you through some of the most splendid scenery. Although these are generally short walks, some require climbing and are mildly strenuous. However, those who make the effort will be rewarded with sights and information that will make their trip unforgettable. For 50 cents, at trailheads or in visitor centers, you can purchase a guide containing an informative map of the area and explanations of the surroundings. If you value recycling and don't wish to keep the guide, simply return it and pay no fee when you've walked the area.

Self-guided trails in Yellowstone include Mammoth Terraces, Upper Geyser Basin, Grand Canyon of the Yellowstone, Norris Geyser Basin, Fountain Paint Pots, Mud Volcano, Fort Yellowstone, and West Thumb Geyser Basin. Grand Teton National Park offers interpretive trails at Cascade Canyon, Colter Bay, the Cunningham Cabin, the Flagg Ranch area, Menor's Ferry, and Taggart Lake. Lunch Tree Hill and String Lake have trails with interpretive signs rather than guides. If you have the time to get out of your car, these are terrific opportunities to stretch your legs and enjoy the scenery.

Rangers present talks in various locations around the parks—at visitor centers or remarkable places such as the rim of the Grand Canyon of the Yellowstone, in a field of bison in the Hayden Valley, or on a hike to Inspiration Point at Jenny Lake. Rangers also lead discussions and answer questions on special topics at evening campfires, covering in some depth topics such as wildlife, fires, geology, history, and park activities. Take advantage of as many of these talks as you can. You won't be disappointed.

Hiking in the Parks

You will find many wonderful hiking trails in the parks—more than 1,000 miles of trails in Yellowstone, and more than 200 miles of trails in the Tetons—from level boardwalks to lengthy climbs in the backcountry to wheelchair-accessible paths. Remember, however, that at this altitude even healthy people may become winded. This guide offers brief descriptions of walks that are close to the road and are generally short and easy; many are barrier free. More serious hikers should refer to *Best Easy Day Hikes Yellowstone* or *Hiking Yellowstone National Park* by Bill Schneider (Globe Pequot, 2003). Visitor centers sell topographic maps and trail guides. For your own safety, if you are going into the backcountry, even for a day hike, leave word with a ranger regarding where you are going and for how long, and use the trailhead registers where provided.

Boating

In Yellowstone a boat permit is needed and may be obtained from the South Entrance, Lewis Lake Campground, Grant Village Backcountry Office, or the Bridge Bay Ranger Station. For canoes and kayaks, permits are available at the Canyon, Mammoth, and Old Faithful backcountry offices, the Bechler Ranger Station, West Yellowstone Visitor Information Center, and the Northeast Entrance. All park streams are off limits to boats, except on the Lewis River between Shoshone and Lewis Lakes. Power boating is limited to the main parts of Yellowstone and Lewis Lakes. The lakes remain extremely cold year-round, averaging 41 degrees Fahrenheit in summer, so hypothermia is a real concern if you fall in. At that temperature you would survive less than 30 minutes. A life jacket and protective clothing must be worn when you are on the water. Winds generate large waves upon the lakes with no warning, so boaters may want to stay close to shore. You should avoid crossing large lakes, particularly in the middle of the day, when thunderstorms are common. In spite of all these conditions and warnings, many visitors each summer bring or rent boats and enjoy the serene beauty of these unspoiled lakes.

In the Tetons, for a fee, motored boats are allowed on Jenny and Jackson Lakes; canoes and kayaks may launched on Jackson, Jenny, Phelps, Emma Matilda, Two Ocean, Taggart, Bradley, Bearpaw, Leigh, and String Lakes. Permits are obtained at the Craig Thomas Discovery Center at Moose, Jenny Lake, or Colter Bay Visitor Centers. A permit from one park is accepted by the other, but all vessels must be registered at each park.

Both Yellowstone and the Grand Teton National Park are making a concerted effort to stop aquatic hitchhikers, or unwanted nuisance species of plants and animals—in particular, species of mussels—that are not native to the parks. In Wyoming new regulations require that boats are cleared through watercraft check stations, where a sticker is issued when your boat passes inspection. If you're planning to boat, please help with this effort.

Information Sources

Several organizations devote themselves to providing information about these two special parks. The Yellowstone Association, a nonprofit organization, operates bookstores throughout the park, offering myriad books, maps, posters, and other educational materials. Proceeds from purchases and memberships help finance The Yellowstone Institute, park exhibits, ranger programs, web videos and podcasts, and the park's research library. The tax-deductible price of an annual membership in the association allows you discounts on purchases at all Yellowstone Association stores throughout the park, as well as at Xanterra gift shops and Yellowstone General Stores, and on Yellowstone Institute field courses. Ask for more information at visitor centers, or visit the association's website at www.yellowstoneassociation.org.

The Yellowstone Park Foundation, another nonprofit partner of the park, helps fund programs and projects to enhance your experience here. More than half of the funding for the Old Faithful Visitor Education Center was given by the YPF (www.ypf.org). Donations to these two organizations help to ensure maintenance of the integrity of the park.

The Grand Teton Association (formerly the Grand Teton Natural History Association) operates bookstores in visitor centers throughout the Teton area as a part of its educational mission. A modest tax-deductible fee for an annual membership offers the benefit of discounts on merchandise at affiliated Grand Teton stores. Profits from sales and memberships support educational, scientific, and interpretive programs in the park (www.grandtetonpark.org). The Grand Teton National Park Foundation provides financial support for programs and projects focused on education, wildlife research and protection, and preservation of the precious resources of the park (www.gtnpf.org). The Teton Science Schools (www.tetonscience.org) and The Murie Center (www.muriecenter.org), two other

Layers of mountains dominate the view from Dead Indian Overlook on the Chief Joseph Scenic Byway.

organizations integral to the education mission of the park, offer courses, lectures, and experiences supported by professionals in the areas of science, conservation, and preservation. Each of these entities is nonprofit and worthy of your support.

Driving Tips

Before you begin your trip, make certain that your car is in good working order and equipped with a spare tire. While driving through the parks, pay particular attention to other vehicles, bicyclists, and pedestrians. Roads are narrow and winding, often climbing or descending steep grades. With all the scenic distractions, it helps that traffic moves at a slow pace. Animals may wander near or even on the roads. They, too, present hazards. Every year hundreds of large animals are hit and killed in the parks. Running into an 800-pound elk or 1,200-pound moose usually causes as much damage to the car as to the animal. In emergencies call 911 any time of day or seek the help of a park ranger. Automobile service stations, equipped to deal with small emergencies such as repairing flat tires or replacing belts, are spaced throughout the parks at major junctions. Should you need more extensive repairs to your car, a full-service auto repair station is located at Fishing

Bridge in Yellowstone National Park, and near Grand Teton National Park in Jackson, Wyoming.

Following the Maps

Maps are included for each drive described in this book. With the help of state maps, found at chambers of commerce or available through state tourism offices, these drives should be easy to follow. Only one—the Kelly–Gros Ventre Slide drive described in Scenic Route 28 in the Tetons—is off the beaten path. Maps provided by the National Park Service or the Forest Service may include details such as side roads for the adventurous and additional trails for hiking.

Highway designations are indicated in this book by initials followed by numbers. "US" indicates a federal highway; "ID" means Idaho routes; "MT" means Montana; "UT" means Utah; and "WY" represents Wyoming roads. "FR" designates a forest road, and "I" means interstate. Whenever possible, I measured drives by using the green mileage markers on the sides of the highways; when they were not present in the parks or in Wyoming, I used odometer readings. These readings vary from car to car and trip to trip, so they are fairly, but not totally, accurate. Use them as approximations of distance rather than exact measures. Watch for landmarks mentioned throughout the narrative as well as mileage indicators, and the going should be good.

After all is driven, written, explored, and studied, the glaring fact remains that you can never really know these parks entirely. This is good news for the adventurous. There will always be more to explore. Naturalists, scientists, historians, and archaeologists continue to piece together and interpret what is here. This book attempts to clarify what you see as you drive to and through the parks and how it came to be, as well as give you some tips to simplify your journey. I hope you have as much fun as I have in my wonderful summers of driving.

YELLOWSTONE
NATIONAL PARK

Overview

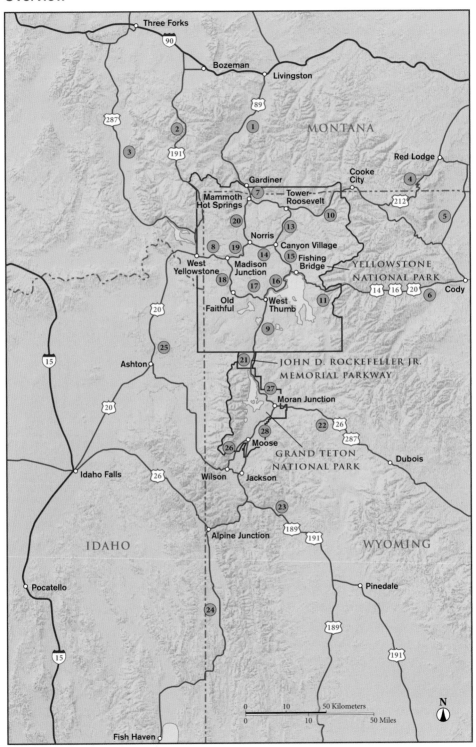

YELLOWSTONE NATIONAL PARK

Two million years of volcanic eruptions have built up the plateau that is Yellowstone. The second greatest of these, a cataclysmic explosion just 600,000 years ago, was so intense that it blew fragments of rock from this area as far away as the Gulf of Mexico, Saskatchewan, Iowa, and California. The blast left a crater 47 miles across, which, over time, collapsed back in on itself, filled with molten lava and ash, and cooled to form a fragile crust about 3 to 5 miles thick. Thus was formed the Yellowstone caldera, the world's largest crater valley, which was shaped over hundreds of thousands of years.

The caldera was sculpted and refined by an ice age 13,000 years ago, a wisp in geologic time. Melting glaciers carved broad, sloping valleys and left scattered debris as they retreated. The dramatic Yellowstone landscape is a result of these two phenomena, fire and ice, and their creative effect is alive today.

This extraordinary land of geothermal features, canyons, waterfalls, lakes, and high valleys has beckoned people for the past 8,500 years. Yellowstone's rugged beauty, its unpredictability, and its everlasting mysteries are gifts to those who visit.

Normally the earth's crust is about 10 times thicker than it is here. The magma, or molten rock, at work just a few miles beneath the earth's surface heats the park's geothermal features, creating the natural fountains and startling configurations of geyserite or sinter. The area is still so seismically active that more than a thousand tremors are recorded annually. The creative forces that forged the earth manifest themselves throughout the park today, allowing visitors a chance to experience ongoing geologic processes.

Imagine the reaction of the first visitors to encounter this awesome landscape. Although evidence of human life here spans centuries, this was an area more traveled through than inhabited. Perhaps it was the eerie thermal features or the hostile extremes of weather and geology that kept people from settling here. Only one native tribe, a small band of Shoshone Indians called the Sheepeaters, is known to have lived in Yellowstone year-round before the land was set aside as a national park. One group of Sheepeaters was so cloistered in a small northern valley, near what is now known as Swan Flats, that when they accompanied members of an early exploration party to the Firehole Basin about 30 miles away, they were surprised and awed by the mysterious thermal features.

Yellowstone was largely untouched, even by Native American tribes, until the Lewis and Clark expedition brought explorers west at the beginning of the 19th century and paved the way for others to follow. Even then, only a few adventurers made their way through the mountains of southern Montana and northwestern Wyoming. Jim Bridger described a place "where hell bubbled up." Known for his tall tales, he wove stories of the thermal features and surrounding area that made skeptics of all who heard him. Osborne Russell, a trapper who kept a detailed and eloquent diary, left one of the first written accounts of the territory. The vivid, daunting descriptions of those who initially explored and mapped the region on foot were full of wonder. Over the next half century, tales about the strange land made their way back east to the centers of commerce and power, where interest in the reports was tempered with disbelief.

The first expedition that came specifically to explore the Yellowstone area, the Folsom-Cook-Peterson expedition of 1869, was made up of three men from Montana who wanted to check out rumors of a land that " . . . was smoking with the basins and boiling from springs, and the burning with the gases from small craters." Their verification of the rumors led to a slightly larger band of investigators the following year. The Washburn-Langford-Doane expedition of 1870 came to map and explore for commercial opportunities. The 19 military and civilian men of this expedition wandered through the territory, charting features and leaving their mark on the landscape by bestowing many names still in use today. The intensity of expression by the men of both expeditions convinced the US government that a serious effort was needed to protect the land. As David Folsom of the 1869 expedition later wrote, "We knew that as soon as the wonderful character of the country was generally known outside, there would be plenty of people hurrying in to get possession, unless something was done." In 1871 the US government commissioned the Hayden Survey expedition—a group of 31 men, including artist Thomas Moran and photographer William Henry Jackson—to venture into this wilderness to map, draw, paint, and record its features. The result of this expedition convinced a reluctant Congress to pass the National Park Act, especially in light of the fact that no money would be required for such a project. On March 1, 1872, Congress designated the first "national park" with a proclamation that "set apart as a public park and pleasuring ground for the benefit and enjoyment of the people" the land now known as Yellowstone. Actually, one other selling point for preserving the land was that Congress thought the area so remote and desolate that it was useless anyway.

Because Theodore Roosevelt was such an enthusiastic naturalist and adventurer, he is the president most frequently associated with the park. His visit in 1903 to dedicate the Roosevelt Arch as the official park entrance was vividly recorded by the press and historians. However, it was actually Ulysses S. Grant who, in what could have been the greatest act of his presidency, signed the National Park Act into law about 30 years prior to Roosevelt's appearance.

Early scamps and hucksters had a lively "go" at the park, trying to figure ways to profit from it. When poaching and vandalism made evident the need for park protection, the US Army came to the rescue between 1886 and 1918. As World War I called the military elsewhere, the National Park Service was created. Today park rangers act as teachers, interpreters, resource managers, protectors, and staff. Although controversies and problems still swirl around the park and its management of resources, the concept of the national park shows the American mind at its creative best.

The designation as a national park allowed the preservation of Yellowstone's beauty and wildness. Today's visitors are able to enjoy and marvel at the process of ongoing creation. Volcanic eruptions of the magnitude of the Yellowstone eruption happen perhaps once every 100,000 years, but the aftereffects remain. As Rudyard Kipling wrote after his visit to Yellowstone, "the park is just a howling wilderness of three thousand square miles, full of all imaginable freaks of a fiery nature." This wilderness—majestic mountains, imposing canyons, pristine mountain lakes and forests, bubbling outbursts of water and steam—covers 3,472 square miles, or 2.2 million acres. Almost 10,000 thermal attractions sputter and spew in the park. In winter the cold air gives the resultant steam an ethereal quality found few other places on earth.

Either through the diminution of time or our lessened capacity for wonder, these features do not look as frightening or imposing as once they might have, but they remain amazing. Today, although we can scientifically explain the "blue flame and molten brimstone" mentioned by the early prospector, the four kinds of thermal features found in the park create an extraordinary effect.

Hot springs, mud pots, fumaroles (steam vents), and geysers, the four kinds of hydrothermal features found in the park, require the same three environmental factors to sustain their activity—a plentiful water supply, an underground source of heat, and cracks and fissures in the earth that conduct water to that source of heat.

At Yellowstone's elevation, an average of 8,000 feet, the annual snow and rainfall guarantee an abundant water supply. The magma that lies just below the earth's surface provides the superintensive heat source required. The plumbing system with its intricate cracks and tunnels, although ever shifting because of ongoing seismic events, transports water close to the magma, allowing it to become superheated. The superheated water must escape and be released back into the atmosphere.

High pressure caused by cooler water bearing down through the underground plumbing allows water close to the magma to heat to temperatures of more than 520 degrees Fahrenheit without boiling. When the superheated water does boil, it surges back through underground channels to the earth's surface with tremendous force, and vents as geysers. This process takes about 500 years: Rain that falls today will reappear in the steam vents and geysers about half a millennium from now.

Heart Spring is one of hundreds of thermal features in the Upper Geyser Basin.

Hot springs, the most common thermal feature in the park, appear where water can easily rise to the earth's surface and accumulate, allowing it to boil or evaporate at a rate fast enough to prevent an explosion. Many of the hot springs in the park are colored by various types of bacteria or algae that grow in the high temperatures of the pools. The kind of algae, bacteria, or mineral presence in the water determines the colors of the pools, ranging from yellow and orange to blue and even black.

Mud pots are created when acidic water collects, but not in enough volume to create a hot spring. They are usually found at slightly higher elevations than hot springs. As the surrounding soil is mixed with the moisture, a bubbling cauldron of mud simmers and percolates, forming weird stews of clay and sulfur. The presence of minerals in the water often colors it various hues, leading to the name "paint pots." As you watch the mud pots, picture the small bubbles as tiny volcanic eruptions breaking through the surface and filling back in with viscous material. This is a microcosm of the volcanic action that formed Yellowstone.

Fumaroles, also known as steam vents, are literally that—vents of steam. These occur in areas of high heat and low water content, enough to collect but not enough to erupt or overflow. A plentiful water supply would help cool fumaroles, but they are usually found at higher elevations or on hillsides, away from accumulated groundwater. Steam vents are the hottest of Yellowstone's geothermal features, with recorded surface temperatures reaching more than 284 degrees Fahrenheit (at the Black Growler steam vent in the Porcelain Basin at Norris). Often steam spews with such force that it hisses as it emerges from the ground.

Geysers are identified by their eruptions, caused by accumulating pressure from cooler water pressing down on the superheated water in pools beneath the earth. Geysers generally have small, constricted vents. Great force is required to push the water up to the earth's surface, back through the small openings, to produce the eruptions. Most geysers erupt unpredictably, rather than in a regular pattern. A majority of the world's geysers are found in Yellowstone, including Steamboat, the world's tallest (very unpredictable), and Old Faithful, the world's most famous (quite predictable). Most are found in the Upper Geyser Basin near Old Faithful.

Geothermal features in the park are as colorful and varied as their names— Morning Glory Pool, Castle Geyser, Dragon's Mouth Spring, Emerald Pool, and Splendid Geyser. There are enough surprises here to endlessly entertain visitors. The unexpected wonders in the park are the ones you will remember, so take time to explore if you can.

Keep in mind that the geothermal features, rare natural occurrences, are delicate. Please help care for them by observing the park's regulations. Also remember that in thermal areas boiling water might be right under the ground's surface. A false step could cause serious injury. Not only could you be hurt, but mineral deposits hundreds of thousands of years old could be damaged if you step off the trails. Be careful not to deface or harm these fragile ancient creations. Walk only on the boardwalks or pathways.

A second major attraction of the park is its varied wildlife. With 58 species of mammals, from moose and bears to squirrels, marmots, and weasels, as well as 318 species of fish, birds, reptiles, and amphibians, Yellowstone has the largest concentration of free-roaming wildlife in the lower 48 states. The park is home to the last wild bison herd in the country. Coyotes set off a chorus on midsummer evenings. Wolves prowl and hunt in the early morning meadows. Bison and elk dramatically rut in fall. The spectacle of life surrounds you here.

The Yellowstone fires of 1988 were a part of this spectacle—disasters in a sense, but natural and necessary to the proliferation of life. Without fire, Yellowstone would be a lodgepole pine "desert," and the varied habitat required by diverse species would be absent. Although lightning fires occur in the park every year, 1988 was a particularly notable year. More than 1.2 million acres were burned or scorched. Evidence of this appears on almost every drivable route in the Park. Wildfires of this magnitude, necessary to the health of the forest, occur every 200 to 400 years. Upon entering Yellowstone, visitors today notice almost immediately the charred remains of thick forests, particularly at park entrances.

However, many interpretive signs along the way tell of the positive effects of the fires, in places that at first look so devastated. Of all the animals in the park, only one species, the red squirrel, was severely affected by the fires, because so much of its habitat was destroyed. Otherwise, new food supplies and environments were opened to the many animal species of Yellowstone. Although park officials now monitor conditions that might produce massive fires, lightning-caused fires are considered natural events, and they often are allowed to burn themselves out as they did for thousands of years prior to the arrival of man.

The 1988 fires in Yellowstone burned hottest near the West and Northeast Entrances to the park. The North Fork fire, which burned more than 385,000 acres near the West Entrance, began outside the perimeter of the park on July 22, when a spark flew from a logger's chainsaw. Although firefighters fought the blaze, it burned out of control for more than 6 weeks. The North Fork, one of eight major fires that summer, spread north to Mammoth Hot Springs and southeast to Old Faithful, coming within 0.5 mile of West Yellowstone and 0.25 mile of the famous Old Faithful Inn. Ultimately, 1,608 firefighters, 39 fire engines, 22 bulldozers, and 6 helicopters battled this fire, but it was not until an early light snowfall blanketed the park on September 11 that nature did what man could not. Firefighters continued their work until October, but the gentle force of nature had controlled the raging fires.

Many factors contributed to the severity of the fires. The winter of 1987–88 had been very mild and dry; a spring with heavy rainfalls in April and May had fostered the growth of unusually lush grass. But by the end of May, the deluge had dwindled. A lightning strike caused the first fire of the summer on May 21. It burned itself out by the afternoon of the same day. But on May 23 and again on May 25, two more lightning strikes ignited fires that began to spread. June came and went with only 20 percent of the normal precipitation. In July no rain fell; the thick grasses dried and, along with dead trees in the park, provided plenty of kindling for the flames. During July, August, and September, a cold front swept the Yellowstone Plateau, bringing winds of 60 to 80 miles an hour that fanned the fires and carried the embers great distances very quickly. On August 20, a day now called Black Saturday, the fire spread over 160,000 acres. While firefighters, often more than 9,000 at a time, bravely dug trenches and attempted to douse the blazes, the fires traveled swiftly, jumping canyons, geyser basins, and other natural barriers. All together, nearly 800,000 acres in the park burned. Aerial photographs show how the fires hopscotched through the park, leaving large areas untouched. Canopy fires, reaching the treetops and killing entire trees, accounted for 41 percent of the burn; 35 percent were ground and canopy fires combined; and the remaining 24 percent were areas that were lightly forested or meadows. More than 25,000 firefighters from the US and Canada took part in the battle for the park.

Enjoy the peaceful, narrow span of Yellowstone Lake's West Thumb, from Grant Village.

It was the most expensive firefighting endeavor in history, involving the most firefighters using the most sophisticated techniques and the most modern equipment. Yet, as Park Ranger Holly Bartlett put it, "A humbling quarter-inch of snow accomplished what people could not."

Now, more than two decades later, allow your focus to shift from the burned trees to the new green growth and the wildflowers flourishing at the base of blackened trunks, covering the hillsides, and lining the riverbeds. It will take about 60 to 80 years for the new trees to reach their mature height, with the strongest, the ones reaching fastest for the sunlight, winning the race to the sky. Lodgepoles, which make up about 80 percent of the park's forest, need sunlight to grow. As the hardiest grow tall, they block the sun from the smaller seedlings, thereby culling the new crop of trees and blocking other species from taking root. The landscape you see now will change over the next decades, as growing trees again block the contour of the landscape and the rich fields of wildflowers disappear from the thickening forests.

The land reaped great benefits from the fires. Normally it takes 60 to 80 years for dead trees to rot and return their nutrients to the soil. Fire accomplishes the same thing in one afternoon, enriching and replenishing the earth. Lodgepole pines, uniquely adapted to fire, have two types of pinecones. One type, the serotinous cone, is sealed with a resin that opens only when exposed to extremely high temperatures. The forces of wind and fire burst the cones and scatter the seeds. An estimated 50,000 to 1 million seeds nestle into each acre of ash-rich soil—instant newly sown land. Historically, fires of the magnitude of the 1988 fires occur in lodgepole forests every 200 to 250 years. The last large-scale fire in Yellowstone is believed to have burned in the early 1700s, and perhaps the next will not occur until the year 2200 or beyond.

A few last practical notes for your trip through Yellowstone . . . unless you plan to drive the entire Grand Loop: What features you see will depend on where you enter and exit the park. It's difficult to calculate trips by mileage, because so many stops and side trips cause you to retrace your route. Look for features mentioned in the route descriptions instead. In this book the Grand Loop drives begin at the northernmost point, Mammoth Hot Springs, and continue in a clockwise direction. If you are traveling in the other direction, read the description from back to front, feature to feature. Don't worry about driving the same road twice; if you are driving in different directions, you will notice different features and be doubly rewarded.

In many places the roads in Yellowstone were built with no proper base on top of old wagon routes. Road improvements, long overdue, are almost finished, but you may still encounter construction delays. Updates and schedules are listed in the park paper you receive upon entering, *Yellowstone Today*, or you can call the number given in Appendix A under Yellowstone National Park road updates. If waiting in line offends you, you might want to plan around this schedule. However, as one park visitor said to me as he stepped out of his car and wandered and waited for the line of traffic to move, "It beats being stuck in traffic in Baltimore."

Pets are not forbidden in the park, nor are they encouraged. Pets must be kept on a leash and are prohibited on trails and boardwalks. Caring for them in the park is difficult at best, so if possible, leave them at home.

The Grand Loop is organized so that facilities are clustered near the major attractions. Lodging or campsites can be found at all major junctions. The park is sometimes criticized for its rustic accommodations, but imagine this wilderness with motel-like facilities scattered throughout and you will be grateful for the efforts made to keep things simple.

Driving Yellowstone is one of the country's greatest touring adventures. Don't just see the park, but feel it in the spray of the geysers, the heat of the thermal features, the cold of the evenings, and the dark solitude of starry or stormy nights; hear it in the hissing of steam vents or the waterfall of geysers, and the bubbling of mud pots; smell it in the sulfur of the geothermal features or in the clear fresh mountain air. Let the park engage all your senses. If not for some visionary explorers more than a century ago, this is an experience that would be lost to us. We must try to have the same vision and wisdom today to enjoy and protect what each year becomes more precious.

1

Livingston, MT, to the North Entrance

General description: A pleasant 51-mile drive north to south that follows the course of the Yellowstone River through Paradise Valley. Flanked on the east by the high Absaroka (Ab-SOR-kee) Mountains and on the west by the Gallatin Range, the drive continues through a short canyon to Gardiner, Montana, and the North Entrance of Yellowstone National Park.

Driving time: About 1 hour, if you make no stops.

Special attractions: Historic Livingston, fishing access to the Yellowstone River, hiking trails in the Gallatin National Forest, Yankee Jim Canyon, Mount Cowen (11,206 feet), Emigrant Peak (10,960 feet).

Location: Southwestern Montana.

Drive route names & numbers: US 89.

Travel season: Year-round. The snow might be flying by mid-autumn, but the road is well maintained, and the area is a playground for many winter sports.

Camping: Mallard's Rest (20 sites), Pine Creek (24 sites), Mill Creek (10 sites), and Canyon Campground (15 sites) are directly off the highway. Carbella Campground (off Tom Miner Road, 20 sites), Tom Miner (16 sites), and, off the beaten path, a campground at Dailey Lake (35 sites).

Services: Full services in Livingston and Gardiner; restaurants and service stations in Emigrant. Cabins, RV parks, and other lodging all along the corridor. Cell service along most of this drive.

Nearby points of interest: Chico Hot Springs, windsurfing and fishing on Dailey Lake, the ghost town of Jardine, and the remnants of a petrified forest.

For more information: Livingston and Gardiner Chambers of Commerce, USDA Forest Service, Livingston Ranger District, Chico Hot Springs (Appendix A).

The Route

Begin the drive in the small, very western town of **Livingston**—home of artists, movie stars, and a jumble of other people who love the Montana outback. For turn-of-the-century architecture, art, history, saloons, and good eating, Livingston is a treasure trove. Bordered on the north by the Crazy Mountains and on the south by the Absarokas, Livingston is a picturesque place where it is easy to trace history by walking through town.

In the early 1880s the Northern Pacific Railroad sent scouts to this area to find a place for a railroad supply store and destination. By the 1890s a raucous, thriving Livingston was home to merchants, railroad workers, and miners, with their attendant saloons and bawdy houses. Martha Jane Canary, better known as Calamity Jane, once lived in a cabin on Main Street. She frequented the **Livingston Bar and Grill,** still operating today. One of the area's more notorious

Livingstone, MT, to the North Entrance

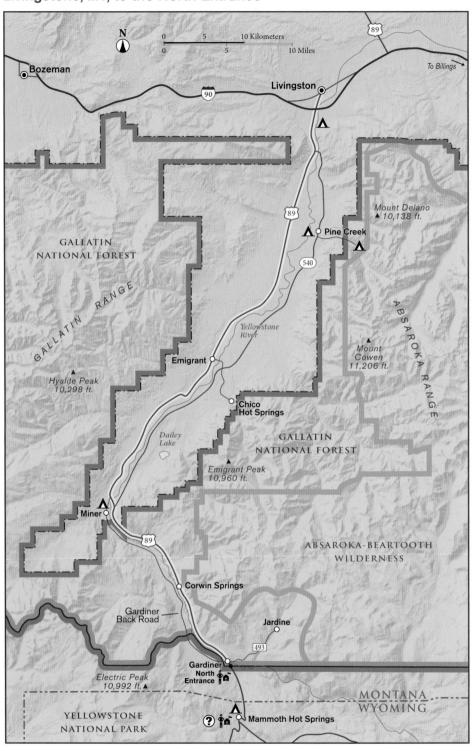

N

0   5   10 Kilometers
0   5   10 Miles

Bozeman

90   Livingston

To Billings

89

89

Mount Delano
▲ 10,138 ft.

GALLATIN
NATIONAL FOREST

Pine Creek

540

GALLATIN RANGE

ABSAROKA RANGE

Yellowstone
River

Emigrant

Mount
Cowen
11,206 ft.

Hyalite Peak
10,298 ft.

Chico
Hot Springs

Dailey
Lake

GALLATIN
NATIONAL FOREST

Emigrant Peak
10,960 ft.

Miner

89

ABSAROKA-BEARTOOTH
WILDERNESS

Corwin Springs

Gardiner
Back Road

Jardine

493

Gardiner
North
Entrance

Electric Peak
10,992 ft. ▲

MONTANA
WYOMING

Mammoth Hot Springs

YELLOWSTONE
NATIONAL PARK

madams, Kitty O'Leary, also known as Madame Bulldog, for years ran a lean and mean establishment in Livingston. Although she herself was not lean, topping the scales at more than 190 pounds, she was mean enough to physically toss Calamity Jane out of her place a time or two. Today the feel of the Old West survives. Numerous historic landmarks, such as the old **Murray Hotel** and the **railroad depot** on the edge of town (circa 1902—now housing the informative and entertaining railroad museum), stand as testimony to the town's beginnings. Another good museum stop is the **Yellowstone Gateway Museum,** about two blocks north of the Depot. Housed in a three-story school building, this museum exhibits collections of archeology, geology, pioneer life, and stories of the Wild West. Currently this attraction is open from Memorial Day through September.

After exploring the town of Livingston, its museums, galleries, and eateries, head toward Yellowstone by going south on US 89. The drive begins at the underpass exits where I-90 (west from Billings or east from Bozeman—exit 333) intersects with US 89. To reach this point travel through the outskirts of Livingston, past commercial establishments, camping and RV parks, motels, and shopping plazas.

About 3 miles south of the interstate underpass on US 89, cross Carter Bridge and the first fishing access on the drive. Fishing access signs posted along the highway indicate easy spots to park your car and get to the river for the area's favorite pastime—fly fishing on the Yellowstone. Most fishing access spots have boat-launching ramps.

Heading into Paradise

US 89 borders the Gallatin National Forest and follows the general course of the Yellowstone River as it flows north to join the Missouri River, just beyond the northeast corner of Montana, in North Dakota. The river, along with ancient glaciers, carved this valley that leads to Yellowstone National Park. Look to the left (east) to spot **Livingston Peak,** site of many winter vision quests by Crow Indian braves. The vision quest was a fasting vigil lasting several days, held in solitude in remote locations, in which a brave would seek mystical visions and guidance from the Great Spirit.

At mile marker 48 the road passes through a small rocky canyon into what Montanans call the **Paradise Valley,** aptly named for the beautiful mountains that surround it and its peaceful atmosphere. The Yellowstone River, one of the prime fly-fishing rivers in the country, never wanders far from the road. The 30-mile-long Paradise Valley holds acres of good ranchland and sagebrush-covered fields fed by the river. Mountains to the right are fronted by colorful hills of orange, red, and yellow rock dotted with pines.

Emigrant Peak keeps its head in the clouds.

Trail Creek Road, a side road to the west beyond mile marker 45, is a dirt road that covers part of the same route as the old Yellowstone Trail, the road by which early tourists came to the park. The Yellowstone Trail, originally marked by simple black arrows painted on a yellow background, pointed the way for early adventurers from as far away as Plymouth, Massachusetts, through Chicago, Minneapolis, and on to Yellowstone. Occasionally, people still find remnants of these painted markers.

About 0.5 mile beyond mile marker 44, Pine Creek Road branches left (east) to a fishing access and Forest Service campground. This turnoff for fishing is followed shortly by Mallard's Rest fishing access. Remain on US 89 and you find numerous places to get out of your car and entice the fish.

As you drive through this lightly populated valley where the river teases the road, the landscape becomes more rural. Throughout much of the year, blue mountains in the foreground are backed by snowcapped peaks that hint at a very cold paradise.

The road, a mostly straight two-lane highway, is monitored for speed by the Montana Highway Patrol. The Montana speed limit, once famous for its nonexistence, now requires drivers of passenger cars to adhere to a speed limit of 75 miles an hour on interstates day and night, 70 miles an hour on other roads during the day, and 65 miles an hour on other roads at night. A speed of about 60 miles an hour is probably best. Don't be in a hurry, and your day won't be ruined by a conscientious officer of the law. The rules are usually well posted.

As the valley widens a bit near mile marker 37, another Forest Service campground is to the left at Mill Creek Road. Look to the east for **Mount Cowen,** elevation 11,206 feet, one of the highest peaks in the Absaroka Range. A road to the east leads to Pray, Montana, now sparsely populated, but once the site of an early mining camp. More than a century ago, the area around Pray, Emigrant, Chico, and Jardine fired prospectors' hopes. The mountains gave up their gold for a few years and then the miners moved on.

At mile marker 31 you reach **Emigrant,** a sleepy place with a store, a good restaurant, a gas station, and the ever-present community saloon. In Montana many ranch towns are little more than a saloon and post office, and it's not unheard of to find the post office located in the saloon. Saloons were gathering places for ranchers and cowboys in need of socializing, and this old western tradition continues.

In 1862 prospectors discovered the first gold to be found in this valley not far from here in **Emigrant Gulch.** The natural hot springs of the area supplied bathing and laundry facilities to more than 300 early miners who built Yellowstone City 10 years before the national park was founded. By 1866 Yellowstone City was abandoned; the miners had moved on to richer lodes elsewhere. Today nothing remains of this settlement.

Chico Hot Springs

Hot springs in the area still provide recreation, most notably the **Chico Hot Springs** resort, 3 miles from Emigrant. **Chico,** a historic mining settlement nestled in the foothills of a little draw, is now famous for its rustic and not-so-rustic lodging, invigorating hot-springs swimming pool, gourmet restaurant, and rowdy bar with good stomping music on the weekends. Room rates are modest to moderate, depending on your needs; many rooms in the old lodge, built circa 1900, have no sink, bathroom, or shower, but these amenities can be found down the hall. Newer rooms offer some in-room plumbing and modern western decor. If you are in the vicinity of Chico and want to overnight, this quintessential Montana resort is definitely worth the stop. Reservations are almost always necessary, but drop-ins are worth a try.

To get to Chico Hot Springs, turn left at the only junction in Emigrant and cross the Yellowstone River. Drive about a mile to the junction with Route 540 and a stop sign. Turn left onto East River Road. After about another mile a sign points you to a right turn for Chico. Beware of the speed bumps as you near the lodge.

Chico is open year-round and provides activities that include swimming (the pool is open 6 a.m. to midnight, and guests are welcome to stay and swim after checkout), horseback riding, mountain biking, and hiking. Fishing trips, Yellowstone Park tours, wilderness pack trips, hunting, and rafting can be arranged at the reservation desk, as can dogsled treks, scenic flights, or massages. So potent is the Hot Springs pool that it begins draining every night at 11 p.m. and is refilled by about 10 a.m. the next morning. When staying here, you may find yourself dining with the rich and famous, who come both for the great food and the low-key atmosphere. Chico, a not-too-well-kept state secret, is a favorite retreat for many.

After visiting Chico, return by East River Road to the junction with Route 540. To continue to Gardiner on US 89, turn right (north) to retrace your steps to the Emigrant junction, where you should again head south. Another option is to remain on East River Road for a 10-mile side trip to **Dailey Lake,** a spring-fed lake with excellent fishing, located next to an elk refuge. On a well-marked side road, the pavement ends shortly beyond this junction, and the road becomes more primitive the farther south you go. If you choose not to go to Dailey Lake but prefer a back road to the interstate, you could continue south on East River Road, which is paved, to about 20 miles north of Gardiner, where the route rejoins US 89.

If you choose to take the main route from Emigrant, US 89, after turning south you will find meadows and flat scrubby lands, ranches, and fishing spots. In the next 5 miles the valley narrows a bit and the road draws closer to the river, providing a lovely spot for the small meditation chapel on the left.

The terrain begins to change, as rock outcroppings testify to the early volcanic activity in the valley. Between mile markers 29 and 28, watch for the dark rock quarry to the west. About 8 million years ago, a large basalt lava flow passed through this part of the valley. Although the river has cut through this rock, about 30 to 40 yards above the road you can still see the vertical columns formed when the liquid lava hardened and compressed. Farther down the road, white chalky bluffs consist of hardened ash from an eruption about 30 million years ago. To the west of the river between mile markers 23 and 22, look for a dark volcanic dike, a vertical wall formed when a fracture in the earth's crust filled with magma.

Shortly beyond Point of Rocks fishing access, at about mile marker 22, you cross the Yellowstone River. On the left you pass the point where East River Road joins US 89. The valley continues to narrow, and barren scrub-colored hills dominate the scenery. To the east the view of the Absaroka Range is among the prettiest on this drive.

For another side trip, an access road heading west at Tom Miner Basin leads you about 8 miles on a dirt road to a campground. This area was rich in petrified wood until tourists and collectors gathered the samples available within easy reach. Today, if you are willing to climb, you can still see the petrified trees that remain from lava flows 35 to 55 million years ago. One of the largest specimens—the **King of Ramshorn**—is a redwood 12 feet in diameter. This species of tree was plentiful here during this valley's more tropical prehistory.

Back on US 89, enter narrow **Yankee Jim Canyon** at about mile marker 16. Yankee Jim was a cranky gold prospector named James George, who built his own road to the Yellowstone country and charged a lucrative toll. His monopoly—and mood—was ruined forever when his buffalo rifle couldn't hold off the Northern Pacific Railroad. The company finagled a right-of-way from Yankee Jim by agreeing to build him another road on higher ground, which they did in exchange for use of his road as a railway bed. Yankee Jim's route quickly became secondary, and he never forgave Northern Pacific for intruding on his monopoly.

The railroad ran into another problem a few miles down the road at **Cinnabar Mountain** when Mrs. McCutcheon, owner of the land a few miles north of the park, refused to grant right-of-way. Cinnabar Station became the terminus of the railroad, and travelers disembarked to board six-horse stagecoaches that carried them the rest of the way to the park.

US 89 climbs slightly as it enters 3-mile Yankee Jim Canyon. The steep, rocky landscape here replaces the wide Paradise Valley, and you can picture the difficulties of putting a primitive road through here. A scenic overlook into the shallows of the canyon provides an interpretive display about the cutthroat trout, which, like so many other native species, now live in only a fragment of their historic range. The canyon provides opportunities for camping at Canyon Campground in the surrounding Gallatin National Forest, and for whitewater rafting on the Yellowstone River rapids. These rapids are challenging, so only experienced rafters should try the canyon without a guide.

Watch for wildlife, mainly deer and elk, between the end of the canyon and Gardiner. Wildlife crossing signs mark the spots where animals most often come into contact with traffic. The tiny community of **Corwin Springs** is near the Cinnabar Mountain winter range for elk, deer, antelope, and bighorn sheep. Cross the bridge at Corwin Springs and head south on the unpaved Gardiner Back Road, also known as the Old Yellowstone River Trail, for a good vantage point for wildlife viewing, particularly from October through January. In winter bald eagles fish along this segment of the river. The Gardiner Back Road, also a popular route for hikers and cyclers, reconnects to US 89 beyond the town of Gardiner, near the Roosevelt Arch at the North Entrance, or you can backtrack to US 89 to continue to the park on the highway.

Back on US 89 at about mile marker 6, **La Duke Spring** picnic area is to the right. Steam rises from the river, evidence of the thermal spring. To the right

The modern town of Gardiner, MT, shows its evening light.

(west) on Cinnabar Mountain, **Devil's Slide,** an easily recognizable vertical strip of red shale, was exposed about 200 million years ago when the Rockies tilted upward during their slow formation. The mountain was named for its red color, as it was mistakenly thought to contain cinnabar, or mercuric sulfide, the main source of mercury. Instead, iron tints the slide and rock of the surrounding area.

Pass a small rodeo grounds on the right, and you are nearing **Gardiner,** population around 2,100, a town that looks pretty much the same today as it did 15, 20, or perhaps even 40 years ago. Named for another scamp of the Old West, mountain man Johnson Gardner, the town is a rough-and-tumble haunt for tourists, sportsmen, ranchers, and park employees. Gardiner is full of motels, cafes, saloons, and souvenir shops.

The town of Gardiner is a base for one more side trip. The mining ghost town of **Jardine,** about 6 miles up Bear Creek Gulch east of town, is still home to a good collection of mining relics. To get there, turn left onto Jardine Road, across the street from the Cenex gas station, before you cross the bridge over the Yellowstone River. The road to Jardine shortly turns unpaved, but it's a lovely drive in summer.

During winter (after hunting season) and spring, elk and bison looking for food pour into Gardiner from Yellowstone. Nothing green is safe. Elk, who live year-round in Mammoth about 5 miles away, find Gardiner a feasting spot. Bison, on the other hand, have been targeted by the state of Montana as dangerous because of the brucellosis bacteria they sometimes carry. If transmitted to cattle, the bacteria can cause the state to lose its "brucellosis free" status. State and federal policies have, in the past, allowed buffalo to be shot when they wander out of the park in search of winter range through this natural corridor. The policies are still a cause of great conflict and controversy between the National Park Service, the USDA Forest Service, the state of Montana, ranchers, and various animal-rights and environmental groups.

To reach Yellowstone, follow US 89 through Gardiner and take a well-marked right turn through town. At the end of this short road, a U-shaped curve leads to the **Roosevelt Arch,** the oldest official entrance to Yellowstone Park, dedicated by Teddy himself in 1903. The Old Yellowstone River Trail intersects here. Gardiner is the only entrance to Yellowstone National Park that is open to automobile travel year-round.

2

Bozeman, MT, to the West Entrance

General description: A scenic, 89-mile drive through the Gallatin River Canyon, with the Gallatin Mountains to the east and the Madison Range to the west.

Driving time: About 1.5 to 2 hours.

Special attractions: In Bozeman: Montana State University, Museum of the Rockies, American Computer Museum, and Gallatin County Pioneer Museum. Gallatin Canyon and National Forest offer fishing, hiking, and whitewater rafting. In West Yellowstone: the Grizzly and Wolf Discovery Center, Yellowstone IMAX Theater, and Museum of the Yellowstone.

Location: Southwestern Montana.

Drive route names & numbers: I-90 to MT 85 (the Belgrade exit on the interstate), connecting with US 191.

Travel season: Year-round, but the Gallatin Canyon can be treacherous in a snowstorm.

Camping: Commercial camping beyond Four Corners with setups for RVs. Forest Service campgrounds include Spanish Creek (8 miles off US 191; 3 sites, primitive), Greek Creek (14 sites), Swan Creek (1 mile off US 191; 13 sites), Moose Creek (13 sites), and Red Cliff (63 sites)—all open from the end of May to the middle of September. They are both small and popular. Reservations, which can be made online, are recommended. Near West Yellowstone: Forest Service campgrounds, Madison, Beaver Creek, Cabin Creek, and Baker's Hole, KOA, and other commercial camping available.

Services: Full services at Bozeman, Gallatin Gateway, Big Sky, and West Yellowstone. Restaurants, cafes, and lodging along the route. You lose cell service in the Gallatin Canyon but pick it up for a while around Big Sky.

Nearby points of interest: Skiing at Bridger Bowl and Big Sky Ski Resort, Lee Metcalf Wilderness Area, Gallatin Petrified Forest.

For more information: Bozeman, Big Sky, and West Yellowstone Chambers of Commerce; Big Sky Ski Resort; Gallatin Gateway Inn; USDA Forest Service, Gallatin and Bozeman Districts.

The Route

Bozeman, MT, was named for John Bozeman, a wagon master, adventurer, gold seeker, and trail guide who paved the way for settlement in the Gallatin Valley in 1864, when he led travelers north from the Oregon Trail on a path that bore his name. The wide valley gave access to easy travel and led to the establishment of a supply stop for miners and emigrants. When gold was discovered near here, the rush was on. Travel continued on the Bozeman Trail for 3 years, until Sioux and Cheyenne Indians closed it by attacking the flow of settlers into the area. Bozeman was murdered in 1867 on the banks of the Yellowstone River. His murderer's identity remains a mystery, although theories implicating a business partner,

Bozeman, MT, to the West Entrance

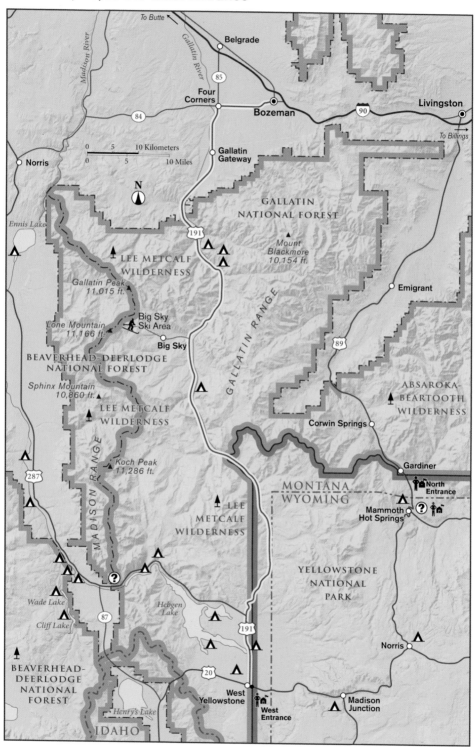

To Butte

Belgrade

Madison River

Gallatin River

85

Four Corners

Bozeman

90

Livingston

84

To Billings

Norris

Gallatin Gateway

0   5   10 Kilometers

0   5   10 Miles

N

191

GALLATIN NATIONAL FOREST

Mount Blackmore 10,154 ft.

Ennis Lake

LEE METCALF WILDERNESS

Emigrant

Gallatin Peak 11,015 ft.

Big Sky Ski Area

89

Lone Mountain 11,166 ft.

Big Sky

BEAVERHEAD-DEERLODGE NATIONAL FOREST

GALLATIN RANGE

ABSAROKA-BEARTOOTH WILDERNESS

Sphinx Mountain 10,860 ft.

LEE METCALF WILDERNESS

Corwin Springs

Koch Peak 11,286 ft.

Gardiner

287

MADISON RANGE

North Entrance

LEE METCALF WILDERNESS

MONTANA WYOMING

Mammoth Hot Springs

Wade Lake

Hebgen Lake

YELLOWSTONE NATIONAL PARK

87

Cliff Lake

Norris

20

West Yellowstone

BEAVERHEAD-DEERLODGE NATIONAL FOREST

191

West Entrance

Madison Junction

Henry's Lake

IDAHO

Indians, or a jealous husband all have their advocates. I-90 and the rail route through Bozeman Pass east of the city parallel the early Bozeman Trail. Mountain man Jim Bridger also journeyed through here in 1864, leaving his name on the mountains to the north.

The Bozeman area was home to native peoples for thousands of years. Tribes who have lived and hunted in the area include the Shoshone, Nez Perce, Blackfeet, Flathead, and Sioux. Meriwether Lewis's journal left the first known written description of the valley, as seen from a vantage point to the west. In his journal he noted that "a distant range of lofty mountains ran their snow clad tops above the irregular and broken mountains which lie adjacent to this beautiful spot."

The city of Bozeman has been described as "Livingston with an attitude." This upscale western town has always strived for an aura of civilization in surroundings that were not always the same. Begin your drive with a visit to this small city, home to **Montana State University.** The university sponsors the **Museum of the Rockies,** a wonderful place with a first-class dinosaur exhibit in the Siebel Dinosaur Complex. Jack Horner, a renowned paleontologist and the expert adviser for Steven Spielberg's movie *Jurassic Park,* serves as curator of paleontology at the Museum of the Rockies and is the Regents Professor of paleontology at the university. Volunteers in the Bowman Fossil Bank at the museum demonstrate fossil recovery techniques and answer questions about current Montana digs, where workers continue to find fossils such as the recently discovered Maiasaur nests, with fossilized eggs and embryos intact. This exceptional Museum of the Rockies collection, along with excellent exhibits about native peoples, the geology of the Rockies, artifacts of the Old West, and the Taylor Planetarium—laser shows included—can be seen in the summer from 8 a.m. to 8 p.m. daily; and the rest of the year from 9 a.m. to 5 p.m. Mon through Sat, and Sun from 12:30 to 5 p.m.

To experience Bozeman's early history, spend time in the **Gallatin County Pioneer Museum** in the 1911 jailhouse at the west end of Main Street. An authentic 1870s log cabin, a model of old Fort Ellis, a hanging gallows, and an exhibit about John Bozeman and his contemporaries take you through more than 100 years of history of the Gallatin Valley.

For pioneer history of another kind, the **American Computer Museum** is a winner. The advance of technology and the history of the Information Age from Cro-Magnon times to today are presented in a way that even non-techno buffs can understand. In downtown Bozeman, western shops, art galleries, and good restaurants dominate Main Street. Finish your tour by stopping at the old **Baxter Hotel** at the west end of Main Street for a look and perhaps a meal in one of the hotel's two restaurants.

Leaving Bozeman

To begin your journey to the park, follow Main Street west for about 9 miles until you come to Four Corners. You will pass a shopping mall, car dealerships, and fast food restaurants on your way out of town. Turn left at the light at Four Corners (recognizable by its antler art dealership on the northeast corner, the Grateful Shed, kitty-corner) onto US 191, the route to West Yellowstone.

If you leave Bozeman via I-90, drive west to the Belgrade/West Yellowstone exit (298), turn south, and drive 6 miles through obviously unzoned territory to arrive at Four Corners, the first stop light you reach. Within a mile of leaving the interstate, you'll find parked in front of a campground an interesting collection of old wagons, buggies, and farm implements that almost make a museum in themselves. If you reach Four Corners in the early morning, consider stopping at the **Kountry Korner,** a cafe popular with the locals, which does a robust breakfast business serving plain food and lots of it.

Head toward Gallatin Gateway, 6 miles south of Four Corners. Street signs say you're on Jackrabbit Road, which shortly becomes Gallatin Road. The **Bozeman Hot Springs** on the west side of the road is always good for a relaxing dip in a warm pool. Beyond this point the outskirts of Bozeman gradually give way to country scenery. Fields are a little larger, homes are spaced farther apart, and mile markers begin a few miles beyond Four Corners.

You pass the Cameron Bridge fishing access and the Axtell Bridge fishing access in quick succession. Fishing and camping opportunities line this route, along with hiking, kayaking, and whitewater rafting. US 191 is outfitter heaven.

Twelve miles south of the I-90 exit (6 miles south of Four Corners), look for **Gallatin Gateway Inn** on the right (west) side of the road. A hotel built in 1927 by the Milwaukee Railroad as a stopover for folks traveling to Yellowstone, the inn is a grand sight, both inside and out. The small hotel contains only 37 rooms (as well as 2 cabins for larger parties) because the railroad expected its patrons to sleep in Pullman cars. When the automobile replaced the train as the most popular means of touring, the hotel languished. An excellent historic restoration in 1986 saved the beautiful inn, which features mahogany woodwork and exquisite craftsmanship throughout. Wander through the ballroom, lounge, and dining area to enjoy this fine example of Spanish colonial architecture, with its wide arches and airy spaces. Inn and dining room rates are at the moderate to high end of the scale, but a stay here is something special. Gallatin Gateway Inn serves wonderful gourmet meals, accompanied by extraordinary service.

Through the Gallatin Canyon

As you leave the Gallatin Gateway area, you begin the main leg of the drive to West Yellowstone. In summer the approach to the mountains is quite colorful; moss-green and brown fields to the left are backed by deep purple rolling hills, possibly snowcapped, topped by blue sky. In winter the palette changes to white and gray. As you approach the canyon, where the road gently curves to the right, look for deer on the scrubby hills to the west. Start watching about 1.5 miles beyond the Little Bear access road. Deer are slightly harder to see on the hills than in open fields, but once you're attuned to them, spotting them will be easy. Occasionally, black bears have been known to approach the highway here from the eastern hills.

The entrance to the canyon is just beyond mile marker 71, where the Gallatin River makes its exit, flowing north to Three Forks where it joins the Madison and Jefferson Rivers to form the mighty Missouri. Lewis and Clark named these three tributaries for Thomas Jefferson, president at the time of the Louisiana Purchase and the Lewis and Clark expedition; James Madison, Jefferson's secretary of state; and Albert Gallatin, secretary of the treasury. Many other geographic features and localities scattered throughout the Pacific Northwest have names bestowed by Lewis and Clark during their expedition in 1804.

US 191 hugs the river at the canyon's entrance, where open fields are exchanged for sagebrush-covered hills and rocky cliffs. Pass over a bridge, placing the river on your left. The road crosses the river repeatedly between here and West Yellowstone.

Beyond the Spanish Creek access road, the rocky **Gallatin Range** to the left hints at the canyon's volcanic origin. Hills of quartz, feldspar, and silica jut sharply up in yellow, red, and pink rock formations. These colorful layered walls lead into the **Gallatin National Forest.** No glacier flow shaped this closed valley; its narrowness indicates that it was cut by the Gallatin River over millions of years.

The 20-mile drive from the canyon entrance to Big Sky follows the twisting path of the Gallatin River. The drive through the canyon can be slow, depending on the flow of traffic and the weather. This no-passing area demands a leisurely speed; 45 to 55 miles an hour should be safe. As with all scenic routes, don't be in a hurry to reach your destination. Numerous hiking, camping, and picnicking areas line the road, encouraging visitors to take their time. Several pullouts along the road allow slower traffic to pull over so that others may pass. This courtesy permits everyone to have an easier drive.

Fishing in the Gallatin River is a year-round activity. You may see fly fishers standing in the river in waders and parkas in the middle of February, pursuing the elusive trout. Places to park and get out your gear are found along the road, even in this narrow canyon. Because of the flow of tourists, lodging on this route is plentiful and diverse. When this two-lane highway was built in 1930, it changed the way people traveled to Yellowstone Park, and introduced tourism to an area that before had been sparsely populated. Campsites, cabins, lodges, motels, and dude ranches are readily available, but reservations are always a good idea. Contact the chamber of commerce in Big Sky for more information.

Many tributaries of the Gallatin River—notably Swan, Deer, Cabin, Porcupine, and Buck Creeks—give their names to hiking trails. The number and variety of trails are exceptional along this route. Between mile markers 65 and 64, Indian Ridge and Hellroaring Creek Trails both lead back toward the **Spanish Peaks** and **Lee Metcalf Wilderness Area,** beautiful spots for serious hikers to explore.

Between mile markers 63 and 62, where both sides of the canyon are thick with pines, begin to watch for moose by the river. Frequently in the mornings or evenings, a thirsty moose will avail itself of the mountain stream. Sightings aren't guaranteed, but they happen often enough that nearby Moose Creek and Moose Creek Campground are aptly named. In spring watch for surprising cascades of melted snow on canyon walls. This segment of the river is a great place for kayaking and whitewater rafting in the summer. Even the kayakers push the limits of the season. I have seen them struggling upstream as early as April, when the river is beginning to surge with newly melted snow.

Three campgrounds are located just before mile marker 58 and in the next few miles—**Greek Creek, Swan Creek** (about a mile up Swan Creek Road to the east), and **Moose Creek** to the west. Check with the USDA Forest Service for opening and closing dates, and note that sites fill early, so plan ahead. As with most of the campgrounds along this route, there is no garbage service. If you pack it in, please pack it out. All Forest Service rules apply and are posted at campgrounds.

As the road follows the winding path of the foothills, the speed limit lowers to 35 miles an hour. For the next few miles, there are several pullouts available for slower traffic. Near Portal Creek, beyond mile marker 54, experienced rock enthusiasts will recognize gneiss to the west that is about 2 billion years old.

The terrain changes as you approach the end of the canyon, just beyond mile marker 48, where a junction points the way west to Big Sky Ski Resort. A watch for wildlife sign posted before this turnoff alerts you to the sometime presence of bighorn sheep, often close to the road during the winter and frequently seen on summer evenings as they come to the creek by the road to drink. Although most western states have bighorn sheep herds, Montana and Wyoming have the largest populations. While driving through this area, be as wary of hitting a roadside photographer as of running into an animal.

Sign up for great year-round activities at the Base Camp in Big Sky. Imagine skiing from Lone Peak in the winter.

Big Sky Ski Resort, one of the premier ski havens in the West, becomes a retreat for golfers, bikers, hikers, and other vacationers in the summer. It's a favorite spot for travelers heading to Yellowstone. With all there is to do here, a triple zip line, a bungee trampoline, downhill bike paths, a high ropes course, and a climbing wall add to the fun. Big Sky has become almost as popular as a summer destination as it is a winter draw. **Lone Mountain,** the main peak, rises 11,166 feet and boasts 21 ski lifts to its slopes. With one of the country's highest vertical ski drops at 4,350 feet, it's worth the drive to Big Sky to take in the 360-degree view from the summit, and maybe to hike or bicycle down from the peak.

The resort was the dream of newsman Chet Huntley, a native Montanan. Upon retiring from broadcasting, he concentrated on the development of Big Sky, which opened for its first ski season in 1973. Huntley Lodge at Lone Mountain bears his name. With 5,300 skiable acres, 85 miles of named ski trails, and 21 available lifts, long lift lines are rare at Big Sky. Billing itself as the Basecamp to Yellowstone, Big Sky truly offers something for everyone. If your plans allow you the time, this is a good place to begin your Yellowstone adventure. To get to the resort, turn right at the intersection of US 191 and Big Sky Road and drive west 9 miles. Though it involves several hairpin turns, the road is well maintained and very drivable.

To continue to West Yellowstone, return to US 191 and again head south. **Soldier's Chapel,** near mile marker 48, was built in 1955 to honor fallen soldiers from this area who served in World War II. Chet Huntley is buried in the small cemetery here. For a short while the road goes through a small valley, more open than the canyon and dotted with dude ranches, restaurants, and outfitters. Gasoline prices here are higher than in Bozeman but lower than in West Yellowstone, so fill up if necessary. **Ophir School** to the right, the local elementary school, is named for a biblical word that means "land rich in gold," one of the many reasons Montana, nicknamed "the Treasure State," attracted its original settlers.

Hiking and camping opportunities continue. Twin Cabin, Porcupine Creek, Cinnamon Creek, Sage Creek, Specimen Creek, Bighorn Pass, and Fawn Pass Trails all invite hikers into the backcountry. The **Fawn Pass** area provides a great starting point for cross-country skiers. The closer you draw to Yellowstone Park, the more likely it is that creeks may have hot springs, identifiable by their rising steam. If you're hiking, go ahead and enjoy, but first check the water temperature to avoid scalding! Buffalo Horn, Teepee Creek, and Specimen Creek trailheads direct you far back into the Gallatins to a petrified forest. A volcanic eruption about 50 million years ago covered this area in lava and ash, smothering the vegetation but leaving much of it standing. As the lava cooled it filled the trees' cells with quartz, thereby preserving them as stone. Many species are identifiable, including the giant redwood. On the **Specimen Creek Trail,** one petrified redwood near the top of the first ridge is more than 12 feet in diameter. The hike in is challenging, but well worth the effort.

By mile marker 42 forested canyon with rocky outcrops again dominates the scenery. This colorful segment of the drive is highlighted by the **Red Cliff** area. Red Cliff campground is one of the larger camping spots along this route. Still, reservations are recommended. Around mile marker 33 begin to watch again for wildlife, including moose, bison, and the occasional black bear. Black bears belie their name, as they are not necessarily black. A cinnamon bear is actually a black bear with a light brown coat; because of its color it is sometimes mistaken for a grizzly, but there is really no comparison. A grizzly bear, much larger, can be identified by the hump that rises behind its shoulders, by the slope of its face from forehead to nose, and by its prominent ears, if not by size alone. A grizzly sighting in this portion of the canyon would be rare; black bears are much more common.

Moose feed in rivers and in any low marshy spots where willows grow from the banks or stream bottoms. Slow, meandering streams with lush vegetation look like diners to a moose. Several such spots exist on the remainder of the drive. Also watch for bison that might have strolled out of Yellowstone. Though bison were plentiful here at one time, the Yellowstone herd was diminished by about two-thirds during the long, hard winter of 1996–97. This was due in part to the weather and in part to the state of Montana's policy, since revised, of shooting buffalo that migrate out of the park. During the winter of 2008, 1,500 bison were sent to slaughter, but in 2009 close to 500 were hazed back into the park when they left looking for winter forage. Still, you may see the occasional bison grazing or lolling by the side of the Gallatin River. All wildlife should be respected and watched from a distance. As with all animals in the parks, if you are close enough to draw their attention, you are too close. A telephoto lens and patience produce many amazing photographic results.

The Part of the Park That's Not in the Park

Around mile marker 31 the road cuts through a small parcel of Yellowstone National Park that extends for the next 20 miles. A stone structure on the right (west) side of the road marks the park boundary. The speed limit changes to 55 miles an hour, fishing is catch-and-release only and requires a Yellowstone license, and a sign proclaims elk crossing for the next 10 miles. All park rules apply here.

A couple of miles inside this border, **Black Butte** to the east provides a good example of a 50-million-year-old lava deposit. Beyond, the meadows to the west of the road for the next several miles provide good feeding opportunities for those aforementioned black bears, and therefore good viewing opportunities for travelers. We've spied them more than once along this route. Between mile markers 23 and 22, evidence of forest fire damage begins to appear on the hills to the southeast. The fire that caused this damage was actually one of eight fires that burned out of control in the summer of 1988, destroying timber throughout Yellowstone but reaching few surrounding areas. Although the dead and downed trees are terrible reminders of the destructive force of nature, the forest is regenerating, as smaller evergreens take root and flourish.

As hills close in toward the end of this park section of the drive (around mile marker 13), watch again for moose, which are often sighted here. We once saw a moose standing right next to the sign that reads WATCH FOR BISON, but we weren't fooled. The sign at mile marker 11, noting the entrance to Gallatin National Forest, indicates that you're exiting this brief segment of Yellowstone.

Shortly after leaving the park, the road climbs. At the top of a rise, the valley opens up, revealing a beautiful view of the **Yellowstone Plateau.** On a clear day you almost can see forever. From this perspective all mountains and rock within view are lava and ash from the past 200 million years. As you descend toward West Yellowstone, 9 miles away, be prepared to meet bison on the road. No fences surround the park, so buffalo often wander outside its borders.

The rest of the way to West Yellowstone is a straight dash downhill. The Madison Arm of Hebgen Lake is to the west at the junction with US 287, offering opportunities for fishing and other water sports. Baker's Hole and Madison Campgrounds, popular stopover points for those staying outside the park, and Hebgen Lake day-use area for boating and fishing can all be found off US 191. Camping is permitted only at developed campgrounds.

West Yellowstone

West Yellowstone is a small western tourist town, with all that that implies. A rapid growth in motels, fast food restaurants, T-shirt shops, and entertainment services has not much altered this colorful stop. Aided by the growing popularity of snowmobiling in the area, West Yellowstone, once a seasonal destination, has become more of a year-round vacation spot. Good restaurants are beginning to appear in town, and we had a great dinner at **Sydney's Mountain Bistro.** Thanksgiving through April, snowmobilers seek out the nine trails in the **Gallatin National Forest** and the close to 1,000 miles of groomed trails that explore parts of Montana, Idaho, and Yellowstone National Park, using West Yellowstone as their base. However, many motels close in spring, when the roads through the park are just beginning to be plowed. For information about lodging and amenities, check with the West Yellowstone Chamber of Commerce or with the Visitor Center at the intersection of US 191/287 and US 20 (Appendix A). While there, pick up the brochure of the historic walking tour you can take through town. Twenty historic markers give you a great sense of the place and a bit of history to boot.

At the south end of Canyon Avenue (US 191/287), three notable attractions, all within two blocks of the Visitor Center, might entice you to investigate. First, the **Yellowstone Historic Center,** located in the train depot built by the Union Pacific Railroad in 1909, focuses on the history of travel to this remarkable place called Yellowstone. Native Americans, trappers, and adventurers all have made their way to and through the park by various conveyances. The story of the railroad alone is worth the modest price of admission. The museum operates from mid-May through mid-Oct.

The second attraction, an **IMAX theater** open year-round, shows a wonderful film on its six-story screen entitled (what else?) *Yellowstone,* as well as other current IMAX thrillers. The theater complex has a store and also a food stand that offers an irresistible 50-cent soft-serve ice cream cone.

The third attraction, located next to the IMAX theater, is the **Grizzly and Wolf Discovery Center,** a not-for-profit wildlife park and education facility. This preserve provides shelter for grizzlies deemed unable to live in the wild, either because they were problem bears that repeatedly traveled too close to populated areas, or because the animals were orphaned before they could survive on their

Claws with a cause—he's digging for dinner at the Grizzly and Wolf Discovery Center.

own. The center also houses two gray wolf packs separated by the naturalist cabin, which has glass walls through which you can view the animals in their habitat. This is my family's favorite stop in West Yellowstone. Films relating to grizzlies, wolves, and other wildlife show in the museum theater, including one on staying safe in bear country. Talks and exhibits are ongoing in the central museum. The Discovery Center takes very seriously its mission to educate, and it does a terrific job of it. Wonderful programs for children are both innovative and interactive. For a very modest fee, a child over the age of 5 can purchase a keepsake button that is her entrance token to help feed the bears in their habitat. While the grizzlies are otherwise (and elsewhere) engaged, children with buckets of food, accompanied by the center's naturalists, enter the habitat and hide the food so that the bears can forage for it at feeding time. When every child is accounted for outside of the enclosure, one or two grizzlies enter to hunt, sniff out, and dig for their meal. Watching a grizzly overturn a large rock or log is indeed awe-inspiring. Naturalists are available at all times to answer questions or give presentations. If you are lucky, your visit will include watching a grizzly test a bear-proof container. Companies use the center to test their latest designs, and the bears are given an hour to try to open the darned thing. Sometimes their persistence pays off, sometimes it doesn't.

Before you leave the center, take note of one other animal that is obvious here: the raven. This fascinating, very intelligent, and crafty bird is everywhere, keeping eyes on both the grizzlies and the wolves. As omnivores, ravens eat the same food as bears, and it's fun to watch them try to find the food in the grizzly enclosure before the bears can get to it. Ravens are pretty adroit at avoiding bear swats when they get too close. Because they eat the same food, ravens also have a relationship with wolves; they can often show you in the wild where a dead carcass may be located, luring wolves and bears to feed. Ravens often hang around wolf packs, and when they are startled and fly away, their action warns the wolves that danger is near. You can learn more about the interrelationship between these birds and the large predators at the center.

Although many people have reservations about keeping wild animals in captivity, the Grizzly and Wolf Discovery Center saves these animals from extermination and shares good science-based information that promotes, rather than hinders, understanding of two magnificent creatures of the wild. A third exhibit, an eagle aviary, has been added to the center's offerings, but it is seasonal and not open in the winter. All in all, if you have the time, or if you're tired of touring and want to stretch, this is an excellent stop to make.

To get to the park from West Yellowstone, turn left (east) at the end of US 191/287 onto US 20 and follow the signs straight ahead to the West Entrance to Yellowstone National Park.

Three Forks, MT, to the West Entrance

General description: A 110-mile drive through the Jefferson River Valley to the broad Madison River Valley, strikingly framed by the Madison and Tobacco Root Ranges.

Driving time: Between 1.5 and 2 hours, if you make no stops.

Special attractions: The Jefferson River Valley, the Madison Range and River, the town of Ennis (Fly Fishing Capital of the World), the Madison River Canyon with Quake and Hebgen Lakes, Sphinx Peak (10,860 feet), Koch Peak (11,286 feet), and a variety of opportunities for camping, fishing, hiking, biking, and enjoying the western scenery.

Location: Southwestern Montana, beginning at exit 274 of I-90.

Drive route names & numbers: MT 2, US 287.

Travel season: The road is maintained year-round, but as with all Montana routes, use extra caution in winter weather.

Camping: Missouri Headwaters State Park (17 sites) and Lewis and Clark Caverns (40 sites), Madison River (10 sites) near Cameron, Beaver Creek (62 sites), Cabin Creek (16), and more within a short driving distance. KOA and other commercial campgrounds as well as Forest Service campgrounds at Madison Arm and Baker's Hole are available near West Yellowstone. For a complete listing, send for the travel planner offered by the state of Montana.

Services: Frequent along the route. Full services at Three Forks, Ennis, and West Yellowstone. Service stations and food at I-90, exit 274, by Wheat Montana deli. Other cafes and guest ranches are found along the way, near and beyond Ennis. Cell service along most of the route.

Nearby points of interest: Missouri Headwaters State Park, the Madison Buffalo Jump, the fly fisher's dream—the Madison River, Bear Trap Canyon, Lewis and Clark Caverns, Virginia City and Nevada City ghost towns.

For more information: Virginia City, Ennis, and West Yellowstone Chambers of Commerce; Madison Ranger District; Lewis and Clark Caverns State Park (Appendix A).

The Route

On July 22, 1805, Captain Meriwether Lewis wrote, "The Indian woman [Sacagawea] recognizes the country and assures us that this is the river on which her relations live, and that the three forks are at no great distance. This piece of information has cheered the sperits [sic] of the party who now begin to console themselves with the anticipation of shortly seeing the head of the Missouri yet unknown to the civilized world."

In the Three Forks area, the interstate intersects with Montana lore and history. Before you head to Yellowstone, two side trips of historic significance are worth your time; each is within about 10 minutes of exit 274 of I-90. The first is

Three Forks, MT, to the West Entrance

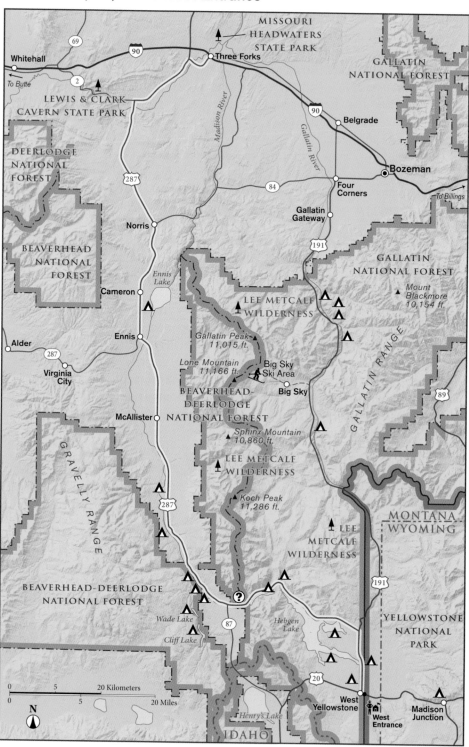

the **Missouri Headwaters State Park** at the confluence of the three rivers that Lewis and Clark identified on July 27, 1805, more than a year after they began their journey in St. Louis, Missouri. Here Sacagawea (Sa-CO-ga-wee-ah) recognized the land as the place where a few years earlier the Gros Ventre (Groh-VONT) Indians had attacked her people and taken her captive. Later sold to a French Canadian fur trader, Toussaint Charbonneau, she helped guide the expedition to the Pacific Ocean.

Captain Lewis wrote of the three rivers that form the Missouri, "Both Captain C. [Clark] and myself corresponded in opinion with respect to the impropriety of calling either of these streams the Missouri . . . we called the S.W. fork, that which we meant to ascend, Jefferson's River in honor of that illustrious personage Thomas Jefferson . . . the middle fork we called Madison's River [after Secretary of State James Madison] . . . And the S.E. fork we called Gallitin's [sic] River." This in spite of the fact that Abraham Alphonse Albert Gallatin, secretary of the treasury, did not favor what he called the "waste of time and money" that was the Lewis and Clark expedition.

From this juncture near the town of Three Forks, the Missouri River travels through seven states before it reaches the Mississippi River north of St. Louis. Picnic spots, interpretive trails for hiking, and biking trails mark the area where the three streams join. You can camp or reserve the tepee or cabin that is available for travelers. For a special treat on a pretty day, take along breakfast rolls, a deli sandwich, or homemade soup from the nearby **Wheat Montana** deli—always great fare—and take advantage of the picnic sites at the state park. If you have time, climb the small butte that rises to the northeast of the confluence for a wonderful view of the patterns the rivers form as they come together.

To get to Missouri Headwaters State Park from Wheat Montana (exit 274 on I-90), go 4 miles east on I-90 to exit 278 and take the frontage road east for 3 miles, then turn left (north) onto Secondary Road 286. Follow the signs or the bike trail 3 miles to the Headwaters of the Missouri River. (From the town of Three Forks, drive 3 miles east on US 10, then 3 miles north on Secondary Road 286.)

Buffalo Jump Site

This region is not only rich in Lewis and Clark history but in Native American history as well. The Gallatin Valley, where wildlife and vegetation proliferate, supported many tribes at different times. The wide valley was a microcosm of the Old West, with hunting grounds, battlegrounds, and homesteaders' settlements. When you are ready to continue experiential history with your second side trip, backtrack to I-90 exit 278, continue east to exit 283, and drive 7 miles south on the

Pioneer cabins hint at a hardscrabble life.

graveled Buffalo Jump Road to one of the prime Montana archaeological areas: the **Madison Buffalo Jump.** Before Indian tribes had horses for hunting, they would stampede bison over the steep ridge, or pishkun, to their deaths on the rocks below. The buffalo jump was a relatively easy way to kill large numbers of bison, the animal upon which so much of the native way of life depended. Food, tools, housing, and clothing came from the buffalo; no part of the animal was wasted. Archaeological digs indicate that this area was probably used as a buffalo jump for about 4,000 years, at different times by Shoshone, Crow, Salish, Blackfeet, Nez Perce, Pend d'Oreille, and Flathead tribes. Signs at the site point to remaining tepee rings, which can still be seen along the top and base of the ridge. A short walk will lead you to them. After exploring the Madison Buffalo Jump, retrace your steps to the highway. Continue east to enjoy the museums and other attractions of Bozeman, described in Scenic Route 2, or return west to I-90 exit 274 and begin your trip south to Yellowstone.

If you choose the latter and turn south on US 287, you soon connect with MT 2. A drive of 5 miles and a left turn will take you on a side trip to the town of Three Forks, once a destination point for the Milwaukee Railroad. If you're interested in old hotels, explore the **Sacajawea Inn,** built in 1910 and listed on the National Register of Historic Places. Its recent restoration and the addition of a top-notch dining room make this a perfect place to stay, for a while or a night.

Back on MT 2, continue heading south. This road will take you all the way to West Yellowstone. The route begins by the Jefferson River, the stream Lewis and Clark followed west while searching for a Northwest Passage to the Pacific Ocean. However, the Jefferson swerves westward within a few miles, and your route south will pick up the famous Madison River farther along the drive.

Beyond, to the southwest, rise the **Tobacco Root Mountains,** fronted by ranch land and expansive wheat fields. A couple of old outbuildings grace the landscape. One of them, the pioneer **Parker Homestead,** used to greet you with a sign that stated YOU ARE ENTERING THE HOME OF THE PRAIRIE RATTLESNAKE. The cabin, now under private ownership, no longer welcomes visitors, much to the rattlesnakes' relief. Back on the road, the scenery soon breaks up into small scrubby buttes and dry ravines. When you come to a Y intersection, follow US 287 left across the steel bridge over the Jefferson River to head to Ennis and Yellowstone.

For an interesting side trip in the summer, rather than turning left, remain on MT 2 to visit the spectacular **Lewis and Clark Caverns** about 5 miles to the west. Open May 1 through September 30, these magnificent limestone caverns were discovered in the 1840s by local ranchers. Rainwater traveling through cracks in the rock formed and eroded the caves over the past million years. In the 1930s the Civilian Conservation Corps mapped the passages and chambers of the caverns and constructed a system of stairs and ladders, creating easy if sometimes narrow pathways through the labyrinth. Reaching the opening of the caves involves a walk of about 0.75 mile on a paved path, up a slope. Rubber-soled shoes are recommended for the guided tour, as passageways are damp. Layers of clothing are also a good idea, since the temperature in the caverns remains a cool 50 degrees Fahrenheit. The tour covers 2 miles and takes about 2 hours, but it's time well spent. The Lewis and Clark Caverns trek takes about 1.5 hours, but is considered to be one of the best cave viewing experiences in the country. Facilities at the caverns include a gift shop, campground, picnic sites, and information center.

Continue your drive to Yellowstone by backtracking to the junction of US 287 and turning right (southeast). Pass through **Harrison,** a one-street town named for Henry C. Harrison, who raised Morgan horses here, far from their origins in Vermont. At the southern edge of town, a turnoff to the west leads to the small town of **Pony,** an old mining town that is now nearly a ghost town. Once home to more than 1,000 people and called the "Metropolis of the Madison Valley" by the local newspaper, Pony now consists of summer residences, ranches, and a pastiche of old buildings and Victorian-era homes.

Back on US 287, proceed southeast across vast ranch lands surrounded by mountains and through a broad winding valley to **Norris,** another ranch town, named for Alexander Norris, owner of the original ranch in this territory. **Norris Hot Springs** is open for a soak Wed through Sun, about 10 miles to the east.

Beyond Harrison the view opens to an interesting mixture of mountains, rolling hills, fields, and mesas, all verdant and lush in June. After Norris the road crosses several arroyos. A sign indicating a chain up area is startling because the hill doesn't appear to be that steep or difficult. It hints at the fierce winters that often assail the range.

Just beyond mile marker 61, a historical marker calls attention to a portion of the **Bozeman Trail** on a rise to the west. Traveled by miners and other settlers between 1863 and 1868, the route fell into disuse when Indians opposed to the intruders continually attacked travelers. Forts Reno, Joe Kearney, and C.F. Smith were built along the Bozeman Trail for protection against these attacks, but they were ineffective and subsequently abandoned. If you look closely at the western hill, you can still see signs of the trail more than 100 years after its last use. An interpretive map on the historical marker shows the Oregon Trail leaving from Independence, Missouri, and the Bozeman Trail Cutoff, which headed north to Montana.

The next town, **McAllister,** lies close to **Ennis Lake,** east of town, which offers good camping, but better swimming than fishing, as the water gets too warm to sustain fish. Between McAllister and Ennis, watch for pronghorn antelope along the strip of land between the highway and the lake. The **Ennis Fish Hatchery** welcomes visitors to tour the operation of raising trout for stocking rivers and streams throughout the country.

Five miles beyond McAllister, another junction yields yet one more side trip. Turn right on US 287 to visit the ghost towns of Virginia City and Nevada City. **Virginia City,** a National Historic Landmark and open-air museum, was the first town incorporated in Montana and the original capital of the Montana Territory. It was founded as a result of a gold discovery by six prospectors in nearby Alder Gulch in 1863. The subsequent rush to the area soon drew about 18,000 people. In the 5 years gold was mined in Alder Gulch, prospectors took away close to $40 million worth from its placer mines. One and a half miles farther down the road is **Nevada City,** a collection of period buildings placed on the site of the earlier mining town. Check with either Chamber of Commerce to see if the **Alder Gulch Short Line Railroad** is operating between the two sites. For a low fee you get an unusual and fun ride on an original old train. Other entertainments present themselves in the area. Virginia City's musical theater produces popular shows every summer for enthusiastic audiences, stage coach rides are offered downtown, and the old-fashioned penny candy store on main street is enough to lure me. If you make this side trip, small **St. Paul's Episcopal Church,** one block south of town (102 E. Idaho), houses several beautiful authentic Tiffany windows. Don't miss them. Camping and lodging are available in the area.

Ennis–Fly Fisher's Dream

Return to the junction with US 287 and to **Ennis,** one of Montana's most popular fly-fishing areas. Ennis was named for one of the first three settlers in Madison County, William Ennis, a man whose children were said to be the first white children to see Yellowstone, in the year 1863. He was shot and killed in Virginia City by an angry neighbor who claimed, according to the local paper, that Ennis had "maligned his character."

Ennis is an almost one-street town, with touristy shops, most related to fishing and hunting. Wooden boardwalks lead to antique shops, outfitters, tack shops, and the inevitable saloons. The **Continental Divide** is the most noteworthy restaurant in town, serving excellent food. Cross the Madison River via the Varney Bridge to leave Ennis. Those heading north will see a sign declaring POPULATION 840, 1 MILLION FISH. This clarifies the real attraction of the area.

As you leave town, look toward the southeast to see **Lone Mountain** (elevation 11,166 feet) and the back side of Big Sky Ski Resort. Head south through the wide, green Madison River Valley with its farmland and ranches, fishing lodges, log homes, access bridges, and many campgrounds. Several motels adorn this sporting stretch of the road.

From Cameron, a wide spot in the road, you can see **Sphinx Peak** (elevation 10,876 feet), a mountain of limestone conglomerate, to the east. Named by geologists for its vague resemblance to the Sphinx of Giza, it is more notable for its red rock, the only such rock in this mountain range. Watch for wildlife, as the **Bear Creek Wildlife Management Area,** also to the east, provides a 3,458-acre habitat for elk, mule deer, black and occasionally grizzly bears, as well as grouse, sandhill cranes, and other varieties of birds. From Cameron to Quake Lake, six easily accessible campgrounds appear, one after the other, and the fee for camping is modest.

Occasional buttes and ridges begin to break up the flat landscape. By the McAtee Bridge and Recreation Area, you have a good view of **Koch Peak,** the highest peak in the Gallatin Range at 11,286 feet. A little farther on, about mile marker 27, to the right (west) of the road, a herd of pronghorn indicates the **Wall Creek Wildlife Management Area,** more than 7,000 acres of year-round wildlife habitat. You can often spot raptors (including eagles, hawks, and ospreys), and occasionally a black bear lumbers into view. Beyond Wall Canyon the road begins gradually to veer southeast, and the terrain becomes hillier. Turnoffs to the right (west) for Cliff and Wade Lakes will take you to more campsites in popular recreation areas that are a little off the beaten path.

At the junction of MT 87 and US 287, you have the option to proceed to Jackson Hole, Wyoming, via Henry's Lake and Ashton, Idaho. This route is

Sphinx Peak was obviously named by someone with an active imagination.

described in the Grand Teton section, Scenic Route 25, "West Yellowstone, MT, to Jackson, WY."

Beyond the junction you approach the **Madison River Canyon Earthquake Area.** The drive through this canyon passes a dozen interpretive signs that detail the story of the cataclysmic quake that occurred on August 17, 1959, at 11:37 p.m. A severe but quick earthquake measuring 7.5 on the Richter scale convulsed the canyon for about eight seconds. The quake's immense magnitude broke apart a section of the south valley wall and loosed about 38 million cubic yards of rubble. Close to 80 million tons of rock tumbled from the mountain, creating a natural dam about 1 mile long and 0.75 mile wide, instantly burying at least 26 campers and leaving a lake where before there had been none. A memorial visitor center on the north side of the road marks the area. The earthquake was so severe that it caused a large tidal wave through the canyon. Winds as high as 175 miles an hour were created by the falling rock, and groundwater levels reportedly fluctuated throughout the US. The geological effects of the jolt are still visible. As you drive through the Gallatin National Forest toward Hebgen Lake, notice the 15-foot fault scarp on the northern side of the canyon, where the Madison Range was thrust sharply upward. In the 5 to 8 seconds the quake lasted, the northern shore of Hebgen Lake dropped 10 feet while the southern shore rose; consequently, parts of the old road were submerged, as were camps and houses. Several boat ramps to the lake today are actually sections of the old road. A road across from Cabin Creek Campground near the east end of Quake Lake leads to the remnants of a buried village—buildings swept downriver by the floodwaters.

Now, once again, **Hebgen Lake** and its public campgrounds are in demand with campers, boaters, and anglers. Beaver Creek and Cabin Creek remain popular throughout the season. This summer recreation spot offers easy access to Yellowstone as well as a host of activities of its own.

Seventeen miles from the Quake Lake Visitor Center, US 287 joins US 191, and a right turn at the junction will lead you 9 miles south to West Yellowstone, which is discussed in the previous route, "Bozeman, MT, to the West Entrance."

4

Red Lodge, MT, to the Northeast Entrance via the Beartooth Highway

General description: A 65-mile drive that climbs through national forest to a 10,947-foot plateau overlooking mountain ranges of two states. The famous Beartooth Highway, a National Scenic Byway, crosses the highest elevations in both Montana and Wyoming accessible by automobile. Panoramic vistas of alpine meadows, glacial lakes, and mountains.

Driving time: 2.5 to 3 hours. You could possibly drive this route in 2 hours, if you avoid the temptation to stop at overlooks or to take pictures. However, it will probably take closer to 3 hours. In a hurry? Don't go this way.

Special attractions: In Red Lodge in August, the Festival of Nations; the Beartooth Highway through Rock Creek Canyon, the Beartooth Plateau, and Clarks Fork Valley; Granite Peak, Montana's highest mountain; endless wildflowers; the Absaroka-Beartooth Wilderness.

Location: South-central Montana and northwest Wyoming.

Drive route names & numbers: Beartooth Highway/US 212.

Travel season: Summer. Beartooth Pass is usually open from Memorial Day weekend through Sept, but it may open late or close early because of snow accumulation.

Camping: A number of campgrounds line the route: Ratine (5 sites), Sheridan (7 sites), Parkside (23 sites, wheelchair accessible), Limber Pine (13 sites), Greenough Lake (18 sites), M-K (10 sites), Chief Joseph (6 sites), Fox Creek (33 sites), Colter (23 sites), and Soda Butte (23 sites, RV). More are located farther back on Forest Service roads, for those willing to drive a few miles on dirt.

Services: Full services in Red Lodge, Cooke City, and Silver Gate. Top of the World has a small store for gas, groceries, and camping and fishing supplies. No cell service.

Nearby points of interest: Meeteetse Wildlife Trail, Grasshopper Glacier and pink snow, the Chief Joseph Scenic Byway, downhill skiing in winter at Red Lodge Mountain ski area, Silver Run Cross-Country Ski Area.

For more information: Red Lodge Chamber of Commerce, Clarks Fork Ranger District, Custer National Forest, Beartooth Ranger District, Shoshone National Forest District, Gallatin National Forest District.

The Route

The high-country drive from Red Lodge, MT, to Cooke City on the border of Yellowstone takes you across a beautiful mountain plateau. The **Beartooth Highway,** also known as the All-American Road, built in the 1930s and restored in 2005, is an engineering feat that still astonishes today.

Red Lodge, MT, to the Northeast Entrance via the Beartooth Highway

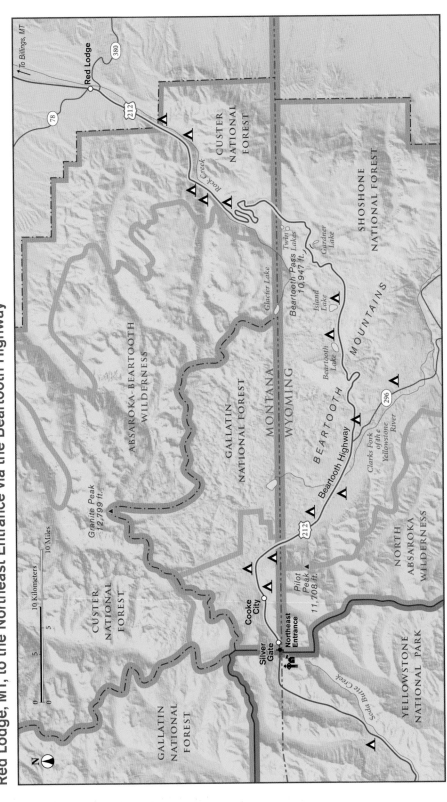

Begin the drive in **Red Lodge,** named for the Crow Indians' custom of decorating tepees with red clay from the nearby mountains. The history here is typical of the Old West; Indians, raucous settlers, miners, ranchers, and entrepreneurs all left their marks. Red Lodge became the county seat of Carbon County after coal-mining ventures drew settlers from all over the world. The **Festival of Nations,** a major celebration lasting 9 days every August, commemorates the town's diverse ethnic heritage. Free food samples and music of many nations are offered on the streets of town during the festivity, which draws festival goers from all over.

Red Lodge is a year-round tourist destination. Winter lends itself to skiing at nearby **Red Lodge Mountain Ski Resort;** spring attracts hikers, bikers, and campers; summer belongs to Yellowstone tourists and travelers looking for spectacular scenery; and fall brings a profusion of hunters.

Local attractions include the **Carbon County Museum,** which contains the homestead cabin of John Johnston, upon whose life the movie *Jeremiah Johnson* was very loosely based. Johnston, the first constable of Red Lodge, was also known as Liver Eating Johnston, a nickname bestowed when he took a gruesome revenge on Indians who killed his wife.

Many buildings listed on the National Register of Historic Places line the main street of Red Lodge. A self-guided walking tour, put together by the Carbon County Historical Society, takes about 40 minutes to complete. It includes visits to the **Pollard Hotel,** a building of historic and architectural interest built in 1893, and the old **Carbon County Bank Building,** robbed by the Sundance Kid in 1887 after he escaped from jail in Belle Fourche, South Dakota. The sheriff pursued the Kid for 80 miles, caught him, and sent him back to Belle Fourche to be reincarcerated, whereupon he again escaped.

In 1919, when coal mining began to dwindle in this area, Dr. J.C. Siegfriedt of Red Lodge envisioned a road through the neighboring high country that would attract tourists to this territory. After a lengthy lobbying effort, residents persuaded Congress to supply the $2.5 million required to build the Beartooth Highway. The road took 5 years to complete, from 1931 to 1936. On one unannounced day each summer, town residents still celebrate the accomplishment by greeting tourists along the route with free coffee and soft drinks. On occasion, rock slides that block or damage the road cause closings for repairs. In this event, the **Chief Joseph Scenic Byway** (Scenic Route 5) offers a wonderful and equally thrilling alternate route to the park from Red Lodge.

Before leaving Red Lodge, if you like driving for adventure, a street sign at the southern end of town will direct you to the **Meeteetse Trail.** The street shortly turns into an unpaved road that transverses high desert terrain, seemingly in the middle of nowhere, and terminates on Montana's Route 72 near the Wyoming border. This trail was utilized by the army for years to reach Cody and beyond.

The road requires four-wheel drive or a truck and is best driven in dry summer weather, but it's an amazing drive, and wildlife sightings are common.

The Beartooth Highway

Begin monitoring your odometer at the turnoff to Red Lodge Mountain Ski Resort on the south end of town. The mile markers at the side of the road mark the distance to Yellowstone's border. In the first 15 miles of this breathtaking route, you will climb almost 4,000 feet in elevation. Several rock slides to the east mark the narrow entrance to **Rock Creek Canyon,** whose walls of Precambrian granite are some of the oldest rocks on earth, dating back about a quarter of a billion years. As a result, the canyon attracts paleontologists, geologists, and archaeologists, as well as hikers. Terrific but challenging trails lead far back into the mountains. As the highway climbs, you pass through yellow and red rock outcroppings, palisades of white limestone, and pine-covered hills nurturing sagebrush, aspen, cottonwood, and Douglas fir.

Several campgrounds appear in short order, as the **Custer National Forest** is rich in sporting opportunities. In and near Red Lodge are resorts and lodges for those who would rather not "rough it." There is no other lodging along this route until you arrive at Cooke City.

As you begin this drive, Rock Creek tumbles along the right-hand side of the road. Looking back to the north you can see the U-shape of the valley, caused by glaciers carving their way through the rock. Lake Fork Road to the right, across from mile marker 59, leads to the first of literally hundreds of lakes accessible from this route. Lodgepole pines, cottonwoods, and Douglas fir line the creek. As the road curves left, you can easily recognize **Black Pyramid Mountain** (elevation 8,608 feet) looming straight ahead.

Beyond Parkside Campground occasional pullouts provide opportunities to enjoy scenic views and allow slower vehicles to pull over and let traffic pass. This is especially helpful if you are driving a van or trailer, which will indeed take its own time climbing to the top of Beartooth Pass. As the mountains grow more rugged and rocky, and the rolling foothills fall behind, the road inclines more sharply. Even in August it's not unusual to find snow patches glistening in sunlight atop the relatively low peaks here.

Hairpin turns switch back almost upon themselves, and profuse wildflowers line the way. Surprisingly, you must be alert for bicyclists, who are attracted by the challenge of this steep, beautiful road, even though it has no shoulders. By the time you reach the second hairpin curve, you will be able to look back for an incredible view of the road's course. Traveling speed as you climb is between 20 and 25 miles an hour as the road hugs the mountain's slope. As you go around a curve banked by rock outcroppings, you will see a small cascade to the left that spills toward the river. Engelmann spruce occasionally dot the rocky landscape, and in the valleys the woods are interspersed with burn areas.

You reach the first overlook, **Rock Creek Vista,** at mile marker 49 on the road's left side. This is a perfect opportunity to look back and see where you've been. The elevation here is 9,190 feet, compared to 5,555 feet in Red Lodge. A wheelchair-accessible path leads across a rocky ledge to interpretive signs and an amazing panorama. You can look back to the north and west toward Rock Creek, Glacier Lake, and the Hellroaring Plateau. The signs point out spots where mountain goats and bighorn sheep often tarry. It is worth this stop to stretch your legs and fill your lungs with crisp mountain air.

Hairpin curves, U-curves, S-curves, and other extravagant configurations continue to carry you upward after you leave the overlook. Several false summits present themselves, but the road continues to climb. Toward the timberline, subalpine firs dot the hills. Everyone who writes about this road, including me, quotes Charles Kuralt, who said in a piece for his *Sunday Morning* television show, that the Beartooth is "the most beautiful highway in America."

As you near the Beartooth Plateau, the road straightens enough to include a passing lane. Notice the snow markers beside the road; these not only measure snowfall, but enable those who clear the pass to find the road under the heavy blanket of white. Within 3 miles of Rock Creek Vista, the ascent becomes more gradual. Watch for mountain goats along the plateau's rock outcroppings. At mile marker 45 you leave Montana at the highest point of elevation reached by automobile, 10,350 feet, and are welcomed to Wyoming.

Panoramic Views

For the next several miles, views of nearly 360 degrees come and go. **Twin Lakes Overlook** to the right reveals double cirque lakes. The Precambrian metamorphic rock of the **Beartooth Plateau,** at about 3.2 billion years old, is among the oldest exposed rock in the world. Points on this plateau make even the most nonmusical want to burst forth with "The Hills Are Alive . . ." Long stretches of fragile, low grass stippled with delicate wildflowers span the tops of these mountains. The temptation to picnic or walk about is strong, but be careful where you tread. Fine tundra growing above the permafrost has a tenuous foothold, is easily destroyed, and takes years to regenerate. In the short summer of these peaks, only a few inches of topsoil thaw, leaving frozen ground underneath year-round. Above the timberline the climate is too harsh to support much vegetation. As snow and ice melt in the summer sun, the surface water forms pools that can't permeate the frozen ground, creating the many glacial ponds of the area. Because the water cannot

trickle into the earth to form a water table as it does at lower elevations, topsoil in the groundwater has filled pool basins over hundreds of thousands of years, creating the flatness of the plateau. Be on the lookout for fields of pink snow, caused by algae that grow in the summer "heat." When they die, the dead algae turn the snow pink.

As the descent begins, a sign at about mile marker 43 announces the **Beartooth Loop and National Recreation Trail,** a 10-mile hiking trail for experienced backpackers. Many trails web out from the top of the plateau. Gardiner Lake, Lake Trailhead, Little Rock Creek Trail, Losekamp Lake Trail, and Camp Sawtooth are a few of the reasonable hikes you may take that originate from this height. Hiking will cause shortness of breath at this elevation if you are not accustomed to it, so take your time and hike in the company of others. Also, this is grizzly country, so take all precautions. Remember that strong scents attract animals; lock away food, utensils, and personal items. These peaks also attract snowboarders year-round, as evidenced by the telltale snowboard tracks.

As you descend, watch for the solitary glacial horn known as **Bear's Tooth Peak,** rising in the distance ahead of you. A turnoff to the right gives you a wonderful view of the solitary tooth, carved by glacial ice, for which this pass is named. A mile or so farther, you reach the West Summit turnoff, the drive's high point both figuratively and literally. Turn right (north) 0.25 mile on a spur road to view the Bear's Tooth; look north from the overlook to view Montana's highest mountain, **Granite Peak,** jutting above the landscape to 12,799 feet. Numerous other glacial horns soar above the horizon along the Beartooth Plateau. The elevation of the road here is 10,947 feet, the highest point on Wyoming's highways. The limestone cliffs of the **Beartooth Range** to the north sedately rise above the timberline.

The course of the descent winds in switchbacks, with pink granite and gneiss contributing to the landscape. Cliffs and ravines on the left (south) side of the road front sloping grassy hills. About a mile from the West Summit Overlook, you can see the red-rocked **Beartooth Butte,** backed by the tall spires of Pilot and Index Peaks to the left. As you descend the Wyoming side of the pass, overlooking craggy mountains and high meadows, the vistas grow broader and more spectacular.

The diverse and impressive details of the panorama—a waterfall at the side of the road, a small cascade of snowmelt, frequent glacial ponds—catch the eye. Descend to the timberline, where twisted juniper, pine, and fir trees begin to appear, seeming rather like small shrubs. Severe winds and weather have stunted their growth and distorted their shape. Only the hardiest of the species survive at this altitude.

As you descend the Beartooth Highway, notice that even in August snow remains on the slopes.

Little Bear Lake is one of hundreds tucked in the Beartooth Mountains.

The road does straighten out and offer pullouts for many hiking trails. Hauser Lake Trailhead, Jeep Road, and Dollar Lake Trailhead follow in quick succession. Lakes appear at every turn, many of them stocked with cutthroat, brook, and rainbow trout. **Long Lake,** near the summit, covers nearly 80 acres. You do need a license to fish, and Wyoming licenses may be purchased at **Top of the World,** a few miles south of here. Little Bear Lake, to the right, and Chain Lakes Viewpoint, to the left, post signs reminding you that you're still in grizzly country. The **Island Lake Recreation Area** in the Shoshone National Forest has a campground with a trailhead, a good point from which to hike to many of the tiny icy lakes that grace the hillside. South of the highway at Island Lake, a web of gravel roads leads to other ponds, including **Beartooth Lake,** a good spot for camping, picnicking, and boating.

Beyond the lake, forests of pine and spruce dotted with lupine line the highway. Beartooth Butte rises high above the lake's far shore. The large dark spot on the butte contains innumerable plant and fish fossils, while the hummocky ground between the lake and the ridge is a large landslide area, now refoliated. A small turnoff to the right affords a view of **Beartooth Falls.** Look to the left of the road for Index and Pilot Peaks, two high glacial horns that dominate the scene. Spreading out to the north and west of here is the **Absaroka-Beartooth Wilderness,** almost a million acres of refuge for wildlife and recreation for hikers, campers, and anglers. With close to 1,000 small alpine lakes and more than 700 miles of hiking trails, the Absaroka-Beartooth Wilderness is the fifth largest wilderness area in the United States.

At Clay Butte Lookout divert your course on a spur road that goes to the right about 2 miles. From here a panoramic view to the west allows you a great view of Granite Peak. About 27 other peaks in this area rise above 12,000 feet. From this vantage point, at an elevation of 9,811 feet, fire spotters used to watch for lightning strikes. To the southwest, the Absarokas, 50-million-year-old mountains that form Yellowstone's east boundary, were created by giant volcanic upheavals.

Shortly beyond Clay Butte, another turnoff, this time on the left, provides a view of the **Clarks Fork Valley,** the escape route for Chief Joseph and his Nez Perce people as they fled to Canada in 1877. Chief Joseph Campground close to Cooke City gives an account of their journey.

Pass Lake Creek Falls on the left and travel about 4.5 miles from the Clay Butte turnoff to the next wonderful viewpoint, the **Pilot Index Overlook.** A turnoff to the right leads back about 0.25 mile to a point where you can look on both **Pilot Peak** (11,708 feet) to the left, and **Index Peak** (11,313 feet) to the right. Dark strips of dikes and sills are prominent on the mountainsides. Both peaks were formed by melting, retreating glaciers that eroded away the hillside, leaving the pinnacles pointing toward the heavens.

Shimmering aspens line the drive to the junction with the Chief Joseph Scenic Byway, which heads through Sunlight Basin toward Cody, Wyoming. On the far hills, signs of areas burned during Yellowstone's 1988 fires appear. Much of the damage you see along this stretch of road was purposefully caused when firefighters built backfires in their efforts to save both Cooke City and Silver Gate, towns on the border of the park.

Good Camping

Crazy Creek and Fox Creek campgrounds offer more chances for playing in the Shoshone National Forest. Cross Crazy Creek, which roars and cascades down the hill. The splendid scenery of this lower country contrasts completely with the first two-thirds of the route, but is every bit as enjoyable. The road dips, climbs, and winds by the side of all kinds of little mountain streams that appear out of the hills to the left. As you pass a valley on the right filled with an old lodgepole pine forest, you cross back into Montana for the remainder of the drive to the park. The road narrows, the shoulders of the Wyoming road disappear, and the Gallatin National Forest replaces the Shoshone. Mile markers miraculously reappear. The road climbs again, passing a rockslide area to the left.

Once you cross a pass, alternately called Colter or Cooke Pass, the road begins to descend. The second Clarks Fork picnic area and trailhead are to the right, directly across from Chief Joseph Campground. Chief Joseph fled east through Yellowstone following the Battle of the Big Hole in Idaho in 1877, taking almost 1,000 tribal members with him. Running from the US Cavalry, which intended to force the group onto a reservation, the Indians surrendered after the 6-day Battle of the Bear Paw in northern Montana, about 30 miles short of their intended destination, Canada. Chief Joseph's stirring speech of surrender—including his famous words "I am tired; my heart is sick and sad. From where the sun now stands, I will fight no more forever"—expressed both the dignity and futility with which they resisted. The campground offers a memorial to Chief Joseph and the Nez Perce tribe with exhibits about their flight. Continue on the route to find other campgrounds, resorts, lodges, and dude ranches as you draw closer to Cooke City.

North of Cooke City one of the more peculiar attractions on this route is within hiking distance for experienced backpackers. A challenging 3-mile trail that begins at Goose Lake leads to **Grasshopper Glacier,** where about 300 years ago millions of grasshoppers were blown onto the ice by an untimely blizzard. Flash frozen, they are now visibly part of several smaller glaciets; as they have melted, the glaciets have left grasshopper carcasses behind. The area of Grasshopper Glacier, once about 4 miles long and 0.5 mile wide, now covers about a mile in length.

Cooke City, Montana, elevation 7,651 feet, was Yellowstone's first border community. Established in 1870, it is older than the park. The town grew out of a gold strike in 1869 that formed a town site called the New World Mining District. It was renamed Cooke City as an attempt to persuade the Northern Pacific Railroad to build its line to this difficult-to-reach location. Jay Cooke was president of the railroad at the time. The name stuck, although the flattery wasn't enough to persuade the railroad to build through the mountains. The high cost of transporting ore from here doomed Cooke City's mining efforts. Mining companies today lust after the gold that remains in the area, but environmentalists fear the effects of mining on Yellowstone's rivers and wildlife.

Old wooden cabins, motels, and cafes edge the town built along the highway. Much wilder looking, primitive, and smaller than Red Lodge, Cooke City is a happening little place, in a curio shop kind of way. Summer and winter visitors sustain the town. In summer, nearby dude ranches enhance the tourist trade, and winter brings snowmobilers. The snow season runs from Thanksgiving to mid-April. With more than 100 miles of groomed trails to explore and more than 200,000 acres of playland, Cooke City and nearby Silver Gate have frequently been test sites for Arctic Cat and Yamaha snowmobiles.

Beyond Cooke City, Soda Butte Creek to the left of the highway leads you less than 4 miles to **Silver Gate,** another small enclave. It is interesting that you must pass through Wyoming to reach both of these small Montana towns. You will find more tourist accommodations in tiny Silver Gate—cabins, outfitters, horseback-riding corrals, pack-trip opportunities, and cafes. At an elevation of 7,400 feet, Silver Gate is, loosely speaking, the last outpost of civilization before you reach the park. The Northeast Entrance (elevation 7,365 feet) is a mile or two beyond Silver Gate.

5

Red Lodge, MT, to the Northeast Entrance via the Chief Joseph Scenic Byway

General description: An alternate road to the Northeast Entrance that takes you from Red Lodge, through a small defunct mining town and beautiful ranch territory, to an 8,000-foot mountain pass with incredible panoramic views of two Rocky Mountain ranges. The route meets the Beartooth Highway Scenic Byway at its southern end and takes you through tiny Cooke City and Silver Gate to the park.

Driving time: About 2.5 to 3 hours, if you make no stops. Stopping, however, is almost inevitable, because of the beauty of the drive.

Special attractions: The Hungry Bear Cafe's "world famous" pie, historic land of the flight of the Nez Perce Indians from the US Cavalry in 1877, Shoshone National Forest and the North Absaroka Wilderness, Sunlight Gorge, Clarks Fork Canyon.

Location: South-central Montana and northwest Wyoming.

Drive route names & numbers: MT 308, to MT 72/WY 120, to WY 296, the Chief Joseph Scenic Byway.

Travel season: Best during summer and fall. Although the road is plowed year-round, snowstorms cause frequent winter closings.

Camping: National forest campgrounds at Dead Indian (10 sites), Sunlight (remote location, 3 sites), Hunters Peak (10 sites), Lake Creek (6 sites), Crazy Creek (15 sites), and Chief Joseph (6 sites, RV) on US 212.

Services: Gas, food, camping, and lodging sporadically along the drive; full services in Red Lodge and Cooke City. Cell service almost nonexistent.

Nearby points of interest: Beartooth Highway Scenic Byway, Sunlight Basin and Sunlight Road, Sunlight Creek Gorge, Clarks Fork Canyon Road.

For more information: Red Lodge Chamber of Commerce, Shoshone National Forest, Clarks Fork Ranger District, Cooke City Chamber of Commerce.

The Route

From Red Lodge, MT, you have a wonderful choice: You can proceed to Yellowstone either by the Beartooth Highway or the Chief Joseph Scenic Byway. Both are high mountain routes with breathtaking vistas. It is the history of the **Chief Joseph Scenic Byway** that makes this an especially compelling route. If you take this road, you won't be disappointed. Personally, it is my favorite route to the Northeast Entrance to the park.

After exploring Red Lodge (described in Scenic Route 4), head south on the main street to the junction of US 212 and MT 308. A left turn toward the town

Red Lodge, MT, to the Northeast Entrance via the Chief Joseph Scenic Byway

of Belfry, 14 miles away, is the first leg of your journey. The road begins to climb almost immediately after making this turn, then levels and dips through plateaus and arroyos. Hills grassy with sagebrush and scrub surround you.

Shortly after the first turnout, you pass through tiny **Washoe,** marked by the site of an old mining disaster. Miners settled here because of the rich deposits of coal in Carbon County. The Smith Mine was active and productive until an explosion on February 27, 1943, caused a fire and methane gas infusion in the underground veins that wound up taking the lives of 74 men. The effect of this, Montana's worst mining accident, led to the end of coal mining here. An interpretive sign on the north side of the road gives details of the event.

The road beyond Washoe cuts through gully bottoms near Bear Creek, shallow in August. Even so, if your windows are rolled down or you're ambling along in a convertible, incredible birdsong may follow you. As you approach the small town of **Bearcreek,** you can learn the valuable lesson about judging a book by its cover. Unprepossessing Bearcreek has a sign stating HOME OF WORLD-FAMOUS BANANA CREAM PIE. If you read William Least Heat-Moon's book *Blue Highways,* you'll recall his system of judging cafes and towns by their homemade pies. This stop would earn a maximum rating. My mother and I entered the **Hungry Bear Cafe** at 9:15 in the morning, she for banana cream, me for coconut, and what a breakfast it was. I would give a lot for their recipe for piecrust, but I digress. The owner of the cafe said that on her best sales day she went through 60 pies, and 48 of them were banana cream.

Bearcreek itself almost looks like a ghost town, although it purports to have about 100 year-round residents. The town lies about halfway between Red Lodge and Belfry, and in 7 more short miles you reach the junction with MT 72. Turn south and travel 11 miles to reach the Wyoming border, where the road designation becomes WY 120. This leg of the drive begins as flat farmland, but shortly the road climbs to scrubby hills. The road parallels the southern end of the Beartooth Range and the Clarks Fork of the Yellowstone River. Several hunting and fishing access roads line the route. On a good two-lane highway lined by juniper and scrub, you draw nearer to the western mountains the farther south you go.

Cross into Wyoming to travel the remaining 20 miles to the beginning of the Chief Joseph Scenic Byway, WY 296. Once you are in Wyoming, the landscape widens. Within a mile you crest the top of a small hill where on a clear day you can see at least 100 miles to the south, and about 30 miles to the west and southwest. You are bordered by the Switchback Ranch for most of this part of the drive. As you cross the Clarks Fork at about mile marker 127, watch for pelicans that frequent the river to the right.

About mile marker 116, at a junction with WY 296, a right turn (west) puts you on the Chief Joseph Scenic Byway/Sunlight Basin Road. This 46-mile stretch

Red rock signifies the beginning of the Chief Joseph Scenic Byway.

of road is accessible year-round, but inclement weather of snow or sleet should make you think twice about the journey. The first 8 miles of the route takes you through the private property of the Two Dot Ranch. The road shortly begins its climb, and the incredible views of the mountain terrain begin. Watch for wildlife—bears, moose, elk, pronghorn, deer, coyotes, and perhaps even wolves—all along this route. At the 45-mile marker (which tells how far it is to the junction with the south end of the Beartooth Highway) the first of many turnouts allows a view of dramatic red buttes and the valley you are leaving behind.

The Quick Ascent

You begin this route with a steady but not steep climb. A speed limit of 45 miles an hour changes to 35 miles an hour, and you'll soon see why. The well-maintained serpentine road passes red sedimentary formations reminiscent of scenery in Sedona, Arizona. A serious climb follows, giving you glances back at the Bighorn Basin to the east. This byway begins with great beauty—windswept hills, red rock formations, and turnouts every 0.25 to 0.5 mile, so you may enjoy the quickly changing scenery. Several signs warn that you are in bear country; if you plan to hike or camp, take all precautions.

The interpretive signs you encounter along this road tell of the flight from the US Cavalry by Chief Joseph's band of Nez Perce (usually pronounced "nez purse") Indians. Much has been written about their journey, but as you cross this high mountain route, imagine, if you can, the next-to-impossible nature of their feat. Various tribes of Native Americans—Shoshone, Crow, Blackfeet, and others— either lived or migrated throughout this area. But the story of the Nez Perce who fled the US Cavalry for almost 3 months in the summer and fall of 1877 colors this route with an amazing narrative that is at once both awe-inspiring and tragic.

Chief Joseph

In 1855 the Nez Perce Indians, led by Old Chief Joseph, Chief Joseph's father, signed an agreement with the United States government that allotted the tribe a large parcel of land that transected parts of Idaho, Oregon, and Washington. In 1877 the government wanted to diminish that land and move the Nez Perce to a much smaller reservation. The Indians, led in part by Chief Joseph, the son, fought against resettlement. Several skirmishes, one in which a few drunken braves killed two white men, led to the government's pursuit of any in the tribe. The fleeing Indians were engaged by the army at the Battle of the Big Hole in Idaho, which resulted in the deaths of many more soldiers.

Led by their chiefs Joseph (In-mut-too-yah-lat-lat, or "Thunder Coming Up Over the Land From the Water"), Looking Glass, White Bird, and too-Hul-hul-sote, more than 1,000 Indians fled for their lives, hoping to meet up with their allies, the Crows, or to reach Sitting Bull in Canada. Pursued by the Seventh Cavalry, they made their way across Idaho and up into Yellowstone, which had recently been set aside as a national park. An unfortunate encounter with tourists camping in the park resulted in two more deaths and a kidnapping, and this only heightened the resolve of the army to stop the tribe.

Led by General O.O. Howard, several companies were enlisted to trap the Indians. The assignment of Colonel Samuel D. Sturgis and others was to block the escape routes to the east of the park. The Seventh Cavalry had been demoralized by General Custer's loss at the Battle of Little Bighorn a year before (where Sturgis's son had been among the casualties). Now they were suffering public humiliation as newspapers picked up the story of the Nez Perce, portraying the army as bumbling and hapless. The Nez Perce had so far eluded capture for more than 2 months. The standoff was portrayed in the press as Goliath fighting David, and public sentiment was clearly with David.

Sturgis's assignment was to stop the Indians at the mouth of Clarks Fork Canyon. However, the Indians, anticipating an ambush and realizing that they were about a day ahead of the army, sent braves, led by Joseph and Little Elk, south to the Shoshone River, where they rode in many directions, creating a confusing trail for the cavalry to follow. They crossed and recrossed the Shoshone, then doubled back to the ridge.

The ploy worked. The cavalry had no idea which way they had headed. Amazingly, the Indians left the mountains through the almost impassably rugged and narrow Clarks Fork Canyon. Their escape seemed nearly assured, but the flummoxed army intensified its pursuit. By this time the band of Nez Perce had diminished to about 600 members, including many women and children. They made their way north, but about 40 miles short of the border, Colonel Nelson Miles overcame them. After the Battle of the Bear's Paw on October 5, Chief Joseph surrendered with the following words:

> Tell General Howard I know his Heart. What He told me before I have in my heart. I am tired of fighting, Looking Glass is dead. too-Hul-hul-sote is dead. The old men are all dead. It is the young men who say yes or no. He who led on the young men is dead. It is cold and we have no blankets. The little children are freezing to death. My people, some of them have run away to the hills, and have no blankets, no food; no one knows where they are—perhaps freezing to death. I want to have time to look for my children and see how many of them I can find. Maybe I shall find them among the dead. Hear me, my chiefs. I am tired; my heart is sick and sad. From where the sun now stands, I will fight no more forever.

It is an incredible story of pride, will, strength, wit, and persistence. Chief Joseph's words are immortal.

The Height of the Pass

By mile 7 of the Chief Joseph Byway scenic route, the high meadows surrounded by pine-covered hills signal the Shoshone National Forest. Near the very windy apex of this climb you reach **Dead Indian Pass,** elevation 8,048 feet. Stories differ about the name, but one version says that Chief Joseph's tribe left a critically wounded brave on this peak during its furtive escape. The cavalry, when they came upon him, killed him. The story is apocryphal, and is only one of many. The incredible view from this vantage point shows a seemingly endless mountain landscape and the swoop of **Sunlight Basin** below.

From this point you begin your long, slow descent toward the junction with the Beartooth Highway and Yellowstone. The beginning descent is steep, and the speed limit slows to 20 miles an hour as you traverse seven switchbacks. Another turnout and overlook appear about 0.25 mile from the summit of the pass. The route offers plentiful opportunities for photographers and scenery gawkers.

About 2 miles from the pinnacle, you come to the **Clarks Fork Canyon** overlook, which offers another good view of the majesty of the peaks of the Gallatin and Beartooth Mountains that overlook beautiful Sunlight Basin. At about mile marker 25, you reach the **Dead Indian Campground** run by the Forest Service, and a mile beyond that you'll find Sunlight Road to the left, which meanders along Sunlight Creek. For a side trip, travel 8 miles back on this gravel road to reach the **Sunlight Ranger Station** and campground. Road maintenance ends 18 miles in, and you'll find you truly are in far backcountry. In bear country. Possibly alone. Even though there are ranches around, this is very close to true wilderness. Activity does pick up in autumn during elk-hunting season.

Back on the byway, within about a mile you reach the scenic overlook of **Sunlight Gorge,** carved by **Sunlight Creek** 110 feet below, and the **Sunlight Bridge,** which spans that drop. This, the highest bridge in Wyoming, provides a dramatic view of the river below and the canyon beyond. The creek has cut a narrow gorge through the granite walls of the mountains. To the north, Sunlight Creek joins the Clarks Fork of the Yellowstone. This overlook presents a good opportunity for a little leg-stretching or picnicking.

As you descend from here the mountains become more forested, and the slopes to the right drop off into a rocky canyon carved by the Clarks Fork. The walls of this canyon rise to over 1,200 feet, and a large herd of mountain goats resides here, although it might take a powerful spotting scope to see them. The terrain changes quickly as you pass from canyon through forest to marshy outcrops. Forty-five to fifty-five miles an hour here should be a safe speed. After a scenic turnout near mile marker 14, you come through to the western slope of the mountain and are suddenly surrounded by aspen stands. Several scenic turnouts grace this part of the route for magnificent views. Another spot for a picnic or stretch appears at the Shoshone picnic area, where **Reef Creek Trail** offers a hike to **Reef Creek** below.

Just beyond mile marker 11, numerous lily ponds and glaciated marshes found on both sides of the road look like good moose habitat. Further on, rock outcroppings appear and the view again opens to mountain ranges, only now you see them from the valley floor rather than from lofty heights.

Guest ranches and outfitters advertise themselves along the road. Cabins and lodges, restaurants and outposts, buck and rail fences signal what little civilization there is. You are nearing the junction with the Beartooth Highway. Take a bridge across the Clarks Fork and pass a sign that advises watching for pedestrians

Sunlight Gorge and the Clark's Fork Canyon afforded Chief Joseph's tribe an escape route in 1877.

and horses. Pass Hunter's Peak Campground to arrive in a small canyon where the lovely spire of **Pilot Peak,** elevation 11,708, dominates the view. When we first drove through here, the top of the pinnacle was lost in the clouds, giving the appearance of a scene from *Lost Horizons.*

The drive from here is a sylvan descent. Another campground at Crazy Creek is about 2 miles from the junction. This drive ends at a high junction with US 212, the southern end of the Beartooth Highway. A right turn at this junction will take you north back over the Beartooth Pass for a return to Red Lodge. Make a left to go on to Cooke City and Silver Gate and Yellowstone Park beyond. The drive from the junction is described on the last two pages of Scenic Route 4, "Red Lodge, MT, to the Northeast Entrance via the Beartooth Highway." Save that drive for another day.

6

Cody, WY, to the East Entrance

General description: A 5-mile drive through town and a beautiful 48-mile route through dramatic rock-ridged Shoshone Canyon and Wapiti Valley and thick pine forest to Yellowstone National Park's East Entrance. Theodore Roosevelt once called this route the "most scenic 50 miles in America."

Driving time: A little more than an hour.

Special attractions: In Cody, the Buffalo Bill Historical Center (and annual powwow in June); Buffalo Bill Dam, Visitor Center, and Reservoir; and Buffalo Bill State Park. Along the route, the Absaroka Mountains, Washakie Wilderness, Fortress Mountain (elevation 12,085 feet), Sleeping Giant Mountain (elevation 11,193 feet), Pahaska Tepee, Shoshone National Forest.

Location: Northwestern Wyoming.

Drive route names & numbers: Buffalo Bill Scenic Byway/US 14/16/20.

Travel season: Summer and fall to Yellowstone National Park. In winter, the road is plowed to Pahaska Tepee, 4 miles east of the park's East Entrance.

Camping: Plentiful. Campgrounds at Buffalo Bill State Park (123 sites), Horse Creek (9 sites), Big Game (16 sites), Elk Fork (10 sites), Wapiti (40 sites), Clearwater 10 sites), Rex Hale (29 sites), Newton Creek (31 sites), Eagle Creek (20 sites, RV), Three Mile (21 sites, RV).

Services: Full services in Cody and Wapiti. Partial services at Pahaska Tepee. Lodging all along the route. Cell service through part of the Wapiti Valley.

Nearby points of interest: The world's largest mineral hot springs in Thermopolis, 84 miles south of Cody; a Red Canyon wild mustang tour 22 miles south of Cody; Heart Mountain Relocation Camp; and Chief Joseph Scenic Byway.

For more information: Cody Chamber of Commerce, Buffalo Bill Dam, Buffalo Bill Historical Center, Shoshone National Forest.

The Route

William F. "Buffalo Bill" Cody, wealthy showman and entrepreneur, was most famous for his Wild West Show, a traveling extravaganza that at different times featured Annie Oakley, Chief Sitting Bull, and Calamity Jane. He first produced the show in 1883 with real cowboys and Indians. It lasted 30 years, toured the entire United States, and spent 10 of its 30 years touring Europe. A tireless promoter, Cody traveled the world spreading tales of the newly settled West. His own diverse and colorful background as a trapper, miner, pony express rider, wagon master, Civil War soldier, and Indian scout gave him plenty of material from which to draw. He earned his nickname by purportedly killing 4,280 buffalo in 18 months for the Kansas Pacific Railroad.

Cody, WY, to the East Entrance

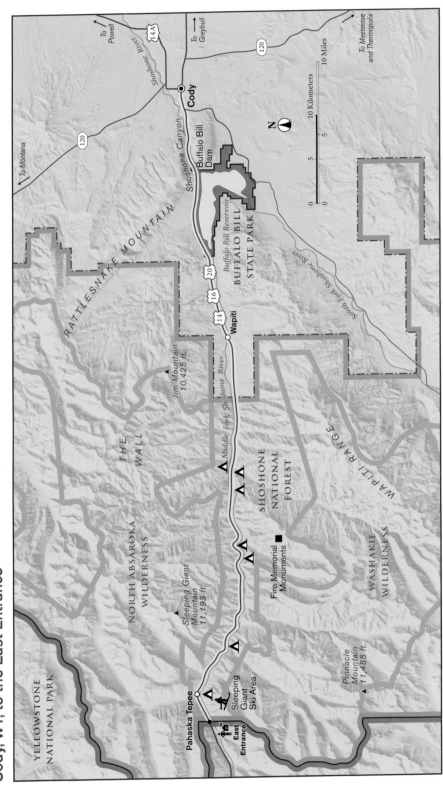

He was also an accomplished self-promoter; the fame he achieved perhaps eclipsed his most remarkable characteristics. In an era when a man's life and word were often cheap, Buffalo Bill respected the Native Americans among whom he worked, and as early as 1879 he cautioned the federal government to "never make a single promise to the Indians that is not fulfilled," recognizing that uprisings were caused by broken promises and treaties. He championed the conservation of the land and its resources, and worked to set aside game reserves and to protect the land's natural beauty. He also employed and promoted women, believing that they should be allowed to do whatever work they wanted, as long as they were physically capable.

Cody long loved this place that bears his name. When, at the turn of the century, two friends wanted his backing to establish a community here, Buffalo Bill became a developer too. The three decided to name the town Cody, because they figured his name would likely attract the needed settlers. Buffalo Bill built the Irma Hotel in town and the Pahaska Tepee, his hunting lodge at the western end of this scenic route, believing that once people realized the beauty of the Wapiti Valley, they would come. He worked diligently to open the East Entrance to Yellowstone National Park, and his imprint remains on the town that bears his name.

Cody, the Town

Cody today reverberates with reverence for its Wild West origins. With nightly rodeos, staged gunfights, and other western folderol throughout the year, the town endeavors to live up to its own publicity. Located in a wide expanse of high desert, it depends on ranching, oil, and tourism for its livelihood. Downtown Cody is a mishmash of boutiques, restaurants, saloons, and motels. Lodging prices are high in the summer months, so shop around and make reservations well in advance. Motels on the town's outskirts seem to be the least expensive, although prices at the Irma Hotel are competitive. A large sign on a local business stating WE SELL BEAR SPRAY gives you a hint of what you are in for. Gasoline prices here are about as reasonable as you'll find anywhere on this drive.

The Cody Visitor Center promotes a historic walking tour that takes about 1 hour to complete. One of its attractions is the **Irma Hotel,** built in 1902 by Buffalo Bill and named for his oldest daughter. The old part of the building has 20 rooms still with their original furnishings; 20 modern rooms are also available. In the dining room the cherrywood bar, made in France, was a gift to Buffalo Bill from Queen Victoria in gratitude for his London performance. Staged gunfights take place each evening in front of the Irma. Stop at the visitor center to obtain tickets to the Buffalo Bill Historic Center, the Cody nightly rodeo, Trolley tours, a cowboy musical revue, and more. If you are heading west through the Wapiti Valley,

Stop at the Old Trail Town in Cody to explore the unsettled, early West.

the center offers a small brochure of the imaginative names of different formations you can see from the drive. Pick one up, and play the name game.

Off the highway in the southwest section of town, near the rodeo grounds, another tourist attraction, **Old Trail Town,** is worth the stop. A reconstructed town from the 1880s and '90s includes authentic historic cabins, garnered from within a 150-mile radius of Cody. A former hideout of Butch Cassidy, the oldest saloon in the area, a museum, and a historical Wyoming cemetery are all part of the display. The buildings for the short walking tour are well documented and interesting.

For a darker side of the area's history, a side trip to **Heart Mountain,** 9 miles north of Cody, offers a new interpretive center for the area where 10,000 Japanese Americans were interred in the relocation camp bearing its name. Photographs, artifacts, and articles about life in the camp are on display at the center.

The best reason to begin your trip from Cody, however, is the **Buffalo Bill Historical Center,** billed as the largest museum between Chicago and Los Angeles. The museum houses one of the best collections of western art and artifacts in the country, including an extensive accumulation of the works of both Frederick Remington and Charles M. Russell. To get your trip off to a wonderful start, begin your tour here at the center of town where Sheridan Avenue turns south.

Five permanent museums comprise the historical center: the Draper Museum of Natural History, the Buffalo Bill Museum, the Plains Indian Museum, the Whitney Gallery of Western Art, and the Cody Firearms Museum. Allot as much time as you can spare to enjoy these outstanding collections. The lobby, presided over by a huge mounted buffalo, is the entrance to five spokes that lead to the exhibits. Outdoor sculpture gardens are an inviting place for a relaxing break on a clear day.

The **Draper Museum of Natural History** dedicates itself to explaining relationships between the animals, people, and geology of the greater Yellowstone area. Wonderful interactive displays of the ecosystems and their inhabitants engage as well as educate. Obviously, the **Buffalo Bill Museum** re-creates the history and time of this most remarkable man, housing an extensive collection of artifacts, including his boyhood home, gun collection, saddles, family letters, Wild West show memorabilia, and other personal belongings. Downstairs, the Harold McCracken Research Library, an extensive collection of resources, historic photos, and microfilm, is available for public use.

The **Plains Indian Museum** explores the rich traditions and histories of the Arapahoe, Blackfeet, Cheyenne, Comanche, Crow, Kiowa, Pawnee, Shoshone, and Sioux tribes. An extensive collection of tribal arts, much of it from the early reservation period, is part of the permanent collection. In addition, the museum sponsors the **Plains Indian Museum Powwow** every June in the Robbie Powwow Garden. If your timing is right, don't miss this cultural event.

In the **Whitney Gallery of Western Art,** paintings, sculpture, and drawings from the 18th century to the present testify to the dramatic changing of the American West. The giants—Albert Bierstadt, John Henry Twachtman, Joseph Henry Sharp, N.C. Wyeth, W.H.G. Koerner, George Catlin, Gutzon Borglum, Thomas Moran, William Henry Jackson, and John James Audubon—are represented here. Special sections devoted to Charles Russell and Frederick Remington display drawings, watercolors, oils, and sculptures. While Russell lived in the West and reveled in its spirit, Remington lived in New York but felt compelled to record the disappearing Indian way of life. Henry Lyons's wonderful bronze of Russell is here, and a huge oil by Harry Andrew Jackson, *The Range Burial,* dominates a gallery. *The Scout*, a sculpture by Gertrude Vanderbilt Whitney, stands outside a wall-size window and is backed by a mountain peak to the northwest, an inspired choice of setting.

The **Cody Firearms Museum** houses the largest American firearms collection in the world as well as European weapons dating from the 16th century to the present. For anyone interested in firearms, the Winchester collection alone is worth the price of admission. All in all, if you are interested in history or art, I guarantee that a stop at the Buffalo Bill Historical Center will be one of the highlights of your trip. Because of the extensiveness of the collections, the cost of your admission is good for 2 consecutive days, so keep your receipt.

Heading West

When you have exhausted your curiosity at the historical center, begin your drive to the park, resetting your trip odometer at the **Stampede Park Rodeo Grounds** at the west end of town on US 14/16/20, about 48 miles from the park. As you leave town, watch to the right for white cliffs composed of travertine, evidence of inactive thermal springs. The Shoshone River, which follows this route, still has four active hot springs along the beginning of the drive, identifiable by their rising steam. John Colter, a member of the Lewis and Clark expedition who later trapped fur in this area, described these bubbling cauldrons to trappers, giving rise to the name **Colter's Hell.** The name is often mistakenly given to the thermal features in Yellowstone. Because hydrogen sulfide in the springs emits a pungent odor, the river was originally called the Stinking River. Cody's image-conscious citizens, wanting a less vivid name, changed the name to Shoshone in 1901.

Enter short Shoshone canyon, cut over the past 3 million years by the Shoshone River through colorfully named **Rattlesnake Mountain,** which was formed when the earth uplifted along a fault about 66 million years ago—about the same time that dinosaurs became extinct. Rattlesnake Mountain rises 3,700 feet above Cody's western end. The road climbs to the **Buffalo Bill Dam.** Slow to 35 miles an hour as you approach two consecutive tunnels, one carved directly through the Precambrian metamorphic rock. The granite canyon walls form a dramatic entrance for this route.

As you leave the tunnels, you near the entrance to the **Buffalo Bill Dam Visitor Center** on the left. Open from 8 a.m. to 8 p.m., May to Sept, on about the same schedule as Yellowstone National Park, the visitor center is an interesting stop. It overlooks the first concrete arch dam in the world, completed in 1910. The dam was actually Buffalo Bill's idea to supply the newly established town of Cody with irrigation and drinking water. A small interpretive center with theater contains displays about area wildlife and the Shoshone National Forest. An entertaining interactive computer program provides travel information on the Yellowstone and Teton areas. Avail yourself of information regarding campgrounds, picnic spots, hiking, horse rental, ranger stations, as well as the Shoshone Project and Buffalo Bill Dam. However, the visitor center's most irresistible offering is the view. From inside the center you look through picture windows across the narrow granite gorge, or over a ledge, straight down to the river. Outside, a catwalk across the dam faces east through the ravine or west toward the reservoir. The North and South Forks of the Shoshone River converge at the reservoir, giving the lake its two-pronged shape. The Shoshone is the largest tributary of the Bighorn River, which in turn is the largest tributary of the Yellowstone River.

Leave the visitor center and resume the drive along the reservoir through **Buffalo Bill State Park,** where camping facilities line the shore for hikers, anglers, and sailboarders. **Sheep Mountain** on the lake's far side, a plateau formed of 300-million-year-old limestone, separates the two drainages, the North and South Forks of the Shoshone River. Toward the west end of the lake, round a curve and get your first glimpse of the sculpted bluffs and weird formations of the Wapiti Valley.

The Wapiti Valley

Refined by wind and water erosion over millions of years, the **Wapiti Valley** is visually stunning, especially on a clear sunny day. The rock formations throughout this valley, with colorful names such as elephant head, laughing pig, kneeling nun, and merry widow, were caused by a continuing flow of ash and lava that contained rock fragments from volcanic eruptions. This breccia, deposited by volcanic mudflows about 40 million years ago, hardened into hoodoos and spires. Watch to the right (north) for the Chinese Wall, a long vertical dike of magma that hardened after filtering into the cracks of the softer limestone of the cliffs. Also watch for pedestrians and horseback riders as you near the core of the valley, a haven for tourists.

Plentiful wildlife attracts hunters and other sightseers to the Wapiti Valley; elk, moose, buffalo, eagles, grizzly and black bears, and mountain sheep are often spotted by careful observers. Wapiti is a Shawnee word meaning "white rump," or "elk." Outfitters still lead hunters on horseback through the backcountry.

The small town of **Wapiti** is about 15 miles west of Cody; fishing, hunting, riding, and dining seem to be the mainstays of the community. As you approach town several tempting restaurants and steak houses advertise along the road. Sagebrush-ridden ranch land brackets both ends of town. The valley narrows, and at the boundary of the Shoshone National Forest, about 21 miles from Cody, the road becomes older, the shoulders disappear, and the speed limit lowers to 55 miles an hour. Head into the canyon, filled with beautiful scenery and dotted with lodges and campgrounds. The Shoshone National Forest contains more than 1,500 miles of hiking trails and about 500 mountain lakes. This is bear country, so if you're hiking in the wilderness, observe all precautions and carry that bear spray you picked up back in Cody. The Shoshone River rollicks along on the right, and on the left wind-carved bluffs rise in astonishing splendor. In certain light, such as after a cloudburst, the bluffs look blue-gray and defiant, but in the sun they are yellow-tinged and glorious. Occasional rock slides make for adventurous driving.

What do you see in the rock formations of the Wapiti Valley?

Within a few miles of entering the canyon, the speed limit is posted at 35 miles an hour, which is good, because shortly you will be gawking at the spires and pinnacles of the easily eroded conglomerate rock. These striking formations were caused by weathering of the vertical cracks in the conglomerate, leaving hoodoos and whatnots.

About 23 miles from Cody, three turnouts are found by the side of the road in short succession. The **Goose Rock Wayside,** named for the visible formation, features maps for sports areas, campgrounds, lodging, and grizzly bear territory. At the **Point of Interest** turnoff, a roadside sign gives a good explanation of the formation of the rocks, along with some whimsical names for several configurations. At the **Wapiti Wayside** turnoff, another map and a ranger station proffer useful information.

Cottonwoods and aspen along the riverbank intermingle with occasional evergreens. The road crosses and recrosses the river, weaving through a pattern of deciduous trees that are gorgeous in the autumn. Here, the narrow canyon has a small slip of land on the other side of the wide river, before the bluffs begin to rise. This is a popular fishing spot, and people in their waders persist in their search for a believable fish tale. The speed limit once again climbs to 50 miles an hour. By mile marker 17 (17 miles from Yellowstone) the road begins to climb as well.

The scenery on the left greens up with undergrowth that is not all sagebrush; small pines tenaciously grow through red rock. At about mile marker 15, a stone memorial remembers firefighters who were killed in 1937 by the Blackwater fire, which flared in a shifting wind and rushed up the side of the mountain, trapping and killing 15 men and injuring many others.

The red rock formations continue as the road climbs. The ascent toward the park is gradual but steady. The **Episcopal Wayfarer's Chapel,** to the right, holds services in this beautiful setting throughout the summer months. As you continue to climb, you'll notice an increase in pines, which hover over a blanket of wildflowers, and grasses replacing the lowland's sage.

Buffalo Bill Slept Here

The road tags along beside the river, which you can glimpse occasionally through the trees. A little more than 2 miles from the park, the **Pahaska Tepee** flaunts its bright green roof and very large flag. The drive ends as it began, in the presence of a western icon. This is Buffalo Bill's old hunting lodge, built in 1905. *Pahaska,* the Sioux word for "long hair," was a name bestowed on Buffalo Bill by his Indian friends. Thus, Pahaska Tepee means Long Hair's Lodge. Pictures of famous guests, princes, and dukes whom Buffalo Bill used to bring here to hunt still adorn the lodge's walls.

The rest of the drive climbs pretty directly toward the park's East Entrance. To the left the canyon drops sharply. The river disappears from view, and the hillside beyond is thickly forested with lodgepole pine. You reach the East Entrance to Yellowstone National Park, elevation 6,951 feet, about 48 miles from the outskirts of Cody.

7

Gardiner, MT, to Mammoth Hot Springs

General description: A 5-mile drive from the oldest official Yellowstone entrance to Mammoth Hot Springs and old Fort Yellowstone, original home of the US Cavalry when it was stationed in the park.

Driving time: About 15 minutes.

Special attractions: Ancient cliffs, the Forty-Fifth Parallel, bighorn sheep, and elk.

Location: Northwestern Yellowstone.

Drive route names & numbers: US 89.

Travel season: This is the only road in Yellowstone open to automobile traffic year-round.

Camping: One National Park Service campground near Mammoth; sites available first-come, first-served (85 sites), open year-round.

Services: Gardiner and Mammoth. Cell service for most of the drive.

Nearby points of interest: The Boiling River.

For more information: Gardiner Chamber of Commerce, the National Park Service at Mammoth Hot Springs.

The Route

Although Yellowstone National Park has always been open to the public, it took 30 years for this remote land to be sufficiently accessible that it required an official entranceway. Actually, it was because people disembarking from the train at Gardiner found the entrance so plain and unappealing that Robert Reamer, architect of the beautiful Old Faithful Inn, designed what has become known as the **Roosevelt Arch.** This 50-foot-high stone structure, erected in 1903, is inscribed "for the benefit and enjoyment of the people," the words the 1872 Congress used when it set aside this land as a public park.

Always looking for an excuse for adventure, President Teddy Roosevelt himself came to dedicate the arch. Speaking to an estimated 5,000 people who had come by rail and coach, he said, "Yellowstone Park is something absolutely unique in the world so far as I know. Nowhere else in any civilized country is there to be found such a tract of veritable wonderland made accessible to all visitors." As you pass through the arch or stop to have your picture taken beneath it, you are using the same historic entrance that has welcomed visitors for more than a century. Although four other entrances lead into the park, the Roosevelt Arch remains the most impressive gateway.

Shortly after passing through the arch, you begin the short, interesting drive through **Gardner Canyon** from the lowest point in the park. The mild climate

Gardiner, MT, to Mammoth Hot Springs

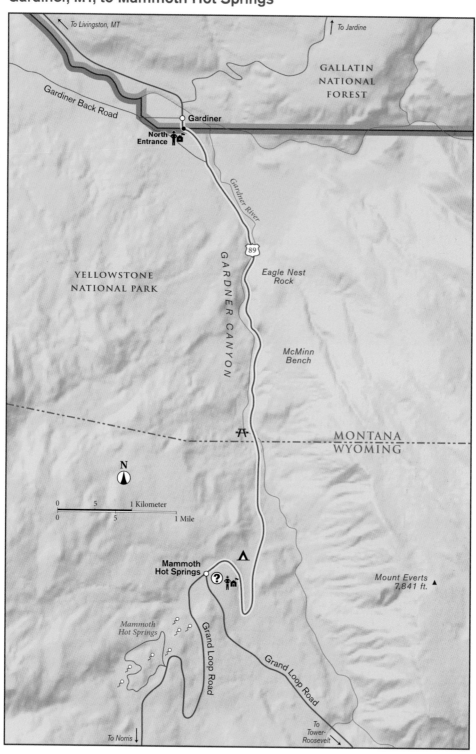

To Livingston, MT

To Jardine

GALLATIN
NATIONAL
FOREST

Gardiner Back Road

Gardiner

North
Entrance

Gardner River

89

YELLOWSTONE
NATIONAL PARK

GARDNER CANYON

Eagle Nest
Rock

McMinn
Bench

MONTANA
WYOMING

N

0   5   1 Kilometer
0   5   1 Mile

Mammoth
Hot Springs

?

Mount Everts
7,841 ft.

Mammoth
Hot Springs

Grand Loop Road

Grand Loop Road

To Norris

To
Tower-
Roosevelt

The Roosevelt Arch is the most recognizable entrance to Yellowstone National Park.

here supports one of the largest elk herds in the country. Watch also for prong-horn feeding in the sagebrush flats to the west of the road, and bighorn sheep scrambling over the rocky cliffs to the east, particularly in the evening. Both animals are initially hard to spot because they blend with their environment, but once you've seen them, it's easier to know what to look for.

The route from **Gardiner** (5,314 feet) to **Mammoth** (6,239 feet) is a constant, though not always steep, climb. The road cuts through rocky Gardner Valley, with sagebrush, Rocky Mountain juniper, cottonwood, and Douglas fir the dominant types of vegetation.

Confusion reigns over the origin of the town name of Gardiner. Although some people think the town and Gardner River are named for two different people, the Gardiner of the town is probably a misspelling of the river's name, which is one of the oldest place names in Yellowstone. Johnson Gardner, a scrappy mountain man of the 1830s, gave his name to the Gardner River and Canyon. Tales of his deeds and misdeeds remain part of the area's lore.

In another case of mistaken identity, Eagle's Nest Rock to the left of the road about 1 mile from the North Entrance actually shields nesting osprey, a different kind of raptor that is also called "fish eagle." It is thought that early coach drivers identified the birds as eagles to park visitors, resulting in the erroneous name.

Halfway Here, Halfway There

About halfway through this drive, a sign on the right marks the **Forty-Fifth Parallel,** the line of latitude midway between the equator and the North Pole, a great place to take a picture. Less than a mile beyond, park your car in the parking area, grab your swimming suit, and take the trail that leads upstream 0.25 mile (about a 5-minute walk) to the **Boiling River,** a stream that empties into the Gardner. Although the tributary itself is off-limits—as are all thermal features in the park—people soak in man-made pools surrounding the confluence. Posted warnings tell you not to submerge your head in the river as bacteria in the water can be dangerous, but wading or sitting and soaking is perfectly safe. This outpouring of hot water is thought to be the underground runoff from Mammoth Hot Springs and is the largest discharging hot stream in the park. A steep trail leads from the Boiling River site to the campground above and the village of Mammoth beyond.

Return to the road and head south again. A campground about 0.25 mile from Mammoth, open year-round on a first-come, first-served basis, is a great place for viewing elk. Beyond the campground, a hairpin curve leads to the top of a hill and the village of **Mammoth Hot Springs,** the first area settled in the park by park personnel. As you approach the top of the hill, a trail to the right allows energetic campers to return to the campground. Look directly east to see **Mount Everts** (7,841 feet), another mistakenly named landmark. Truman Everts, a member of the Washburn expedition in 1870, was lost for 37 days and was nearly starved by the time two mountaineers found him. More than a little delirious, he was not grateful to his saviors and later refused to pay the reward money offered for finding him. Although he was thought to have been rescued on Mount Everts, he was actually found some miles southeast of here on the western side of Crescent Hill.

Driving into Mammoth Hot Springs is often like driving through an elk refuge. Because the climate here is more temperate than in the rest of the park, the animals roam around 12 months of the year and are happily oblivious to tourists and park personnel. That is, unless you get too close. Follow all park rules regarding encounters with wildlife, even these apparently docile ungulates. The elk seem to know that hunters can't touch them here, and they're happy to hunker down near the warm thermal areas during the winter.

Mammoth is the site of **Yellowstone National Park headquarters,** located in the stone buildings that also house the **Horace Albright Visitor Center,** a good first stop in the park. Albright, named superintendent of Yellowstone in 1919, was the first official National Park Service superintendent. The center that carries his name features exhibits about early human history in the park—Native Americans, mountain men, and the people who mapped, surveyed, and explored the area.

This elk enjoys the quiet life of Mammoth Hot Springs, even with its thousands of visitors each day.

Also on exhibit is an especially good collection of Thomas Moran drawings and watercolors, which played an important role in persuading Congress to set aside this special land. The **Yellowstone Association Bookstore** located here sells books, maps, posters, and other materials related to the park and its history. If you join the association for a fee, your first purchase at any YA store in the Park will be 25 percent off, and 15 percent for all subsequent purchases. The Yellowstone Association supports the educational mission in the park through the Yellowstone Institute, and provides books, maps, and other materials in support of preservation here. If you can, take the time to watch the excellent film *The Challenge of Yellowstone,* about the wilderness and its effects on humanity, or *Yellowstone Today,* the park orientation film.

The Albright Visitor Center is located in the buildings of old Fort Yellowstone. When Congress passed the act to create the park, it did not allocate funds for its administration or upkeep. The number of visitors soon was so great that poaching, vandalism, and commercial ventures threatened to destroy the park. With no funds available, the secretary of the interior in 1886 sent a plea for help to the secretary of war, who commissioned the cavalry to Yellowstone to establish law and order and protect the land. The soldiers remained for 32 years.

Construction began on Fort Yellowstone in 1891, and the last stone structures were built in 1913. Today, a pamphlet for an interesting self-guided trail can be obtained from the visitor center for a step back in time around these turn-of-the-century buildings.

In 1916, as the United States prepared to enter World War I, the army could no longer afford to station men at Yellowstone. President Woodrow Wilson signed an act creating the National Park Service, whose mission was to "conserve the scenery and the natural and historic objects and the wildlife therein, and to provide for the enjoyment of the same in such a manner and by such means as will leave them unimpaired for the enjoyment of future generations."

Yellowstone's main post office is located here by old Fort Yellowstone, as are a medical clinic and the Yellowstone National Park chapel. Before you leave Mammoth, walk through the old **Mammoth Hot Springs Hotel,** last rebuilt in the 1930s. The hotel has an excellent restaurant, but the real attraction is the magnificent inlaid hardwood map of the United States, designed by Robert Reamer (architect of the Roosevelt Arch and the Old Faithful Inn), which covers most of one wall in the great room. The map alone is worth the stop at the hotel, if you are interested in true craftsmanship. While you are here, you can register for trail rides or rent a cabin, but reservations are usually necessary for cabin accommodations. The hotel remains open in winter for use by cross-country skiers and snowshoers. Like other hotels and inns in Yellowstone, the Mammoth Hotel has not been ruined by renovation, but if you prefer more amenities than are provided, you may want to stay outside the park's borders.

From Mammoth, begin your tour of the Grand Loop of Yellowstone. For information about the hot springs found in this community, refer to Scenic Route 12, "Mammoth Hot Springs to Tower-Roosevelt," and Scenic Route 20, "Norris to Mammoth Hot Springs."

8

West Yellowstone, MT, to Madison Junction

General description: A 14-mile route along the Madison River, beginning at the most popular entrance to Yellowstone and climbing to the probable birthplace of the idea for Yellowstone National Park at Madison Junction.

Driving time: About 25 to 35 minutes, if you make no stops.

Special attractions: Madison River, Mount Haynes, Mount Jackson, Riverside Drive, Two Ribbons Trail, wildlife viewing (swans, moose, bison, elk, sandhill cranes, bald eagles, and Canada geese).

Location: West-central Yellowstone.

Drive route names & numbers: West Entrance Road, an extension of US 20.

Travel season: By automobile, about May 1 to Nov 1, depending on weather conditions. By snowmobile, Dec to Mar.

Camping: Commercial camping in West Yellowstone; Xanterra campground at Madison Junction (275 sites) available on a first-come, first-served basis.

Services: Full services in West Yellowstone; camping in the park only at Madison Junction. Cell service along most of this drive.

Nearby points of interest: Gneiss Creek Trail, Harlequin Lake Trailhead, Harlequin Lake.

For more information: National Park Service at Mammoth Hot Springs or at West Yellowstone Entrance Station.

The Route

About half of Yellowstone's visitors enter the park through the **West Entrance,** located in southwestern Montana. An ancient route used by Native Americans for thousands of years, the relatively flat valley carved by the Madison River has been the course for horses and wagons, explorers, mountain men, and eventually droves of tourists. As this is one of the first park entrances to open each spring, a board at the right-hand (southern) side of the road at the entrance lists available campgrounds and services, depending on the season. Until the park is fully open in late May, accommodations are limited. However, early spring visitors reap the advantages of few crowds and good wildlife viewing, as animals frequent this lower elevation until summer weather drives them to higher ground.

The route begins on a level two-lane forested road. Except for a few designated one-way drives, two-way traffic is the rule throughout the park. Lodgepole pines, named for their long, straight trunks, which Native Americans used to build lodges and tepees, line both sides of the road at the entrance. However, extreme fire damage to the forest soon becomes evident. Downed trees and skeletons of burned trees litter the hillsides and line the riverbeds within the first 4 miles of the

West Yellowstone, MT, to Madison Junction

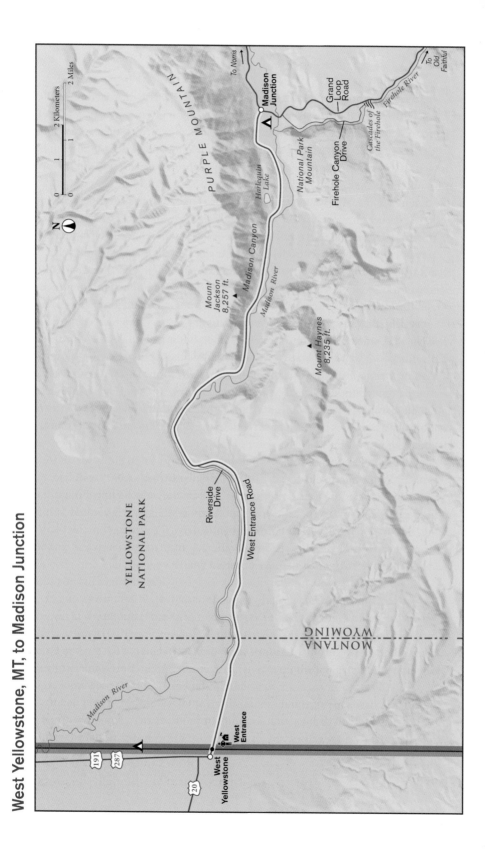

drive. These reminders of the fires of 1988 startle many first-time visitors to the park, but the natural process of burn and reforestation provides many benefits to the ecosystem. Stop and read the interpretive signs provided by the National Park Service that explain this cycle of nature, and you will view the devastation left by fire with a more objective and appreciative eye. More information about the fires is found in the Yellowstone Introduction (page 15).

You reach the Montana/Wyoming border about 1.5 miles from the park entrance. Although slivers of the park lie in Idaho and Montana, the great bulk of Yellowstone is in the northwestern corner of Wyoming. Shortly beyond the border, a scenic turnoff to the left offers a view of the **Madison River** and the meadows beyond. A second turnoff is on the left about a mile farther. Use these pullouts for photo opportunities or wildlife viewing. Many tourists are tempted to stop in the middle of the road when confronted by bison or elk; don't do it. You will block the flow of traffic, particularly at this entrance. Many roadside pullouts have been provided for you to stop to view and photograph to your eyes' content. Occasionally, animals cooperatively pose alongside these pullouts.

About 3 miles from the West Entrance, the **Two Ribbons Trail** on the north side of the road gives access by boardwalk through a burn area. This 0.75-mile interpretive walk along the Madison River demonstrates the effects of wildfire and forest reclamation. It is wheelchair accessible and sets the groundwork for understanding the fires from the park's point of view.

As you continue the drive beyond the Two Ribbons Trail, the Madison River runs to the left of the road through flat terrain with downed trees resembling a giant's game of pick-up sticks. For much of the summer, white-peaked mountains in the background offer a pleasant contrast. At about 4.5 miles, **Riverside Drive,** a spur road to the left, affords an opportunity to drive directly next to the Madison, one of the world's great fly-fishing rivers. You may want to stop and do some catch-and-release fishing, or just take in the view.

Wildlife viewing opportunities abound along this drive. Elk live in the valleys by the water; Canada geese and sandhill cranes harbor here. Rare trumpeter swans endeavor to make a comeback in the protection of the park, but they remain one of the most imperiled birds here. Watch for the occasional moose, coyotes, and smaller fur-bearing animals that sometimes scout or feed along the riverbanks. This temperate water, made up partly of the Firehole River, doesn't freeze in winter, making this a haven for many species of waterfowl. Bison frequently struggle through snow here in spring and winter, but they migrate to the higher valleys in summer. When you come across a herd of bison or elk here, remember, never crowd the animals. This is their space, and you are the intruder, not vice versa. This opportunity to observe nature nearly unintruded upon by humans—with the exception, of course, of the 3 million visitors who gawk annually—is unique.

Casting a line is always tempting along the Madison River.

That's why such an emphasis is placed on leaving the Yellowstone environment as you find it.

At 7.1 miles, the **Madison River picnic site** offers benches and primitive bathroom facilities, a good place for a brief stop. Shortly beyond the picnic area, the road crosses to the left-hand side of the river, and in summer fly fishers happily cast their lines here. **Gneiss Creek Trail** climbs to the left of the road, leading 9 miles back to US 191 as it approaches West Yellowstone from the north. This trail crosses grizzly country, so hikers should take precautions. Bear spray is a wonderful invention.

An interpretive sign in a pullout to the right tells of the attempted comeback of the rare trumpeter swans; this is a protected nesting area in an ideal habitat. In the spring of 1997, to the delight of park naturalists, five cygnets were hatched, the first in many years. However, they disappeared, harmed either by predators or poachers. Now, although 8 to 10 nest attempts are counted each year throughout the park, fewer than a dozen cygnets live to fledge. Swans often mate for life and return to the same nesting spot year after year. Park officials hope for more successful breedings and hatchings and make a special effort to protect any young that may arrive. Please immediately report to park rangers or officials anyone in undesignated or off-trail areas. Poaching is punishable by a large fine and imprisonment.

Those Who Have Gone Before

At the same pullout, an interpretive sign explains the peoples and cultures that used this route before it was a paved park road. Travelers included all three exploration parties whose work resulted in the founding of the park in 1872—the Folsom-Cook-Peterson party of 1869, three Montana citizens who wanted to confirm rumors of a strange geological wonderland to the southeast; the Washburn-Langford-Doane party of 1870, the first official government foray into the territory; and the Hayden Survey party of 1871. The Hayden Survey included artist Thomas Moran and photographer William Henry Jackson, two advocates of the national park idea whose artistic powers of persuasion helped push a reluctant government into setting aside the parks' lands as a national treasure. The route is used not only by humans; recently, it has been adopted by bison in winter. When the road is groomed for snowmobile travel, its surface provides an easy path on packed snow for bison searching for winter forage. Unfortunately, bison traveling out of the park are in danger of being permanently removed. Solutions to this controversial problem are being sought by various environmental, state, and agrarian organizations, but they often have conflicting agendas. For more information about the plight of park bison, park rangers are excellent resources.

The road begins to climb away from the river through a small mountain canyon. About 10 miles from the West Entrance, a pullout to the right offers a boardwalk and some benches, a chance to pause and stretch. This spot overlooks **Mount Haynes,** a rather flat-topped 8,235-foot-high mountain named for F. Jay Haynes, an early photographer of the park and photo concessionaire from 1883 to 1921. Haynes took most of the historical park photos that you see on postcards and in books. He accompanied early tours, including that of President Chester A. Arthur, and wrote some of the first guidebooks to Yellowstone.

Mount Haynes and its companion across the road, **Mount Jackson** (8,257 feet), were created by rhyolite lava flow. Mount Jackson was named for William Henry Jackson, photographer, artist, historian, pioneer, and explorer, who accompanied Hayden on all of his surveys of the southern Rockies.

Harlequin Lake Trail meets the road 11.8 miles from West Yellowstone. This short 0.5-mile trail leads through a burned lodgepole forest to small **Harlequin Lake,** home of various waterfowl as well as a healthy crop of mosquitoes in summer. An interpretive sign near the trailhead explains how the 1988 fires often consumed sections of the forest that were unhealthy, already dying from an infestation of beetles. The dry and brittle trees fueled the fire, making it burn hotter here than in less diseased sections of the forest. As you continue to follow the

Mount Haynes is named for an important, early park photographer.

river, watch for the Madison River elk herd that remains in this valley regardless of the season. Year-round, elk are more certain to be found here than anyplace else in the park. If you don't see them, they are lying hidden in the woods; drive through later, and they'll be grazing again.

Madison Campground is located to the right of the road just before you reach **Madison Junction,** at an elevation of 6,806 feet. The road has climbed less than 200 feet in 14 miles. The campground fills on a first-come, first-served basis. Rangers entertain and inform tourists with great fireside lectures at the amphitheater each evening. From the Madison Junction, a right turn leads to a ranger station, information center, and Yellowstone Association book store. However, no other services—lodging or gas stations—are located here. Information center exhibits include a history of the early explorations and the legend of the beginning of the national park idea, frequently called the best idea America ever had. A path behind the museum takes you a few hundred feet to the confluence of the Gibbon and Firehole Rivers, where they form the Madison. The Madison River was named by Lewis and Clark for James Madison, secretary of state to Thomas Jefferson at the time of the Lewis and Clark expedition, and is one of the three beautiful rivers that forms the great Missouri.

This route ends by 7,560-foot-high **National Park Mountain,** named, as the story goes, for an idea proposed by members of the Washburn party as they sat around the campfire and discussed the extraordinary and awesome features they had seen on their excursion. They discussed staking claims, owning, and profiting from the land—in other words, exploiting what they had seen—but one member of the party wanted to see the land preserved so that all people could enjoy its marvels. Members of the expedition ultimately worked toward that end, publicizing the idea and lobbying for legislation. Yellowstone was finally set aside, partially because lawmakers originally thought the land was useless for any practical purpose. Little did they know.

9

South Entrance to West Thumb

General description: If you approach Yellowstone from Grand Teton National Park via the Rockefeller Memorial Parkway, the South Entrance Road takes you about 22 miles through lodgepole pine forest, by marshy meadows and a high mountain lake, and climbs a steep canyon drive with views of waterfalls and rivers. The drive ends at the West Thumb of Yellowstone Lake.

Driving time: About 40 to 45 minutes, depending on traffic and photo stops.

Special attractions: Moose Falls, Crawfish Creek; Lewis Canyon, Falls, and Lake; Yellowstone Lake; a crossing of the Continental Divide; and Grant Village.

Location: South-central Yellowstone.

Drive route names & numbers: South Entrance Road, an extension of US 89.

Travel season: About May 1 through the end of Oct, depending on weather/snow conditions.

Camping: Lewis Lake (85 sites) and Grant Village (414 sites) are operated by the National Park Service and Xanterra, respectively.

Services: Flagg Ranch on the Rockefeller Memorial Parkway, Grant Village on the West Thumb of Yellowstone Lake. No cell service.

For more information: Grant Village Visitor Center, Xanterra Reservations, Yellowstone National Park Headquarters.

The Route

The drive begins at the **South Entrance** to the park, the second most popular gateway, after West Yellowstone. Visitors coming from or going to Grand Teton National Park may want to make this drive a natural extension of their tour. The elevation at the South Entrance, after a gradual climb from the Teton Valley, is 6,886 feet.

Just inside the park boundary to the right of the road, the Snake River picnic area invites a stop. Although the headwaters of the **Snake River** are in the south-central portion of the park, the river quickly leaves Yellowstone to wind its way through northwestern Wyoming, across Idaho to form much of that state's western border, and on to Washington, where it joins the Columbia River on its way to the Pacific.

The speed limit in most of Yellowstone is 45 miles an hour, so prepare for a leisurely drive through changing scenery.

About 1.5 miles into this route, you reach **Crawfish Creek.** Its temperate waters provide a hospitable habitat for the small lobsterlike creatures. Leave your car by the bridge and cross the road to the creek to look for them in the water warmed by upstream hot springs. Just beyond the bridge, **Moose Falls** cascades

South Entrance to West Thumb

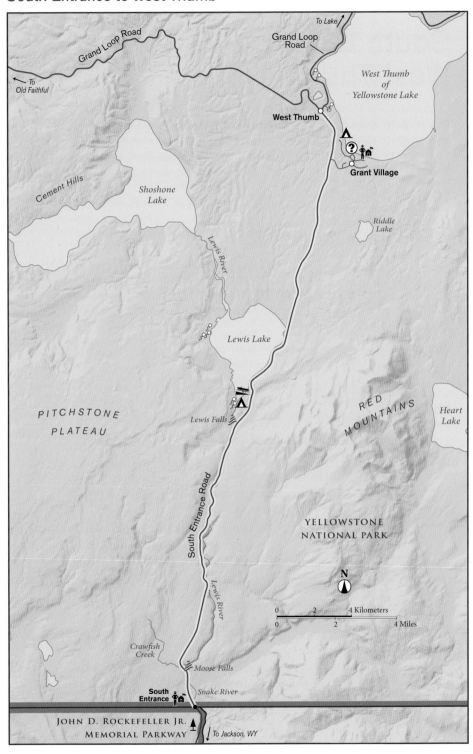

into the Lewis River. Watch closely for the turnout to the right that allows you to park and walk a short distance to view the falls or hike to the bottom. Moose Falls is one of over 200 named waterfalls in Yellowstone.

Beyond the bridge the road begins a slight climb through hills covered with lodgepole pines, tall trees aptly named, as Native Americans used their long, straight trunks as lodge or tepee poles. The **lodgepole** is the most common tree in the park, constituting about 80 percent of the forests. It commonly grows between elevations of 7,600 and 9,000 feet, ideal for Yellowstone.

Dramatic Canyon

Shortly beyond Moose Falls, **Lewis Canyon** appears to the right. Look past the forest to see where the land drops into a chasm. The road climbs to several over-looks of the canyon, beginning about 4.5 miles from the South Entrance. The canyon and river were named in 1875 for Meriwether Lewis of the Lewis and Clark expedition, who never actually saw any part of the park. Lewis River carved the 600-foot-deep, 1.5-mile-long canyon where two rhyolite lava flows poured out of the Yellowstone caldera about 500,000 years ago. The exposed canyon walls, the very edge of the caldera, reveal hardened ash over the rhyolite. While viewing this deep gorge from one of the overlooks provided along the road, you'll notice evidence of the 1988 fires pervading the mountain slopes. Two fires attacked this southern section of the park. The Huck fire burned more than 56,000 acres, spreading southeast into the Teton Wilderness, and the Snake River complex of fires—four fires that joined—burned more than 200,000 acres and occupied more than 700 firefighters. The fires of 1988, really eight large fires, altogether ignited almost 800,000 acres of Yellowstone's forests. High winds here propelled the flames across the 105-yard-wide Lewis Canyon, ignoring the meager 30-yard trenches dug by resolute firefighters. A pullout to the right at about 6.2 miles fea-tures interpretive signs entitled Fire Power. The signs offer further information about the conflagration that tore through this area.

Lewis Falls, to the left (west) as you cross **Lewis Bridge,** plunges 37 feet to the Lewis River. A parking access is inconveniently placed (for those traveling south to north) on the west side of this narrow road. The road continues to climb to the top of **Pitchstone Plateau,** named for the type of volcanic rock of which it is composed. About 8 miles from the South Entrance, this plateau is one of seven that make up the great Yellowstone Plateau. Rock here is about 60,000 years old, the youngest volcanic flow from the caldera. As the landscape flattens, marshy wetlands signal the possibility of sighting a moose, particularly in the early morn-ing or at dusk. Moose frequently linger near or just beyond the forest edge, as its shadowy darkness provides excellent cover for these rather shy animals. As the forest begins to crowd the road, notice the verdant vegetation of its floor, regenerating before your eyes.

Frequent turnouts provide access for hikers, or, as you approach Lewis Lake to the west, for campers and anglers. Several trails cross the road here, including the **Pitchstone Plateau Trail,** which leads to Phantom Fumarole, Phantom campsite, and beyond. If you hike in the backcountry, remember to strive for zero impact and to take precautions for wildlife, especially bears. **Lewis Lake,** a little more than 11 miles from the South Entrance, is the third largest body of water in the park after Yellowstone and Shoshone Lakes. Popular with sailors, canoeists, campers, and anglers, the 108-foot-deep Lewis Lake harbors brown trout and mackinaw, a challenge for those who love to cast a line. The road follows the lakeshore for about 2.5 miles. **Lewis Campground** at the southern end of the lake is a popular camping and picnicking spot. On the far side of the northern end of the lake, a fumarole spews steam into the air. Two trails lead from the road; the eastern trail heads to Heart Lake, and the western goes to Shoshone Lake.

As you journey beyond Lewis Lake, you progress again through an impressive canopy of lodgepoles. Lodgepole pines, uniquely fitted to regenerate from fire, have two kinds of pinecones. One drops its seeds annually as cones fall from the tree; the second type, called serotinous cones, are sealed by resin, which explodes under extremely high temperatures, flinging seeds that would otherwise remain encased and dormant. This scattering gives the lodgepole a head start at regeneration because seeds quickly take root in the mineral-rich soil. Lodgepoles, which need direct sun to flourish, literally race to grab the sunlight and grow. When lodgepole pines reach a certain density, the lodgepole forest thins itself out, as the slower-growing trees cannot compete for sunlight with the faster ones. As the forest thickens, the lack of sun deters other species of tree from taking root, so lodgepole forests tend to be fairly homogeneous.

About 17.4 miles from the entrance, you will make an unassuming crossing of the Continental Divide. If there were no sign here, the crossing would go unnoticed because it is so unremarkable. The land is relatively flat, although the elevation is 7,988 feet. Beyond here, the trees begin to thin and open meadow replaces forest, signaling you to watch for wildlife—particularly elk, moose, and deer.

Grant Village, the newest complex in the park, is east of the road at about 19.3 miles. A right-hand turn at the junction of Grant Village leads to all available services along the West Thumb of Yellowstone Lake. **West Thumb** was named by members of the 1870s Washburn party, who thought the lake was shaped like a hand. Services here include the full-service Lake House restaurant, a gas station, a cafeteria, a Yellowstone General Store, a photo shop, a ranger station, a boat ramp,

Lewis Lake was never seen by the man for whom it was named: Meriwether Lewis.

Duck Lake overlooks both Yellowstone Lake and the Sylvan Pass.

an amphitheater for evening firesides, a post office, and lodging and camping. Next to the campground, showers are available for a fee. The exhibits at the Grant Village Visitor Center provide the most comprehensive and interesting account of the 1988 fires to be found in the park. Take the time to see the excellent film, and you will view Yellowstone through different eyes.

Two miles from the Grant Village turnoff is West Thumb Junction, where a right turn takes you to the Lake Hotel and a left leads to Old Faithful, two spectacular points on the Grand Loop.

Northeast Entrance to Tower-Roosevelt Junction

General description: A 29-mile drive that begins in thick forest and continues through a stark canyon into a river valley formed by glaciers over the past 13,000 years. This valley offers good wildlife viewing, including the possibility (not probability) of sighting a wolf.

Driving time: 50 minutes to 1 hour.

Special attractions: Soda Butte, Buffalo Ranch/Yellowstone Institute, the Lamar Valley, good fishing in the Lamar River and Slough Creek.

Location: The northeastern to north-central segment of Yellowstone National Park.

Drive route names & numbers: Northeast Entrance Road, extension of US 212.

Travel season: The road from Cooke City to Mammoth Hot Springs is the only park road open year-round. However, during the winter, you can travel no farther than

Cooke City from Mammoth. The Beartooth Pass beyond Cooke City is closed from about mid-Aug through Memorial Day, or later, depending on snow conditions. Chief Joseph Scenic Byway is open year-round, but not plowed all the way through to Cooke City. However, those with their own snowmobiles can get there on a groomed trail beyond the terminus of the Chief Joseph.

Camping: National Park Service campgrounds at Pebble Creek (36 sites) and off the road at Slough (pronounced Sloo) Creek (29 sites); available on a first-come, first-served basis.

Services: Cooke City offers full services. Cabins, food, and a general store are found at Roosevelt Lodge.

For more information: Cooke City Chamber of Commerce, the Yellowstone Institute, Yellowstone National Park Headquarters.

The Route

The Northeast Entrance to the park, the most remote gateway to Yellowstone, sits in the Beartooth Range of the Absaroka Mountains. Although tiny **Cooke City** is the least accessible of Yellowstone's entrance communities, it bustles with tourists in the summer and snowmobilers and cross-country skiers in the winter. Nonetheless, the road that leads into the park from Cooke City is one of the least traveled.

The route begins in the thick Gallatin National Forest and winds along a narrow but newly improved two-lane road. Almost from the beginning of the drive, **Soda Butte Creek** runs along the left (south) side of the road. Charred trees on the hills are evidence of the Storm Creek Fire of 1988, which came within a mile of Cooke City.

At Warm Creek, shortly after entering the park, energetic and hungry travelers will find **Pebble Creek Trail** and a picnic area. Beyond Warm Creek the road

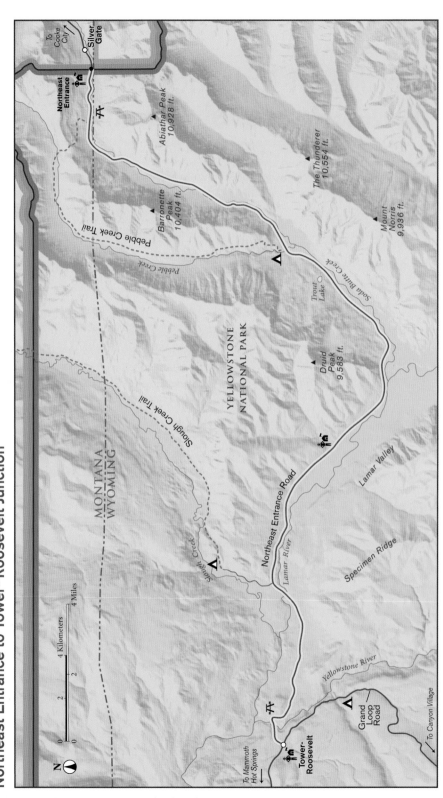

climbs slightly and has several turnouts in quick succession. Use the turnouts to take pictures, view scenery, or pull over to let drivers pass you, particularly if you are in a slower-moving camper or RV. Frequent turnouts throughout the park allow traffic to flow safely and smoothly.

At 1.9 miles from the Northeast Entrance, the road leaves Montana and enters Wyoming. In the summer tall white yarrow and bright yellow arrowleaf balsamroot grow by the side of the road. Although no sign marks the spot, the road crosses the **Forty-Fifth Parallel** about halfway between Warm Creek picnic area and the Soda Butte Creek Bridge. This is the point of latitude halfway between the equator and the North Pole. At 2.6 miles the road descends, curving to the west as it crosses Soda Butte Creek.

You continue between two of the highest peaks on the route, **Abiathar** (10,928 feet) to the left and **Barronette** (10,404 feet) to the right. In spring, Barronette's mountainside is covered in cascades of melted snow. This is one of the few places in the park where, if you're lucky, you might see mountain goats climbing on the rocky peaks of these mountains. The road from here carves its way through a deep ravine and soon enters aptly named **Ice Box Canyon.** The steep slopes block exposure to sunlight and help keep the walls of the canyon icy well into the summer. To your left (east) the peak known as the **Thunderer** (10,554 feet), named for the summer weather patterns that are drawn to it, rises south of Abiathar.

About 9 miles into the drive, a valley begins to open. Several hiking trails lead from or cross the road along this segment, heading into the surrounding backcountry. They are obviously for experienced hikers. On the left side of the road, Pebble Creek joins Soda Butte Creek on its way to the Lamar River, a tributary of the Yellowstone River. To the right **Mount Hornaday** rises above unusual limestone outcroppings in which are embedded 300-million-year-old marine animal fossils. The peak was named for naturalist William Hornaday, who campaigned mightily to save the dwindling Yellowstone bison herd from extinction.

Within 2 miles of Mount Hornaday, a broad expanse of meadow called **Round Prairie** covers the floor of the widening valley. Lava mountain walls give way to green hills bordered by forest. Soda Butte Creek widens as it approaches the butte for which it was named, about 12.5 miles from the Northeast Entrance. The first evidence of hydrothermal activity you see on this drive, **Soda Butte,** was formed by an underground hot spring; the water passed through layers of easily dissolved limestone on its way to the earth's surface. Over hundreds of years the limestone, or travertine, deposits formed the cone now left from this time-consuming process. Although now the spring is mostly inactive, a trickle of water still flows from the back side of the butte. The unmistakable, unpleasant odor of hydrogen sulfide still emanates from other nearby springs. As with all natural features in the park, be careful not to touch or disturb this fragile structure.

The Lamar Valley

Beyond Soda Butte you approach the eastern end of the **Lamar Valley,** one of the release sites of the popular but seldom seen Yellowstone wolf packs. Sightings are not as rare as they were shortly after the release of the wolves, as their increased numbers prove the health of the packs. The possibility of seeing a wolf entices visitors to park along the next 10 miles of the road with their binoculars at eye level, patiently hoping to glimpse these famous canines. People have been known to stay for days, their spotting scopes and cameras at the ready.

In March 1995, 14 captured gray wolves from Canada were released in the park, where the species had once been prolific. The repopulation program was so successful that by fall of 1997 the packs comprised more than 80 wolves, and the program, which was originally to have lasted five years, was suspended because it had already proved a success. At present 97 wolves, 11 packs, and 6 lone wolves make Yellowstone their home. They have spread beyond the Lamar Valley and can be found in most areas of the park, particularly here and in the Hayden Valley. Still, if you have seen one here, you have been given a gift.

The impact the wolves have had on the park's ecosystem is fascinating. The coyote, once "top dog" in the park, quickly realized after the reintroduction that the rules had changed, and deferred to the much more powerful wolf. Yellowstone's huge elk population has been confronted and curbed by the predator. Grizzly bears in Yellowstone, once largely vegetarian, have become more carnivorous, as they freely move in on wolf kills.

Often on summer evenings you can hear the howl of the lobo in the valley. While you watch for wolves or signs of wolves as you continue through the Lamar Valley, make note of the differences in size and conformation between the wolf and the coyote. The wolf is a much larger and stronger animal; check the newspaper you received at the entrance for illustrations and descriptions of the distinctions. People with patience, perseverance, and plain good fortune may catch a glimpse of these much maligned yet romanticized creatures.

About a mile beyond Soda Butte, Soda Butte Creek meets the Lamar River, creating a popular fishing spot. The Lamar Valley is named for Lucius Quintus Cincinnatus Lamar, secretary of the interior under President Grover Cleveland. Lamar mistakenly interpreted the congressional act establishing the national park as intending to create a wilderness preserve. Thus, almost from the beginning the park had a powerful advocate who thwarted development and exploitation of the parklands. This valley was referred to as the "secluded valley" by Osborne Russell, a trapper who kept a journal in the 1830s. Enchanted by this area, he wrote: "I

The banks of rocky Lamar River offer good picnic sites.

almost wished I could spend the remainder of my days in a place like this where happiness and contentment seemed to reign in wild romantic splendor." The valley harbors a bison herd much of the year, and frequent road pullouts allow for buffalo-gazing.

The Yellowstone Institute & Buffalo Ranch

You pass another picnic area about 15.8 miles into the route, almost opposite the Lamar Ranger Station and Buffalo Ranch. The ranch is the headquarters of the **Yellowstone Institute**, an enterprise sponsored by the Yellowstone Association, which offers active educational experiences in geology, wildlife natural history, and the environment. Two- to five-day classes with titles such as "Are Wolves Worth the Effort?"; "Scavenger Hunt: Wolf Scavenger Relationships"; "Three Dog Night"; and "Hot Rocks, Hot Waters, and Great Shakes" are offered in spring and fall. These classes often take place outdoors, rather than in a classroom, depending on the nature of the course. For information about current course selection, go to www.yellowstoneassociation.org/Institute or contact the Yellowstone Institute or the Yellowstone Association.

At the turn of the century, the **Buffalo Ranch** was established at the **Lamar Ranger Station** in an effort to save the park's dwindling wild buffalo herd from extinction. In 1902 plains bison were transported to the park to be bred and raised like cattle. Although at first they were penned at night, in 1915 they were turned loose during the summer to range freely. By 1936 the herd had grown large and healthy enough to roam unprotected throughout the year, but it still received supplemental hay feedings during the harsh winter months. This practice was stopped in 1952, when the current policy of noninterference with nature was implemented. The bison thrived under this policy until the late 1980s, when bison wandering out of the park came under fire (literally) from the state of Montana.

Beyond the Lamar Ranger Station, grass-covered buttes are backed by darkened plateaus. A broad view of the mountains opens to the northwest, as ridge after ridge unfolds in green and purple beauty. Bison wander back and forth through the valley or lie in the wallows created when they roll on their backs in the dust. Often they stay close to the river, which winds its way through the valley, emerging on and then retreating from the road. This is one of the few places in the park where the climate and elevation are conducive to aspen. Like lodgepole pine, aspen also thrive after fire. Aspen grow in stands with interconnected root systems. Throughout the life of the trees, treetops send hormonal messages to the roots that say "we're doing fine." As fire descends on aspen stands, the message changes to "help!" alerting the roots that the trees are in trouble. When that happens, the roots send up more shoots. As long as aspen are not overgrazed after a fire, they actually come back in greater abundance.

Petrifying Facts

Specimen Ridge, to the southwest, is the site of one of the world's largest preserves of petrified trees, many of which still stand upright after close to 50 million years. Geologists believe that more than 40 separate layers of petrified forests exist on the ridge, one on top of the other. Around 50 million years ago, after a large volcanic explosion, living trees were buried in volcanic ash and mud. In the rich and fertile aftermath of the volcano, another forest grew in its place, and then the volcanoes again erupted. The cycle repeated many times, leaving layer upon layer of trees turned to stone when they absorbed silica from the volcanic flow. The petrified forests cover nearly 40 square acres. Trees that no longer grow in this region, such as the magnolia, breadfruit, avocado, redwood, sycamore, walnut, oak, and maple, can be found on Specimen Ridge.

The ridge is inaccessible by automobile and very difficult to reach by foot. The best way to get within binocular distance is to take a guided hike with a ranger. Obtain information about these hikes from the visitor center at Mammoth Hot Springs or from the Tower Ranger Station.

Beyond Specimen Ridge, about 20 miles into the drive, you ascend through **Lamar Canyon.** Its yellow-orange rocks climb away from the river. The canyon road takes you through some of the oldest exposed rock in the park. It dates to the Precambrian era, more than 600 million years ago. At just over 22 miles, a road by the banks of cutthroat trout-filled Slough Creek leads to a favorite campground for anglers. To the right beyond Slough Creek are meadows of mixed grasses and sagebrush, the grass growing in wetter recesses, or kettles, left thousands of years ago by retreating glaciers. The sagebrush grows on the higher land. This valley was formed by glaciers 13,000 years ago during the last ice age; reminders of their retreat are scattered about. Look for large, displaced boulders, known as erratics, which look as if they were tossed by a catapult. They were carried from their origin by glaciers and deposited as the ice melted. Erratics often harbor a single tree that took root in their shelter and thrived. The kettles, or marshy ponds, here are the last lingering remnants of the ice age; as the land becomes increasingly drier, the marshes fill in with silt and gravel carried by the water, and marsh turns to meadow. A marker at about 25.5 miles tells eloquently of the formation of this fascinating land.

At 26.7 miles another picnic spot, called the Yellowstone, offers a stopping point to the left of the road. Beyond, a steel bridge over the Yellowstone River leads to the **Tower-Roosevelt** area, where cabins and horses can be rented, a

Hitch a ride on a stagecoach at Roosevelt Lodge Stables.

lodge offers food and warmth, and a Yellowstone Store sells provisions for the next portion of your trip. The elevation at the junction with the **Grand Loop** is a low 6,278 feet. Go straight across the junction to the Roosevelt Lodge to stretch and explore a little before tackling the Grand Loop. While Teddy Roosevelt never saw the small lodge that carries his name, he did camp near here when he visited in 1903.

The rustic cabins at **Roosevelt Lodge** are a great place to stay for those who love stream fishing, wildlife gazing, horseback riding, and trail hiking into the northeastern section of Yellowstone. Stagecoach rides can be arranged at the lodge. Tower Fall is about 2.5 miles to the south, and the Grand Canyon of the Yellowstone is 16.5 miles beyond the falls. The Tower Ranger Station is less than 0.25 mile to the north, and Mammoth Hot Springs is 18 miles west of the junction.

11

East Entrance to Fishing Bridge

General description: Beautiful 26-mile drive, climbing from the East Entrance through a high mountain pass, past two small lakes, and down to the rocky shoreline of Yellowstone Lake, where the first geothermal features are seen from this approach to the Grand Loop. This region offers good waterfowl viewing as you drive on toward the Fishing Bridge on the north shore of the lake.

Driving time: 45 to 55 minutes.

Special attractions: Sylvan Pass, tiny Eleanor and Sylvan Lakes, shoreline of Yellowstone Lake, Steamboat Point, Indian Pond, Fishing Bridge, and Fishing Bridge Museum.

Location: East-central Yellowstone.

Drive route names & numbers: East Entrance Road, extension of US 20.

Travel season: Approximately the end of Apr to the end of Oct, dependent, as always, on weather conditions.

Camping: The only camping along this short route is found at Fishing Bridge; hook-ups are available for RVs. Operated by Xanterra on a first-come, first-served basis (345 sites).

Nearby points of interest: Lake Butte Overlook, Pelican Valley.

Services: Full-service gas station at Fishing Bridge, as well as a Yellowstone General Store with an ice-cream bar. No cell service.

For more information: Yellowstone National Park Headquarters.

The Route

Begin at the **East Entrance,** at the low point of a canyon with an elevation of just under 7,000 feet. The middle creek of the Shoshone River travels along the right side of the road. Alpine scenery dominates the beginning of the drive as you climb to the summit of **Sylvan Pass,** named undoubtedly for the deep green forest through which it traveled before lightning fires in 2001 and 2003 left their mark.

About a mile into the park, there is an early ranger station that was built in 1904 as a soldiers' station when the US Army was in charge of the park. Pullouts line this portion of the drive, since faster vehicles may need to pass slower traffic on the climb to the summit. The road hugs the slopes of the **Absaroka Ridge,** winding as it makes its ascent. This is a lovely stretch of road, with rocky ledges and wildflower-covered hills to the right and a deep gorge dropping to the left. Wildflowers flourish on both rock and soil; Indian paintbrush, thimbleberry, mountain bluebells, and wild hollyhocks grow profusely in the alpine pass during the short summer months. Roadside waterfalls caused by springtime snowmelt

East Entrance to Fishing Bridge

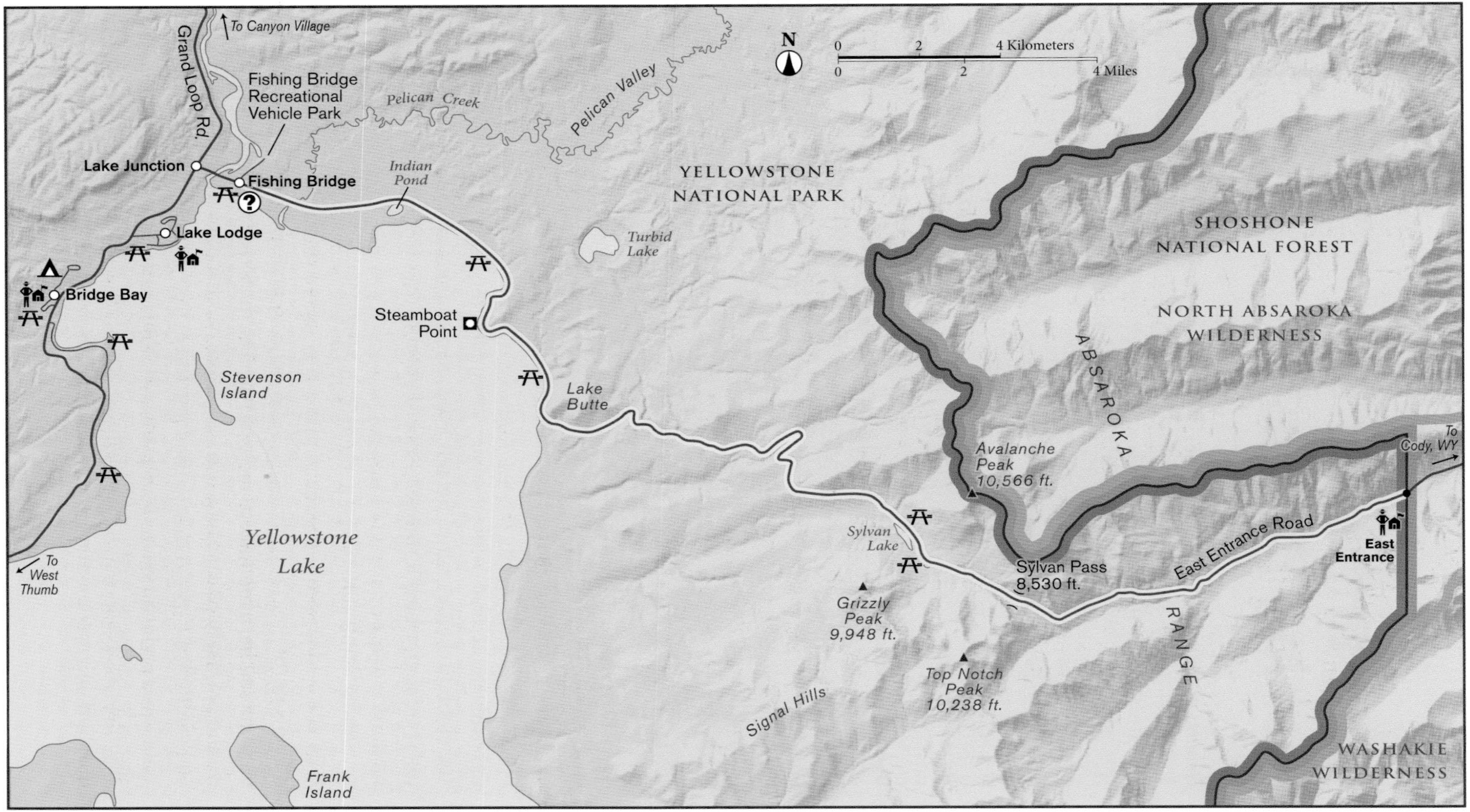

add a startling beauty to these mountain ridges, although snow often stays on the peaks well into August, if not throughout the year. You are traveling on the only park road that crosses the ancient Absaroka Range. A series of volcanoes much older than the Yellowstone Plateau formed the range by depositing lava upon lava.

Hoyt Peak rises to the right (north) side of the road 3 miles inside the park. It was named in 1881 by P.W. Norris, the second park superintendent after John W. Hoyt—doctor, lawyer, educator, and first territorial governor of Wyoming. Actually, Hoyt may in fact have named the peak for himself on an excursion to the park with Norris, while trying to scout an easy route by which Wyoming residents could visit the park.

About 7 miles into the drive, you reach the top of Sylvan Pass, elevation 8,530 feet. Near the top is an avalanche cannon, which is fired in winter to prevent avalanches in the backcountry. The explosion triggers small avalanches, preventing snow buildup that could result in larger, more dangerous snowslides.

About 7.5 miles into the drive, tiny **Eleanor Lake** appears to the left. The lake was named for the 5-month-old daughter of Hiram Chittenden, the road engineer who oversaw the construction of park roads, including this East Entrance Road in 1902. Both Eleanor Lake and Sylvan Lake 2 miles to the west—peaceful ponds, actually—lie at about 8,000 feet elevation. Picnic facilities are available at both spots. Beyond Sylvan Lake, look toward the north to see **Avalanche Peak,** which surges to 10,566 feet in elevation, and is mirrored by **Top Notch Peak** to the south, rising to 10,238 feet.

The road climbs briefly and then descends the western side of the pass. The road, which was sorely in need of repair, has newly added safety shoulders as well as a nice firm foundation. Many of the roads through the park had been built over old carriage roads, and have been improved with the help of your tax dollars. We all thank you.

About 12 miles into the drive, a 90-degree curve slows drivers from 40 to 25 miles an hour. Frequent S-curves and hairpin and horseshoe turns punctuate the remainder of the drive to Yellowstone Lake.

Much of this ridge is still ash-colored, and the odor of sulfur permeates an area where an unseen thermal feature makes its presence known. As you descend the pass to the west, overlooks on the left side of the road afford opportunities to view the southern mountains and catch a glimpse of Yellowstone Lake. At 16.2 miles, **Lake Butte Overlook,** 600 feet above the lake, offers the best panoramic view to the southwest. Take the road to the right, which curves through pine and spruce to a parking lot. From there, a short walk leads to an overlook that, on a clear day, affords a view of the Tetons, about 60 miles to the southwest.

Yellowstone Lake

After returning to the main road, continue downhill for less than a mile to the edge of **Yellowstone Lake.** The road meets the lake approximately at the eastern rim of the great Yellowstone caldera. This rim was formed about 600,000 years ago during the third cycle of immense volcanic eruptions, which produced most of the rhyolite flows throughout the park.

As you drive around the northern shore of Yellowstone Lake, note the steam rising in the distance from **Steamboat Point.** Two fumaroles, Steamboat and Locomotive, vent from this spot on the southeastern edge of Mary Bay. These are the first thermal features you encounter coming from the East Entrance. A tiny rock "island" juts from the water a few hundred yards offshore; Pelican Point is so named because of the natural roost it forms, and the pelicans happily own it. At 18.1 miles you cross **Sedge Creek,** a marshy bog that empties into the lake. Sedge is a family of grassy plants that grow in wetlands and river bottoms, inviting moose and aquatic birds to feast on either them or the bog's inhabitants. At 18.7 miles another view of Pelican Point appears.

From this shore you can see **West Thumb Geyser Basin** 18 miles across the lake to the southwest. The road plays tag with the shoreline as it skirts **Mary Bay.** In 1871, as a member of the Hayden expedition, artist Henry Wood Elliot named the bay for his betrothed, Mary Force. However, upon returning home from Yellowstone, the lout married another. The name persisted and is now official. Mary Bay fills a crater formed when the glacial ice that dammed the waters suddenly drained, allowing extremely hot water underground to turn immediately to steam, causing an explosion that created the crater and bay. A portion of the crater's rim is seen in the semicircle of bluffs to the north.

The rocky northern shore around this portion of Yellowstone Lake is composed of glacial till; the lake formed as water filled the depression left by the blast. One of the world's largest natural freshwater lakes, Yellowstone Lake lies at 7,733 feet. It is the largest lake in the US found at an altitude of over 7,000 feet. The lake covers 137 square miles, is 14 miles wide by 20 miles long, and has 110 miles of shoreline. Its average depth of 140 feet and average temperature of 41 degrees Fahrenheit make swimming dangerous in this water, not only because of the cold but also because quick weather changes can cause turbulent, perilous conditions. Survival time in water this cold is 20 to 30 minutes, at best.

On the other hand, fish, including an indigenous population of cutthroat trout, flourish in the lake. Unfortunately, lake trout, a natural predator of the cutthroat, have also found their way into the lake, threatening the native population of fish. Current park policy allows unlimited fishing for lake trout, which must be kept and killed rather than released. This is just one of the ways park officials are

Peaceful evenings at Mary Bay can change in an instant when a summer storm arises.

trying to rid the water of lake trout before the cutthroat population is decimated to the point of endangerment. How cutthroat, typically a Pacific Ocean waterway fish, came to live in Yellowstone Lake remains a mystery. According to the most current theory, the fish probably crossed the Continental Divide at Two Ocean Pass. The cutthroat is easily identified by the red marking beneath its throat for which it is named.

At the western end of Mary Bay, **Indian Pond** appears to the left of the road. It was created in much the way Mary Bay was—by hydrothermal explosion. Hot springs are still active on the bottom of the pond. In 1880, evidence that this spot was a Native American summer campground was found, including shelter remnants and discarded stone implements. The campground would have been ideally located; its proximity to Pelican Valley would have provided hunting and fishing grounds and convenient quarries for weapon points and other tools.

Beyond Indian Pond, marshy meadows line both sides of the road as it moves away from the shoreline. Cross braided Pelican Creek as it exits Pelican Valley, a rich wildlife habitat even today. Watch for the large white waterbirds that stalk this lucrative fishing spot, or rare trumpeter swans that sometimes nest on nearby waters. Pelican Valley also provides habitat for grizzly bears and is one of the most likely spots in the park to spot the giant bears.

The Fishing Bridge

As you near the Fishing Bridge area, you pass over the **Howard Eaton Trail,** one of the oldest trails in the park. Although it is no longer intact, the trail once nearly followed the Grand Loop, leading foot travelers to many points of interest in Yellowstone. With a little detective work and determination, you can still follow the nearly 150-mile path.

Before you reach the actual Fishing Bridge, you encounter a visitor center to the left, with an exhibition of area wildlife, a Yellowstone General Store, an RV park, and one of the two service stations in the park that can make some major car repairs.

The **Fishing Bridge** itself is built over the northern outlet from the lake, the source of the Yellowstone River. Fishing was allowed from the bridge until 1973, when it was closed to provide a safe spawning ground for the park's population of cutthroat trout. Today tourists can park by the bridge and walk out onto it to view the large fish in crystalline water. After this small trek, continue by car to the Fishing Bridge junction, where a left turn will take you to the Lake Hotel and beyond to West Thumb. A right turn leads toward the Grand Canyon of the Yellowstone.

12

Mammoth Hot Springs to Tower-Roosevelt

General description: About an 18-mile drive along a high road between Lava Creek Canyon and Blacktail Deer Plateau. Scenic overviews are beautiful, though not dramatic.

Driving time: 35 to 40 minutes.

Special attractions: The terraces at Mammoth Hot Springs, Mammoth elk herd, Fort Yellowstone, Albright Visitor Center and Museum, Undine Falls, Phantom Lake, Floating Island Lake, and Roosevelt Lodge.

Location: North-central Yellowstone.

Drive route names & numbers: Grand Loop Road from Mammoth to Tower.

Travel season: This section of the road is open year-round, all the way to Cooke City.

Camping: Mammoth Hot Springs Campground (85 sites)—the only park campground that remains open all year—and Tower Fall (32 sites), National Park Service on a first-come, first-served basis.

Services: All services at Mammoth, including camping. A museum is located at the Albright Visitor Center in Mammoth. Full services also at Tower-Roosevelt, including cabins and a Yellowstone General Store. Occasional cell service.

Nearby points of interest: Wraith Falls, Blacktail Deer Plateau, the only view in the park of a petrified tree that is accessible by automobile.

For more information: Albright Visitor Center, Yellowstone National Park Headquarters, Roosevelt Lodge, Xanterra.

The Route

As you enter **Mammoth Hot Springs,** a village occupied mostly by park employees, the first thing you are likely to notice are the large elk placidly moving about the area. These grand animals, part of the largest elk herd in the park (at least 5,000 animals), live in the temperate safety of this admiring community.

Other surprises await explorers of Mammoth Hot Springs (6,239 feet). The unique Mammoth Hot Springs Terraces as well as a particularly good small museum at the Albright Visitor Center are worth investigating. Many services are located in Mammoth, including a post office, an outpatient clinic, gift shops, stores, and a chapel, as well as Yellowstone National Park administrative headquarters. Housing for many park employees is also located here. In winter the area becomes a haven for those who love cross-country skiing and snowshoeing.

If you're interested in architecture or the ambience of days gone by, begin with a visit to the **Mammoth Hotel,** rebuilt in 1930, the third hotel at this site. The first, erected in 1871, was reportedly beyond rustic, measuring 25 feet by 35

Mammoth Hot Springs to Tower-Roosevelt

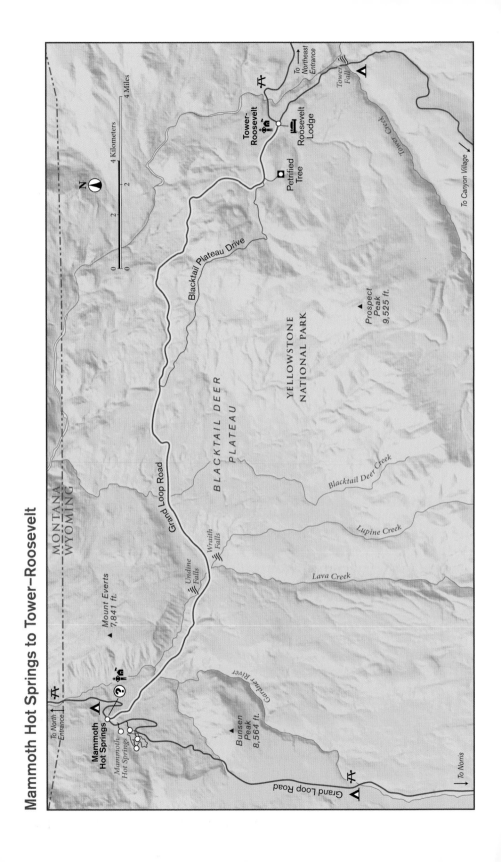

feet, and patrons had to provide their own blankets. According to one Reverend Stanley, the food served was "remarkable more for its quantity than its quality or variety." The hotel standing today, a beautiful old structure with wooden floors and high ceilings, rents simple rooms, many with shower and bathroom facilities down the hall. A walk through the large open lobby leads to the "map room." It is worth stopping to see the magnificent wall-size (10 feet by 17 feet) inlaid wood map of the United States, designed by Robert Reamer, architect of the Old Faithful Inn. Made with 15 luminous hardwoods and composed of 2,544 pieces, this work of beautiful craftsmanship is a true treasure.

From the upstairs windows you can view elk lying in the meager shade of scrappy trees, surrounded by vapor rising from several cordoned-off fumaroles in front of the hotel. Cabins nestle behind the hotel in the foothills, backed in spring by snow-covered peaks of the Gallatin Range. From the cabins, as from much of town, you see steam rising from nearby Mammoth Hot Springs.

To the east of the hotel, a row of stone buildings dating to the early part of the 20th century forms the front of old **Fort Yellowstone.** The fort housed a company of cavalry during part of its tour of duty as park protectorate from 1886 until 1916, when the National Park Service took over administration of the park from the US Army. Park administration buildings, the museum, and the **Albright Visitor Center** are all located in this front row of fort buildings. Behind the stone buildings, the wooden buildings of the fort, built in the 1890s, are still used as housing for park employees. A self-guided walking tour leads through the buildings and grounds of the old fort. A trail guide is available for 50 cents at the Albright Visitor Center, where information on other area hiking trails is also available. As with all trail guides, you may either make the 50 cent donation or use the guide and return it when you've finished the tour. The museum, located in the visitor center, features exhibits about early expeditions to the park, and Native American cultures that have lived or passed through here. Two films, *The Challenge of Yellowstone* and *Yellowstone Today,* are shown on a regular schedule, and an excellent Yellowstone Association Bookstore offers maps, posters, and informative books about all aspects of the environment and history of the national park.

The Hot Springs

From the visitor center proceed 0.25 mile south to the **Mammoth Hot Springs Terraces,** the showpiece of the village. Jim Bridger described the terraces in a letter to a friend as "Great Springs, so hot that meat is readily cooked in them, and as they descend on the successive terraces, they afford at length delightful baths." No longer used as baths, medicinal or otherwise, the hot springs, like all hydrothermal features of the park, are heated by magma, rock so hot it is in a liquid state. The temperature of hot springs is not as high as that of geysers, which prevents them from erupting but does allow them to bubble to the surface. Mammoth's terraces are formed of travertine, limestone that dissolves in the underground water and then solidifies as the water cools on the earth's surface.

The springs at Mammoth are estimated to discharge about 500 gallons of water per minute. About two tons of travertine a day are deposited on the terraces, accumulating in some places at the rate of about 8 inches a year. The travertine buildup, estimated in places to be more than 200 feet thick, extends from the springs clear to the Gardner River beyond the junction that leads to Tower-Roosevelt. Because the fissures, or "underground plumbing," through which the springs reach the earth's surface become clogged with these deposits, the springs constantly change location, emerging wherever they can break through. As cracks in the surface clog or open up, the flow of water moves across the hillside. As a result, these white terraces constantly change shape. Active springs can be identified by their color—red, yellow, orange, brown, or green—which is caused by bacteria and algae growing in the various temperatures of water. The travertine is white as it is deposited but quickly weathers to a smoky gray. Although the locations of the springs change, the water output is nearly constant. The terraces in winter can be enchanting, as the steamy water often freezes as it encounters the extremely cold air, building strange and wonderful ice sculptures on top of the travertine formations.

Before you walk the paths or boardwalks that lead around the terraces, pick up an interpretive guide at the stands located near Liberty Cap, the large formation of travertine at the lowest level of the hot springs. You may use the guide and return it when you are finished with your tour, or pay 50 cents to keep it. Mammoth Hot Springs has both upper and lower terraces and two corresponding parking lots, enabling visitors to approach these magnificent springs from several heights and angles. The boardwalk climb around **Minerva,** the largest terrace, can take 40 minutes to an hour to complete. To the south of the terraces, Mammoth Terrace Drive (described in Scenic Route 20, "Norris to Mammoth Hot Springs") is a one-way, 1.6-mile drive surrounded by springs and travertine formations. If your tour of Yellowstone will not return you to Mammoth from Norris, drive south beyond the Upper Terraces to enjoy this short, uniquely beautiful drive.

After exploring the hot springs, return to the north 0.1 mile to the Mammoth-Tower junction and turn east toward Tower-Roosevelt. As you leave Mammoth, the **Yellowstone National Park Chapel,** built in 1913, is on the left. Worship services are held for park personnel and visitors throughout the year.

The colors of the hot springs here at Minerva Terrace in Mammoth indicate hydrothermal activity.

On to Tower-Roosevelt

This drive begins with a 1.5-mile descent to the **Gardner High Bridge,** where it crosses the **Gardner River.** To the left watch for white buttes, sagebrush, broken ground, and possibly elk or pronghorn antelope. This ravine, part of the **Gardner Canyon,** which extends to the northern exit of the park near the town of **Gardiner,** contains the lowest elevations and the driest climate in the park; as such, it is the only place in the park where you may encounter rattlesnakes. Gardner River and Canyon were named for Johnson Gardner, a tough mountain man and fur trapper of the 1830s known for his skirmishes with Indians and unscrupulous ways.

Beyond the bridge, **Lava Creek** joins the Gardner River from Lava Creek Canyon to the south. The road climbs the north end of the Washburn Range through a forest of Douglas fir and occasional stands of aspen. A good portion of this road to Tower-Roosevelt follows the old **Bannock Indian Trail,** used by the Idaho tribe from about the late 1830s as they traveled east every summer in search of bison, which in their homeland had been hunted to extinction.

About 4 miles into your drive, Lava Creek tumbles over **Undine Falls** to the north. An overlook on the left side of the road allows you to view this lovely

two-tiered gossamer cascade. The upper falls is 60 feet high and the lower falls 50 feet high. The falls were named for mythological water nymphs that lived around waterfalls and could become human if they married a human. The water cascades over basalt, the hard volcanic rock that gives Lava Creek its name. Beyond the falls, the road continues through a mixed spruce-fir forest along a high plateau covered in meadows. Several hiking trails radiate from this segment of the road, and it is a good place for chance encounters with either a coyote or a bear.

Half a mile beyond Undine Falls you will find another falls and another chance to stop. **Wraith Falls** on Lupine Creek is about 0.5 mile from the Lava Creek picnic area, a nice spot by a gurgling creek. A short, easy hike leads through sagebrush and forest to the bottom of the 100-foot-high falls. The picnic area has wheelchair-accessible restroom facilities.

As you continue the drive, you pass several overlooks that afford views of Lava Creek Canyon to the north and the Gallatin Mountains beyond. The nearby landscape of grassy meadows, sage, and charred trees is typical of much of the plateau scenery of the park. Sagebrush, plentiful in Yellowstone with about a dozen species represented, can be identified by its green-gray color and low scrubby growth. A single plant can live for up to 200 years. The forest that grows along this portion of the drive is one of the few in the park dominated by Douglas-fir rather than lodgepole pine.

After about 5.5 miles, boggy meadow terrain appears on the left. This is the ill-named **Blacktail Lake,** really more of a bog than even a pond. Glacial depressions that fill with snowmelt in spring but disappear in the summer heat, the ponds attract waterfowl and the occasional beaver. Scattered erratics (large boulders carried and deposited by retreating ice) and the sweeping slopes of the surrounding hills are clues that this terrain was at least partially formed by a glacier. Park personnel call this area **Shaky Lakes,** because if you walk too close to the ponds you sink into muck.

In another mile willow trees to the right guard **Blacktail Deer Creek.** Between 7.5 and 8 miles the view to the west of the Gallatins is noteworthy for those driving from Tower toward Mammoth. As you proceed east, the road curves around and ascends to high **Blacktail Deer Plateau,** offering views of the valley, rolling meadows, and mountains. A parking area on the left side of the road gives you the opportunity to stop and take in the view.

At about 8 miles you reach the trailhead for an interpretive walk, Features of the Northern Range. The road beyond this point ascends again, and glacial erratics litter the landscape.

Undine Falls

The **Blacktail Plateau Drive** turnoff, to the south at 9.5 miles, leads to an alternate 7-mile, 30-minute to 1-hour route that climbs steadily but not steeply until it rejoins the Mammoth Tower Road less than 2 miles from Tower-Roosevelt Junction. The road is open June to September but closes after rain or snowstorms, and no RVs or trailers are allowed. This is a one-way drive for those with time to spare and a rugged vehicle that has no loose parts. The very rough gravel road parallels the Grand Loop, taking the approximate route of the old Bannock Indian Trail. From the top of the sage-, sedge-, and aspen-covered plateau, profuse with wildflowers in summer, you have a panoramic view of the Gallatin Range. The first time I took this route I thought "There's nothing up here." That is exactly the point, and it has become one of my favorite side trips. The expanse of the view, the wildflowers, and the solitude are all extraordinary. Bears, coyotes, and deer love it here—and if you're very quiet and very lucky, keep your eyes open. You begin descending about 4.2 miles into this drive, and a view of the pattern created by the fires is remarkable from this vantage point. This can be a good drive for people with disabilities, as it is one of the few roads that penetrate the backcountry. As the route rejoins the Mammoth Tower Road, a right turn takes you the last 2 miles to Tower-Roosevelt.

For those remaining on the Mammoth Tower Road, **Phantom Lake,** another glacial depression, can sometimes be seen on the right at about 10.5 miles. It is named for the spring snowmelt that disappears by August; in late summer you can still see its high-water line on the far hillside. Beyond 12.5 miles, you reach the top of the hill with a great overlook of the **Black Canyon of the Yellowstone,** carved by the Yellowstone River. Alpine fir, Douglas fir, lodgepole, and aspen grow on the northern face of the hill by the road. The cone-shaped peak to the north is **Hellroaring Mountain** (8,363 feet), named for Hellroaring Creek, so-called by an early prospector who described the creek ahead as a "real hellroarer." Hellroaring Creek is just inside the park's northern boundary. Several overlooks give you great photo opportunities.

As you wind around downward, you will glimpse occasional views of the high Absaroka Range in front of you to the east. Fireweed, a wildflower that quickly takes root in ash-rich soil following a fire, is still plentiful along these hills. **Floating Island Lake,** to the right at about 15 miles, has an island of floating vegetable matter—moss, bacteria, other plant life, and debris. When I passed, not one, but two floating islands were working their way across the pond; sometimes there are none. As a sign will tell you, this site attracts nesting waterfowl, and human presence around the island disturbs the birds. As in the rest of the park, this delicate spot depends on a careful ecological balance.

For extra wilderness, take the Blacktail Plateau Drive.

Begin a gradual descent through pines and firs, typical western rounded-mountain terrain. Cross tiny Elk Creek, a mere trickle of snowmelt from the Blacktail Deer Plateau in August. This part of the drive offers a good view of the Slough and Lamar Valleys to the east and the glacial hills and the Absaroka Range beyond.

One last marvel is found on this drive. At about 16.5 miles a turnoff on the right takes you to the only **petrified tree** you can see from the road. Do not attempt this narrow side road with a trailer, as there is no turn-around room at the other end. The petrified tree is a relic of a volcanic eruption about 50 million years ago. A giant redwood grew in the subtropical climate of the time, genetically identical to trees today in California, but now preserved as stone. There used to be three petrified trees at this site, but they were peeled away by early souvenir hunters, resulting in the fencing of this remaining trunk. The trees became petrified when an enormous volcanic eruption triggered landslides that buried entire forests in mud, ash, and sand. Before the trees could decompose, silica in the volcanic flow permeated the cells of the wood, turning the trees to stone and preserving them. Although many other petrified trees stand in the park, this one is easiest to access and offers the closest view.

At 16.8 miles a roadside interpretive sign points out a place where the North Fork fire, which began outside the park near West Yellowstone, passed through here in 1988. It burned so hot that it sterilized the soil, killing roots and seeds. Forest regeneration here is behind that of other places in the Park.

Proceed to **Tower-Roosevelt** (elevation 6,278 feet), where **Roosevelt Lodge,** to the right of the road, offers a place to stop, refuel, shop, stretch your legs, take a horseback or stagecoach ride, or arrange to participate in an old-fashioned western cookout. The Roosevelt area is a favorite headquarters for family vacations in the park, as it is low-key and more peaceful and secluded than the area surrounding Old Faithful. The turnoff to Roosevelt Lodge isn't obvious until you are practically there. Although Teddy Roosevelt never stayed at the lodge that bears his name, he camped near here during his visit to the park in 1903. So enthusiastic was he about Yellowstone that he became a lifelong advocate of its preservation. The lodge, built in 1920, is unobtrusive in both location and architecture, a situation the National Park Service has tried to maintain from the beginning. Visitors staying in the surrounding cabins, built in 1916, can choose between accommodations with woodburning stoves but no private bathing facilities, or cabins with propane heaters and private showers.

13

Tower-Roosevelt to Canyon Village

General description: A 19-mile drive through an alpine forest, past dramatic falls, to the top of the highest pass in the park. You descend through meadow and forest to the falls of the Grand Canyon of the Yellowstone. Along this road and in the Canyon Village area are three of the most astounding waterfalls on the Grand Loop tour.

Driving time: Close to 1 hour, if you make no stops.

Special attractions: Calcite Springs, Rainy Lake, Tower Fall, Mount Washburn, Dunraven Pass, Caldera Overlook.

Location: North-central Yellowstone.

Drive route names & numbers: Grand Loop Road from Tower to Canyon.

Travel season: From mid- to late May through mid-Oct.

Camping: Tower Fall, mid-May to late Sept, National Park Service, first-come, first-served (32 sites); and Canyon, from early June to early Sept, run by Xanterra, first-come, first-served (280 sites).

Services: Full services at both Roosevelt Lodge and Canyon Village. Cell service is sporadic.

Nearby points of interest: The Chittenden Road and a chance to sight bighorn sheep on a hike across Mount Washburn.

For more information: Xanterra Reservations, Canyon Visitor Center, Yellowstone National Park Headquarters.

The Route

Head south from the Tower-Roosevelt junction toward the **Grand Canyon of the Yellowstone,** one of the major attractions of the park. If you have visited the Roosevelt Lodge and cabin area, make a right turn to rejoin the Grand Loop. A horse corral on the right offers trail and stagecoach rides, and an opportunity to linger and pretend the Old West lives on. As you begin your drive you pass little Rainy Lake to the left, so named for the hot springs that bubble up under the surface of the water, giving the appearance of rain falling on the pond. Theodore Roosevelt camped here during his 1903 visit to the park. Almost immediately the road begins to climb toward the first spectacle on the drive—**Calcite Springs.** Because this route winds and climbs to the highest points in the park accessible by road, it is not recommended for RVs.

The Calcite Springs stop at 1.5 miles overlooks the northern end of the Grand Canyon of the Yellowstone. Park on the left side of the road and climb a few steps up a small hill for a sensational view of the **Narrows,** the narrowest portion of the canyon. From here it is a 500-foot plunge to the canyon floor. Whitish rock spires composed of basalt rim the top of the canyon like open-air stalactites standing

Tower–Roosevelt to Canyon Village

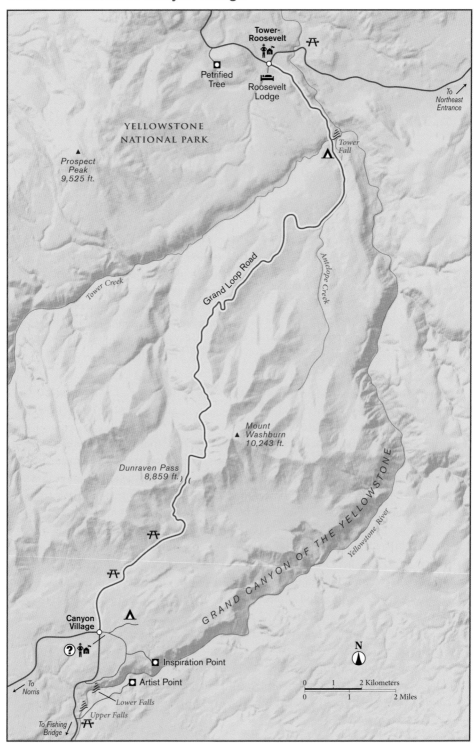

Tower-Roosevelt

Petrified Tree

Roosevelt Lodge

To Northeast Entrance

YELLOWSTONE NATIONAL PARK

Prospect Peak 9,525 ft.

Tower Fall

Tower Creek

Antelope Creek

Grand Loop Road

Mount Washburn 10,243 ft.

Dunraven Pass 8,859 ft.

GRAND CANYON OF THE YELLOWSTONE

Yellowstone River

Canyon Village

To Norris

Inspiration Point

Artist Point

Lower Falls

Upper Falls

To Fishing Bridge

N

| 0 | 1 | 2 Kilometers |
| 0 | 1 | 2 Miles |

sentry over the deep gorge. From this beautiful viewpoint a wooden boardwalk continues downward to another overlook and then loops back to the road. The odor of sulfur wafts upward, and steam rises from geothermal springs far below.

Continuing southward on the road, you can see 45-foot columns of basalt that form the **Overhanging Cliff,** created as lava cooled and cracked about 2 million years ago. Several turnouts on the left (east) side of the road allow you to view these intricate cliffs.

Tower Fall

Cross a small ravine via a stone abutment, Tower Creek Bridge, as you approach the turnoff to **Tower Fall** (6,650 feet). The dark gray rocky draw below the bridge is called **Devil's Den.** It was named by Dr. Ferdinand V. Hayden, geologist and leader of the Hayden Survey parties that first explored Yellowstone for the federal government, for the fateful trap he remembered from the Battle of Gettysburg. Beyond Devil's Den, Tower Creek flows over the falls.

Turn off to the waterfall at 2.5 miles. A large **Yellowstone General Store** here sells souvenirs and ice cream, just the thing for a hot summer day. Begin your sightseeing by taking the short flight of steps to the high overlook of the falls, which tumbles 132 feet through a narrow shaft. A half-mile walk to the foot of the cataract switches back and forth down a fairly steep path leading to the river and a view of the pinnacles that give the Tower area its name. This path used to lead to the base of the falls, but erosion has made it too dangerous to get a view from the bottom. In 1870 Lieutenant Gustavus Doane of the Washburn expedition wrote of Tower Fall, "nothing can be more chastely beautiful than this lovely cascade, hidden away in the dim light of overshadowing rocks and woods, its very voice hushed to a low murmur. . . ." Although many early descriptions of Yellowstone's marvels indicate that some features have quieted or changed over the years, Doane's words still apply to this enchanting attraction.

As you leave the Tower Fall area (after grabbing that ice cream), you begin a long, gradual, and winding climb beside stony **Antelope Creek,** the creek that drains Mount Washburn. Drive through grassy, sparsely forested land, past several burned hillsides. Wildflowers proliferate in the wake of fire, in the rich ash- and mineral-laden earth left in the aftermath. The new growth includes a profusion of yarrow, sulfur buckwheat, fireweed, and wild aster.

For the next mile or so, the first of several overlooks to the left (east) face vast mountain meadows. As you begin the climb to Dunraven Pass, you pass through grassy, rolling, glacier-carved hills scattered with erratics. This innocuous-looking country is really prime grizzly bear habitat. The bears are attracted by the nuts of the slow-growing whitebark pines, which cover the hills. Grizzlies, often thought

of as carnivores, are actually omnivores. They consume huge amounts of pine nuts, berries, and other fruits of the forest, as well as small animals the meadows harbor. Both a predator and scavenger, the grizzly ranges widely and needs hundreds of square miles to sustain it. People park at the road's turnoffs and arm themselves with binoculars to watch for the bears, but they are seldom seen. The aspen and pine forest at the meadows' edges provides them with both camouflage and shelter. During winter many hibernate here on the north slope of Mount Washburn.

The road continues to climb and wind beyond what is called the **Mae West Curve,** so-named by early travelers for the voluptuous actress. A side road that juts off to the left at about 8.5 miles is the **Chittenden Road,** named for Hiram M. Chittenden of the US Army Corps of Engineers, who directed road construction in Yellowstone at the turn of the 20th century. Chittenden also directed the construction of the Roosevelt Arch at the North Entrance and was one of the first park historians.

A Good Hike

The Chittenden Road climbs a mile to a parking area from which hikers can begin a 6-mile crossing of Mount Washburn, the most popular hike in the park. A parking area at the other end of the trail is available for those who wish to hike one way. One of the attractions of this hike is the bighorn sheep that migrate to this high summer range. They often feed close to the trail, surprising and delighting hikers. Be sure to take your cameras and binoculars along, and wear layered clothing, as the weather at the summit is windier and cooler than at either trailhead. Glacial erratics, such as the large granite boulders at the summit, were carried here from the Absaroka Range to the east. The view from the top of Mount Washburn encompasses the whole eastern side of the park, sometimes including the geyser basins to the west and the Tetons to the south.

Whether you begin your hike here at the northern end of the path (Chittenden Road parking lot) or at the southern end on the other side of Mount Washburn, you will climb and descend about 1,400 feet. The elevation change is steady but not steep. At the top, a lookout tower and day-use shelter offer travelers a resting place.

Beyond the Chittenden Road, the Tower Canyon Road progresses to the western face of Mount Washburn, where the landscape changes from grassy hills to forested mountain slopes. Areas of severely burned forest appear at 9 miles, where the North Fork fire that began near the western side of the park blazed through

Tower Fall is a singular attraction.

here on its way to the northeastern border. As you near the top of Dunraven Pass, pull off the road and look back to the north to see not only magnificent mountain views, but the hopscotch effect of the fire on the hills. Note the now visible contour of the land. The fire rushed through here quickly, drawn upward through draws and gullies and swept downhill by rapidly shifting winds, so briskly consuming the forest that often entire stands of trees were bypassed. Notice the taller living trees on the right side of the road and the charred trees on the left. This was one of the most badly burned areas in the park. Now, grasses and pines are growing, and wildflowers—wild asters, yarrow, red monkey flowers, yellow balsam arrowroot, and alpine forget-me-nots—flourish in the aftermath of the blaze.

Many bicyclists can't resist this road. You may see them pedaling up this incline, which is rather steep in places, with no safety shoulders or steel guardrails. Drive with extreme caution.

Mount Washburn, an inactive, 50-million-year-old volcano, rises to 10,243 feet above the western rim of the Grand Canyon of the Yellowstone. It was named for the leader of the Washburn-Langford-Doane expedition, which spent a month exploring the park in the summer of 1870. General Henry Dana Washburn made the first recorded climb of the mountain in August 1870. After serving in the Civil War, Washburn became the surveyor general for the Montana Territory and led one of the most important early explorations of Yellowstone. His party gave names to many geologic features of the park, including Old Faithful.

At about 13 miles, the Mount Washburn/Chittenden Road hiking trail emerges on the southwestern face of Mount Washburn. You are likely to see many cars parked here, waiting to transport hikers. You begin to see glimpses of the Absaroka Range to the left (southeast) and the Yellowstone Plateau to the south. At 13.3 miles, you reach the summit of **Dunraven Pass,** elevation 8,859 feet. This is the highest point you can reach by vehicle in the park. The pass was named for the fourth Earl of Dunraven, who visited Yellowstone several times during sightseeing and hunting trips to the West in the 1870s. Dunraven wrote a book called The Great Divide, which introduced Europeans to Yellowstone and the American West.

At 14.1 miles the **Caldera/Hot Springs Overlook** is on the left side of the road. Round the southern face of Mount Washburn for an excellent opportunity to view the ridge line of the Yellowstone caldera, the result of a volcanic eruption that happened 600,000 years ago. When the crust left by the eruption collapsed back in on itself, it left a circular rim marking the circumference of the blowout. From this viewpoint, steam rising from **Washburn Hot Springs** is also visible in the nearby forest to the east. These extremely hot springs that boil out of the

Stop and smell the wildflowers.

caldera's fracture lines are not accessible by foot because the ground is too unstable and toxic. Signs at the overlook point out the Absarokas, the Grand Canyon of the Yellowstone, Washburn Hot Springs, the caldera boundary, Elephant Back Mountain, Mount Sheridan, and the Teton Range.

The road leads to the eastern slope of **Dunraven Peak,** 9,900 feet high. The Dunraven Road picnic area at 15.6 miles is a pleasant spot in a meadow. There is another picnic spot on the right, and the 2.2-mile Cascade Lake Trail at 16.7 miles leads to a small lake at the base of the Washburn Range. Beyond here the route descends steadily through lodgepole pines untouched by fire. In about 2 miles a sign warning you to reduce your speed signals your entrance to the area known as the Grand Canyon of the Yellowstone, one of Yellowstone's major attractions and scenic wonders.

At the junction with the Norris Canyon Road, elevation 7,918 feet, turn left to explore the museum with its exhibit on Yellowstone's volcanic eruptions and the caldera, as well as Canyon Village Lodge and area amenities. Within a mile south of the junction, two roads lead east for spectacular views of the Canyon. Turn right at the junction with the Norris Canyon Road to reach Norris, thereby crossing on the only lateral road of the park, a short drive that cuts from one side of the Grand Loop to the other. Continue straight to reach Yellowstone Lake area and points south. From the Canyon Norris junction, the Fishing Bridge is 16 miles to the south and Lake Hotel turnoff is 1 mile beyond.

14

Canyon Village to Norris

General description: A straight 12-mile drive that bisects the Grand Loop and crosses the forested Solfatara Plateau. The least interesting drive in the park, but also the most expedient way to pass from one side of the park to the other, with a slight chance of glimpsing a shy, elusive moose along the way.

Driving time: 20 minutes.

Special attractions: The Blowdown Area interpretive stop.

Location: North-central Yellowstone.

Drive route names & numbers: Grand Loop, Norris Canyon Road.

Travel season: Mid-Apr through Oct, weather permitting.

Camping: National Park Service campground at Norris, mid-May to late Sept, first-come, first-served basis (116 sites); and Canyon, operated by Xanterra, early June to early Sept, first-come, first-served (280 sites).

Services: Full services at Canyon Village, no cell service.

Nearby points of interest: A side trip that passes by the 60-foot Virginia Cascade.

For more information: Yellowstone National Park Headquarters, Xanterra Reservations, Canyon Lodge.

The Route

This road traverses the park from east to west, turning the Grand Loop into an asphalt figure eight. The short, straight drive on a newly resurfaced road crosses the Solfatara Plateau, linking Canyon and Norris, two of the most spectacular places in the park.

The **Solfatara Plateau** rises to a mean elevation of 8,000 feet. Twelve miles wide and 700 feet from base to top, it was formed by the progression of thick lava 600,000 years ago. The word *solfatara* means a thermal vent that emits hydrogen sulfide, steam, and other gases. Solfataric areas are characterized by little water, and the plateau is indeed one of the drier places of the park, with white chalky earth frequently seen along this drive. Although no hydrothermal features are found here, several small lakes not visible from the road dot the meadows. Trails to several of these lakes cross the road. Elk, moose, occasional bison, and even grizzlies may be sighted here on summer mornings, and bald eagles are commonly seen in winter.

As you begin this drive across the plateau, you pass meadows decorated with wildflowers. The road begins winding uphill after a mile. From the beginning of

Canyon Village to Norris

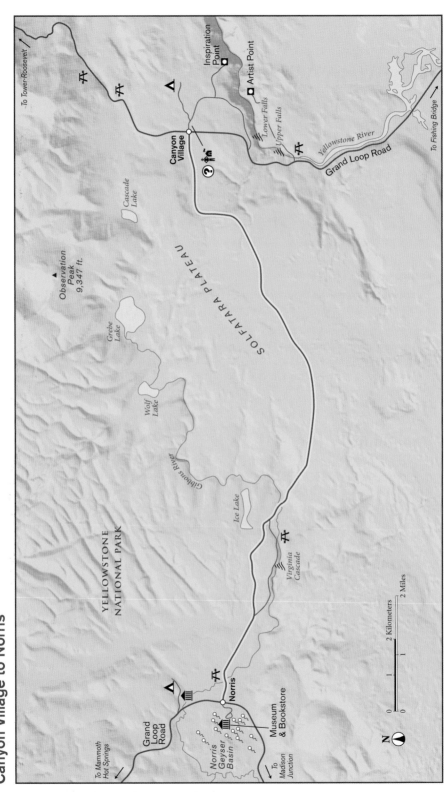

Inspiration Point

Artist Point

Lower Falls

Upper Falls

Canyon Village

Cascade Lake

To Tower-Roosevelt

Observation Peak 9,347 ft.

Grebe Lake

Wolf Lake

Gibbons River

Ice Lake

SOLFATARA PLATEAU

Yellowstone River

Grand Loop Road

To Fishing Bridge

YELLOWSTONE NATIONAL PARK

Virginia Cascade

Grand Loop Road

To Mammoth Hot Springs

Norris

Museum & Bookstore

Norris Geyser Basin

To Madison Junction

N

0   1   2 Kilometers

0   1   2 Miles

this drive, stay alert for wildlife. Frequent "moose jams" are reported near the Canyon Village junction, and elk inhabit the meadows and forests near Norris. You will notice several burn areas, most often on the northern side of the road. Again, the culprit here was the North Fork fire of 1988, which began in the Gallatin National Forest outside West Yellowstone. The road weaves through forest and burn areas, affording occasional glimpses of the Gallatin Range to the west and even the Madison Range beyond; on a clear day the view is spectacular from this high perspective.

By 7 miles the road has begun sloping downhill toward Norris, on the western side of **Blanding Hill,** formed by the flow of thick lava 600,000 years ago. The road crosses the **Gibbon River,** a tributary of the Madison, named for one of the many Civil War soldiers who visited Yellowstone in the 19th century. John Gibbon was a Union general who also fought in the Seminole Indian Wars. Ferdinand V. Hayden, leader of the first official US government surveys of Yellowstone, named several park features after Gibbon, a companion on another western exploration. On Hayden's second surveying journey to the park, he accidentally encountered Gibbon, who with his own party had traveled from Montana to investigate the new park. Gibbon shared with Hayden valuable information he had noted about sights and locations and was rewarded with nomenclature by his friend.

At about 7.5 miles you will pass the first of several turnouts on the southern side of the road that afford beautiful views of the valley below. A trail to the right leads to **Ice Lake,** so named because it supplied ice to the ill-fated Norris Hotel. The hotel burned down in 1887 after only a year of operation.

For either a beautiful view or information, at about 8.5 miles watch for a boardwalk, partially hidden by new growth, to the south. Stop here at the **"Blowdown"** interpretive turnout and stretch your legs. The North Fork fire burned particularly hot here, scorching the earth and making it more difficult for the forest to regenerate. In 1984 a tornado or funnel cloud reportedly swept 22 miles across this plateau, cutting a swath through the lodgepole forest and instantly toppling the trees, particularly vulnerable because lodgepoles are anchored by very shallow root systems. The result of this cataclysmic event was a plentiful supply of dried, brittle ground fuel for the North Fork fire. The boardwalk leads to a unique viewpoint from which you can see the results of the blowdown and fire. Although the sign says that the field may remain a meadow for perhaps 50 years, signs of the new forest are already encroaching on the damaged area.

The best feature along this route is the **Virginia Cascade.** To get to it, take a marked, rather primitive road to the left, at about 9 miles from Canyon; it leads to an overlook of a beautiful waterfall, or more precisely, a kind of downhill rapids. The one-way rugged road winds along the cliff before looping back to the east to the main road, but it affords an excellent view of the narrow rocky canyon of the Gibbon River as the river tumbles 60 feet from the rim of the plateau. The naming

Here's a precursor to a good fish story.

of Virginia Cascade was a fluke. Ed Lamartine, the foreman in charge of initial roadwork in the park, proposed the name to mapmaker Arnold Hague, knowing the map would render the name permanent. Lamartine wanted it named for Virginia Gibson, wife of the head of the Yellowstone Park Association in 1886. Hague did not like to give names of people to park features, but he did believe the names of states were acceptable. Thus, Virginia Cascade made its way onto the map.

Continue to descend toward **Norris.** The Norris picnic area is 0.5 mile from Norris Junction, where you will have a chance to explore one of the finest geyser basins in the park. The Norris area is named for the second park superintendent, P.W. Norris, a native New Yorker with an interest in nature and an eagerness to be a tour guide in the West. As a soldier in the Civil War, he heard rumors of the Yellowstone country from his companions, and he vowed to get to Yellowstone Lake. A trip in 1875 cemented his interest, and he became the second and very formidable park superintendent in 1877. His accomplishments included persuading Congress to provide funds for the park, including money for road construction. Between 1877 and 1882, when he resigned, the miles of park road increased from 32 to 153, and the miles of trails almost doubled. From Norris Junction, Mammoth is 21 miles to the north, and Old Faithful 30 miles to the south.

15

Canyon Village to Fishing Bridge

General description: A 16-mile journey offering a bit of everything that's special about the park: the Grand Canyon of the Yellowstone, wildlife, hydrothermal features, and the largest high mountain lake in the US.

Driving time: 45 minutes, if you make no stops.

Special attractions: Grand Canyon of the Yellowstone, Mud Volcano, Sulphur Caldron, bison and more in the Hayden Valley, LeHardys Rapids, and the Fishing Bridge.

Location: Central Yellowstone.

Drive route names & numbers: Grand Loop Road from Canyon to Lake.

Travel season: Early May through Oct, weather permitting.

Camping: Canyon, operated by Xanterra, first-come, first-served (280 sites); and Fishing Bridge RV park (no tents or trailers), also operated by Xanterra (345 sites).

Services: Full services at both Canyon and Fishing Bridge/Lake area. Fishing Bridge has one of the two service stations in the park prepared to deal with some mechanical problems of your vehicle. Very little cell service.

Nearby points of interest: North Rim Drive to Inspiration, Grandview, and Lookout Points; South Rim Drive to Artist Point; Uncle Tom's Trail; Upper and Lower Falls.

For more information: Yellowstone National Park Headquarters, Xanterra Reservations, Canyon Lodge, Fishing Bridge Visitor Center.

The Route

One of Yellowstone's most astonishing characteristics, both for early explorers and today's first-time visitors, is how unexpectedly many of its most astounding, very diverse features are encountered. No matter how you approach this junction, you see no signs of the marvelous canyon or falls nearby. It's no wonder that early visitors here called the park a "wonderland." From the Norris Geyser Basin, you travel a mere 12 miles to stumble upon the incredible Grand Canyon of the Yellowstone—so different, yet equally amazing. Travel south 16 miles to reach a glistening alpine lake or 8 miles south to see hydrothermal features entirely unlike those at Norris. If backcountry hiking entices you, marvels not included on the Grand Loop await.

As you approach **Canyon Village** (elevation 7,918 feet) from Tower Fall, turn left at the junction to explore this enclave of stores and services—a lodge, backcountry office, fishing and sporting gear, groceries, handcrafts, and more. If you are coming from Norris, go straight across the junction to reach Canyon Village. **Canyon Lodge** offers rooms and cabins with private baths, a restaurant, a gift shop, and a cafeteria. The Yellowstone General Store sells souvenirs, apparel, and

Canyon Village to Fishing Bridge

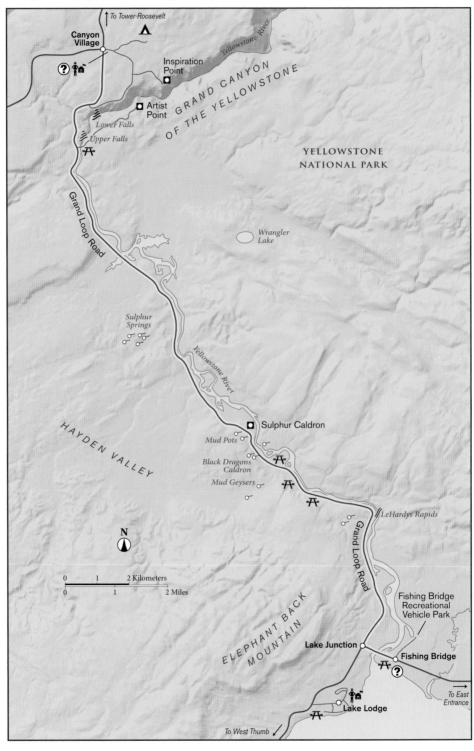

To Tower-Roosevelt

Canyon Village

Inspiration Point

Artist Point

GRAND CANYON OF THE YELLOWSTONE

Yellowstone River

YELLOWSTONE NATIONAL PARK

Lower Falls

Upper Falls

Grand Loop Road

Wrangler Lake

Sulphur Springs

Yellowstone River

HAYDEN VALLEY

Sulphur Caldron

Mud Pots

Black Dragons Caldron

Mud Geysers

LeHardys Rapids

Grand Loop Road

N

0   1   2 Kilometers
0   1   2 Miles

ELEPHANT BACK MOUNTAIN

Fishing Bridge Recreational Vehicle Park

Lake Junction

Fishing Bridge

Lake Lodge

To East Entrance

To West Thumb

other goodies. The service station is available for minor automobile services and repairs, and a post office allows you to mail all those cards you've been hauling around. Reservations are necessary for the campground here.

Corrals at Mammoth, Tower, and Canyon are the only places in the park where trail rides are available. If you have the time, this is a special way to see part of the landscape. A great display in the visitor center here tells of the formation of the natural phenomena that created this land—the volcanoes. A lighted map of the US alarmingly depicts the size of the Yellowstone eruptions. Other parts of the exhibit explain the measurement and monitoring of the hot spots in the park, plate tectonics, geology, lithology, and magma in an easy way for novices to grasp. It's an excellent, informative, and enjoyable exhibit. Rangers, as always, are available to offer helpful information and answer questions, and a Yellowstone Association store sells books, maps, posters, and more.

The North Rim Loop

You don't want to miss exploring the **North Rim** of the Grand Canyon of the Yellowstone. When you leave the visitor center, return to the Grand Loop Road and go south for less than a mile to take a 2-mile, one-way loop road that skirts the small portion of the North Rim that is accessible by road. Three scenic points overlook the majesty of the chasm and falls. The first North Rim overlook is **Lookout Point,** where a half-mile trail leads to the brink of the **Lower Falls.** You can peer over the ledge to watch the water drop 308 feet to the canyon floor. In spring, when snowmelt is at its peak, an estimated 64,000 gallons of water plunges over the falls each minute. From this vantage point you can watch people on the South Rim clambering down the steps of Uncle Tom's Trail toward the bottom of the Lower Falls.

Return to the one-way loop road and proceed to **Grandview Point,** which looks directly across and into the chasm. The **Grand Canyon of the Yellowstone,** 1,200 feet deep at its deepest point and from 1,500 to 4,000 feet across, was carved by the river through hydrothermally weakened rhyolite. Hot, acidic water issuing from fissures and cracks in the canyon walls, and hydrothermal features deep in the gorge here have helped erode the canyon walls relatively quickly. The coloration of the canyon walls comes from oxides and minerals leaching from the hot springs through the rocks. The path to the overlook opens in April, but the wooden steps leading to the rim may be icy in spring or fall, so walk with care.

Turn right to continue on the loop road. To reach the third vantage point, take the short two-way spur road that leads to Inspiration Point, from which you will have a spectacular view of the river and lower falls. On this two-way road, just off the road to the left, you pass a huge boulder, actually a glacial erratic,

surrounded by trees. A retreating glacier deposited the 500-ton rock about 15,000 years ago. Its composition shows it probably was carried from the Beartooth Mountains, at least 40 miles away. Inspiration Point offers a panoramic view of the path the Yellowstone River has carved through the canyon, and a look to the right gives you your last glimpse from the route of the lower falls. A trail, however, begins here and allows hikers to walk about 3 miles back along the rim to the Chittenden Bridge by the Upper Falls of the Yellowstone River.

The loop road winds up back at the Canyon complex and visitor center.

Explore the South Rim

Rejoin the Grand Loop and turn left again to travel the short distance to the **South Rim.** Another left takes you across the Chittenden Bridge over the Yellowstone River. Signs for the brink of the Upper Falls Trail, to the left 0.5 mile beyond the bridge, lead you to the parking area for trails that wind near the top of the **Upper Falls,** as well as to a special view of the Lower Falls via popular Uncle Tom's Trail. After viewing the 109-foot Upper Falls, consider climbing down the 328 steps of **Uncle Tom's Trail,** named for "Uncle" Tom Richardson, a guide who took visitors to the bottom of the falls at the turn of the 20th century. Originally the descent involved 528 steps, many of them on rope ladders (which are no longer used). If time, energy, and health permit, you will have astounding views of the 308-foot falls and the walls of the canyon. The effort is worthwhile.

Drive less than a mile to the next stop, **Artist Point,** where a short walk will take you to one of the most famous views in the park. Interpretive signs here tell of the geology of the canyon. Look carefully at the canyon floor for evidence of geysers or fumaroles, indications that this was a hydrothermal area filled with geysers and hot springs before the Yellowstone River carved the canyon.

Following the River

When you have spent your sense of wonder at the canyon, return to the Grand Loop and follow the course of the west bank of the **Yellowstone River.** At 675 miles long, it is the longest undammed river left in the contiguous 48 states. Proceed south to **Otter Creek,** a good picnic spot 2.9 miles from Canyon junction. Otters frequently splash and play here in the calm waters preceding the falls, and you may see anglers casting their lines. In 1877 tourists camping here were attacked by Nez Perce Indians who were trying to make their way out of the park. The Nez Perce were fleeing from the US Army with Chief Joseph's band.

A young artist works at Artist Point.

A broadening vista at about 4.5 miles signals the beginning of the marvelous **Hayden Valley,** where a bison herd lives year-round. This is probably the best place in summer to watch the animals in all their glory. A bison's coat is light tan at birth, but it darkens as the animal ages, so you can almost tell the age of a calf by the color of its coat. In August, in rut season, a bull will pick out a comely cow and separate her from the rest of the herd, including from her newly weaned calf, by charging any contenders that come close to his chosen. It is an entertaining spectacle. On one of my trips through the valley, bison on the road caused such a buffalo jam that it took 30 minutes to travel 0.6 mile. When a bison jam (or a moose jam, or a bear jam) occurs, rangers quickly arrive on the spot, trying against all odds to protect both animals and tourists, one as problematic as the other. Rangers approach their task with a great deal of calm consideration. Although it can get very hectic, I have yet to see a ranger get testy with the gawkers. Firm, yes. As ranger Mike Hassall said, he tries to remember that the travelers have a kind of "animal intoxication" while watching wildlife at close hand, something he understands. Try to give the rangers your thanks as well as your cooperation. They really deserve it.

This is a great place to hear a ranger talk about the bison herd, the formation of the Yellowstone caldera, or the glaciation of this valley. Check the park newspaper for times and meeting places for all ranger talks. The valley was named for Ferdinand V. Hayden, leader of the federally commissioned survey party instrumental in founding the park. The valley was formed by a retreating glacier about 13,000 years ago. Long after the volcanic activity that formed the caldera, glaciers slipped out of the Absaroka Mountains east of here and flowed across this area. The glaciers were about 15,000 feet thick. They completely covered Mount Washburn to the north and deposited glacial erratics—granite boulders—as they moved.

In contrast, most of the rock of the Yellowstone Plateau is volcanic rock. This area was the edge of a glacial dam that blocked the Yellowstone River for 11 miles, about where Fishing Bridge is located today, and completely flooded the Hayden Valley. The resulting lake left a layer of clay soil that is much more conducive to the growth of grass and sagebrush than trees. And that is why bison love the Hayden Valley. Its wonderful grassland for grazing is part of the singular ecological balance that is Yellowstone.

Warmed here year-round by thermal features upstream, the Yellowstone River attracts many varieties of waterbirds—Canada geese, ducks, pelicans, and even trumpeter swans—which in turn attract small predators such as coyotes. Because the birds are disturbed by the presence of humans, fishing is banned in the Hayden Valley. At 5.8 miles an overlook allows a good view of the braided river, enhanced by small creeks all along the valley. Alum Creek, source of many

"This is my parking spot!"

tall tales, is reputedly so astringent that it will pucker anything that happens through it. At 8.9 miles a roadside exhibit explains the formation of the Hayden Valley, and Grizzly overlook marks a spot from which you can sometimes see the enormous bears on the open sloping meadows across the river to the east. In fact, the last time I drove through here, wolves and a grizzly were battling over the same bison carcass. The Hayden Valley is Yellowstone's most obvious ongoing pageant.

The Mud Pots

At about 10 miles you encounter the first hydrothermal feature on this route— **Sulphur Caldron,** a malodorous collection of mud pots burbling up through fragile ground. **Mud pots** are formed when small amounts of hot water, not enough to make a hot spring, simmer through the claylike soil. The pH of the Sulphur Caldron, 1.2, is nearly as acidic as battery acid. Visitors should stay on designated trails near all thermal features, since the ever-changing landscape makes the crust of the earth here unexpectedly thin. Each year, accidents occur when people ignore warnings and break through the surface into scalding water. A wall cordons off the mud pots and a fumarole, a steam crater, about 10 to 12 feet across.

Mud stew, anyone?

The **Mud Volcano** complex lies a little south of the Sulphur Caldron. Here again, mud springs and fumaroles containing sulfuric gases and steam dissolve the clayish earth. The features here bear colorful names like Dragon's Caldron, Devil's Grotto, Sizzling Basin, Grizzly Female, Dragon's Mouth Spring, and Sour Lake. In 1896 the area was described as "the most fascinatingly loathsome thing in the world." Pick up a park brochure describing the sights along the 0.66-mile trail that circles this area of hydrothermal wonders. Part of the trail is wheelchair accessible. The brochure costs 50 cents if you want to keep it, but is free to use if you return it after the walk. As you're walking, you do get used to the rotten-egg smell of the hydrogen sulfide. In 1870 members of the Washburn party reported that the noises coming from Mud Volcano could be heard a mile away, but this is no longer true.

Because the ground here is continually warmed by the thermal waters, bison winter around the Mud Volcano area. Paths may be closed in spring if grizzlies awakening from hibernation are attracted by carcasses of bison that died during the winter.

Back on the Grand Loop, a couple of picnic grounds are far enough beyond the Mud Volcano that the atmosphere is not spoiled by the scent of sulfur. You are enough of a distance from Hayden Valley that catch-and-release fishing is once again allowed, so several places are provided to pull off the road and break out the fishing gear. Just beyond 11 miles, the **LeHardy Trail** exits the woods. Travel 0.5 mile farther to the parking area on the left side of the road and follow the wooden boardwalk to **LeHardy Rapids.** In June and July you may see cutthroat trout leaping high into the air, on their way to the spawning beds upstream. LeHardys Rapids were named for hapless Paul LeHardy, a topographer on expedition in 1873 with the US Army Corps of Engineers, who toppled from his boat while rafting through here. He survived, as does his memory.

Beyond LeHardys Rapids, at the outlet of the Yellowstone River from the northern end of the lake, the water becomes wide and still. Tall lodgepole pines shade both sides of the road, temporarily hiding the river in forest. At 14.5 miles you reach the **Fishing Bridge** junction. Turn left to visit the bridge and watch the great cutthroat trout, and the pelicans that watch the tempting fish with thoughts similar to those of fishermen everywhere. Until 1973 park officials allowed fishing from the bridge. The activity was prohibited when they realized the importance of this spot to both cutthroat trout and the grizzlies that feed on them in spring.

Facilities across the bridge include a visitor center with a really good wildlife exhibit, a Yellowstone General Store, an RV park, and one of two service stations in the park that can handle some automobile repairs.

Fishing Bridge itself is built over the Yellowstone River where it leaves the northern end of Yellowstone Lake. The turnoff to the beautiful Lake Hotel is 2 miles south of the Fishing Bridge junction. West Thumb is 21 miles to the south, and Cody, Wyoming, is 81 miles to the east.

16

Fishing Bridge to West Thumb

General description: A visit to a beautiful old hotel in a pristine setting, and a 21-mile tour along the forested western shore of Yellowstone Lake to a fascinating geyser basin nestled along the shoreline.

Driving time: About 45 minutes.

Special attractions: Old and elegant Lake Hotel, Bridge Bay Marina, and West Thumb Geyser Basin.

Location: South-central region of the park.

Drive route names & numbers: Grand Loop Road from Fishing Bridge to West Thumb.

Travel season: Early May through Oct or early Nov, depending on weather conditions.

Camping: RV park at Fishing Bridge, operated by Xanterra, first-come, first-served (345 sites); campground at Bridge Bay, also Xanterra, reservations required (420 sites); and a Xanterra-operated campground at Grant Village just beyond West Thumb, first-come, first-served (414 sites).

Services: Full services at Lake Village, including a hospital. Full services also at Grant Village, just south of West Thumb. Sporadic cell service along this drive.

Nearby points of interest: Natural Bridge, Stevenson Island.

For more information: Fishing Bridge Visitor Center, Lake Hotel, Xanterra Reservations, Yellowstone National Park Headquarters.

The Route

Lake Hotel is a compelling attraction just 2 miles south of Fishing Bridge. Its beauty, history, and setting near the lake make it an outstanding place for a walk or a stay. Turn left onto the road marked for the hotel to reach a complex that includes a hospital, Yellowstone General Store, ranger station, cabins, and lodge complete with laundry facilities and a very good cafeteria. The centerpiece of Lake Village is the elegant Lake Hotel, built in 1891 by the Northern Pacific Railroad. It is the oldest hotel in the park, open late May through late September.

As you drive toward the hotel you don't immediately see the lake. Drive slowly; the speed limit throughout the village is 25 miles an hour. Park in the large lot behind the resort to wander to the lake and through the hotel, which is listed on the National Register of Historic Places. Originally a plain wooden structure, the hotel gained distinction when Robert Reamer, architect of Old Faithful Inn, added Ionic columns and 15 false balconies to the design. It now boasts the most pleasant ambience of any hotel in the park. Piano or chamber music is played in the evening in the large, elegant sunroom/lobby, and fine food is served in the dining room. This hotel was a favorite of early tourists—at least the fortunate few

Fishing Bridge to West Thumb

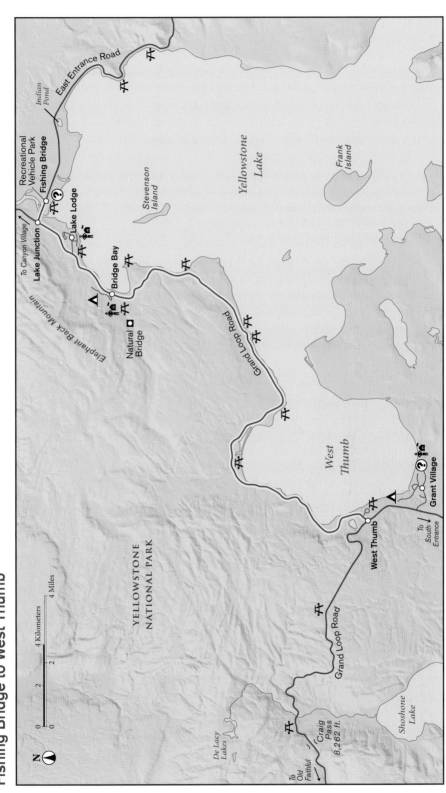

who could afford to travel in style. While many sightseers camped out under the stars and slept on hard ground, Lake Hotel guests arrived at the porte-cochere in 11 passenger coaches, toured by coach and boat, dressed for evening meals, and on occasion danced to live orchestral music. President Calvin Coolidge and members of European royalty were counted among its guests.

In the lobby read the posted histories gleaned from the letters and journals of travelers. At the registration desk you may arrange for scenic bus tours, car audio tours, stagecoach tours, Old West cookouts, and fishing and boating excursions. Free historic tours are conducted every evening at 7:30 p.m.

The second-largest wood-frame building in North America, Lake Hotel had fallen into disrepair by the 1970s, but a concerted 10-year effort by the park concessionaire restored the building to its previous glory. Now, each year, 500 gallons of yellow paint refresh its exterior. Facing the lake to the southeast, the hotel overlooks beautiful sunrises that are mirrored in the clear, cold water. A stroll in front of the hotel along the lake offers wonderful views of the Absaroka Range to the east and Mount Sheridan, rising to 10,308 feet, on the opposite shore.

To reach **Lake Lodge,** travel beyond the hotel for about 0.5 mile. The lodge also has a great view of Yellowstone Lake from the northwestern shore. Register for the cabins in the lodge's lobby, where the information desk is flanked by a huge fireplace. With its tables and chairs set out for reading, game-playing, and relaxing, Lake Lodge has the feel of a community hall at summer camp. Cabins here are more like 1950s motel rooms than cabins. On the rainy day I was there, the fireplace doubled as a dryer, with wet clothing and gear hanging from furniture and other improvised clotheslines. The lodge's large front porch is lined with rocking chairs for sitting and admiring the view, planning tomorrow's tour, or just whiling away time.

Yellowstone Lake

The road that passes in front of Lake Hotel loops by the ranger station and the Yellowstone General Store, which is nicely equipped with lakefront picnic tables. With all the beautiful picnic spots found along this lakeshore drive to West Thumb, consider grabbing some deli so that you'll be ready to stop and enjoy the view. Paths lead to the shore for a peaceful walk by the water. **Yellowstone Lake,** 20 miles long and 14 miles wide, has an imminently changeable nature. Because of its high elevation, 7,733 feet, and the mountainous terrain surrounding it, sudden storms appear, which can violently stir the lake from glassy stillness. With a surface area of about 137 square miles, the lake remains cold—an average of 40

A chipmunk has a picnic by the lake.

degrees Fahrenheit—so even on the warmest summer days swimming is not recommended. Hypothermia sets in rapidly at this temperature, and even the finest swimmers are put at risk. The lake freezes over by mid-December and generally thaws by late May. It eventually drains into the Gulf of Mexico via the Yellowstone, Missouri, and Mississippi Rivers. Although there are 110 miles of shoreline, less than a fourth of it is accessible by road. However, two long backcountry trails—Thorofare on the eastern shore and Trail Creek on the southern—parallel sections of the lake inaccessible by car.

On to West Thumb

To begin the journey to West Thumb, return to the Grand Loop Road and turn left (south). **Bridge Bay** and marina, a fine recreation area, is only 1.6 miles away. Commercial touring and fishing boats leave the marina regularly, and a good number of summer visitors bring their cabin cruisers for lengthy stays. Outboard and inboard motorboats can be rented at the marina, and while water-skiing is not allowed on the lake, sailboarders wearing dry suits have been known to skim the surface on hot summer days. A tour boat leaves from Bridge Bay to make an hour-long cruise around mile-long **Stevenson Island,** the second-largest island in the lake after Frank Island. From Bridge Bay campground you can hike a 3-mile round-trip trail that leads to the **Natural Bridge,** which you can also reach by road from a mile south of the marina. A biking trail begins just south of the marina. Natural Bridge, a rock arch 40 feet high and 30 feet wide, is composed of volcanic rhyolite.

Anglers may fish for and keep an unlimited number of lake trout because the National Park Service is trying to rid the lake of this nonnative predator of the indigenous cutthroat trout. If caught, the fish must be killed. Ask at the Bridge Bay Ranger Station for regulations and permits. There are good exhibits at the ranger station on water wilderness and the geography and natural history of the lake region.

Back on the Grand Loop, you travel along the western shore of the lake. There are a number of places to pull off for lakeside picnics and fishing excursions. At about 5.7 miles a hot spring empties into the lake at Gull Point. From here you have a great view of Lake Hotel across the bay. For a while the road leaves the lake and weaves through forest, but it never strays very far from the shore. At 6.9 miles Sand Point turnoff features bathroom facilities, picnic tables, and plenty of well-fed squirrels.

At about 10 miles an interpretive sign about the forest is worth a stop. While 80 percent of Yellowstone is covered by forest, and 80 percent of the forest is lodgepole pine, this segment of the drive is dominated by Engelmann spruce and alpine fir. The sign explains the competition among the three species for survival. Spruce and fir need shade to grow; lodgepole pine needs sun. In an ongoing saga, wind and fire destroy the shallow-rooted lodgepole, which in turn eliminates the shade needed by the spruce and fir. If natural phenomena would just stay out of the equation, Engelmann spruce and fir trees would probably provide enough of their own shade to take over the park. That, however, is unlikely to happen. What's more, lodgepole has the advantage of having two types of cones for regeneration, one that opens only in the high heat of a forest fire.

Frequent turnouts and picnic spots continue to line the route. At most of these you get a view of **Mount Sheridan,** 20 miles to the south. The mountain is named for General Philip H. Sheridan, who came west to fight in the Indian wars that followed the Civil War. A lover and champion of the park, Sheridan used his political influence and strong personality to fight for the preservation of Yellowstone.

Pumice Point marks the north-shore boundary of the West Thumb of Yellowstone Lake, which was created by a volcanic eruption about 162,000 years ago. On a clear day you can see the Tetons far to the south, and at several points along this segment of the Grand Loop you catch sight of fumaroles venting their steam along the lakeshore to the southwest. The drive through here is relatively flat, making it popular with runners and cyclers.

At about 13.5 miles **Arnica Creek Sandbar,** named for the yellow flower that grows in the park, crosses the northern portion of the bay. On the hottest summer days people stroll or wade across the bar, which creates a kind of two-sided beach.

Between 16 and 17 miles, small **Carrington Island** is visible just offshore. Watch for pelicans, gulls, or other waterfowl, as many of the small islands in Yellowstone Lake make wonderful bird habitats. Bluff Point is the last jutting tip of the shore before you come to West Thumb Geyser Basin. Along the rest of this drive, you may glimpse steam rising through the air from the geysers and fumeroles along the shore. Of the many yarns told about the hot springs in Yellowstone, one of the most oft-repeated claims that anglers could cast their lines in Boiling Spring near West Thumb, hook a fish, and reel it to shore through the spring, already cooked and ready to eat.

Yellowstone Lake is widest—18 miles across—from West Thumb Geyser Basin to the east shore. West Thumb Bay also boasts the deepest point in the lake, at 320 feet. If you are driving from the South Entrance to the park, from Jackson and the Tetons, **West Thumb** is the first of the park's hydrothermal features you will encounter.

As you approach the junction at West Thumb, a fumarole, or steam vent, to the right signals the geyser basin on the left. Pull into the parking lot, from which a hiking trail leads to the west to a spot overlooking both Duck and Yellowstone

Lakes. A portion of the boardwalk circling the geothermal area is wheelchair accessible, and a tour by the water is a pleasant break from a cramped car. The path passes several fumaroles, which by definition emit only steam. However, once while I was walking through here, one clearly marked fumarole seemed to be evolving into a geyser before my eyes. It continually spouted water, not a property of a steam vent, underscoring the changing nature of all geothermal activity in the park. West Thumb geyser basin has quieted in the last few years, but that can change at any time, with ongoing seismic activity below the earth's surface. Even with the slowdown, there are plenty of animated hydrothermal features at this stop.

A massive explosion about 162,000 years ago created this bay and the lingering hydrothermal aftereffects, a conglomeration of geysers, mud pots, bubbling pools, and fumaroles. Magma here is estimated to be about 3 miles below the lake's bottom, and water at the bottom of the lake here still records higher temperatures than in shallower parts. In winter, ice doesn't form over underwater hot springs, making them a perfect place for otters to play and search for food.

From West Thumb Geyser Basin you can continue north and west to Old Faithful via the Grand Loop, or turn left to visit Grant Village and points south.

Stunning colors paint the West Thumb Geyser Basin.

17

West Thumb to Old Faithful

General description: A 17-mile jaunt through forested hills that twice crosses the Continental Divide. Expansive views of lakes, waterfalls, and forested hills; at the end awaits the indomitable Old Faithful.

Driving time: 35 to 40 minutes.

Special attractions: Duck Lake, the Continental Divide, Isa Lake, Scaup Lake, Kepler Cascade, and the Upper Geyser Basin, including Old Faithful.

Location: West-central Yellowstone.

Drive route names & numbers: Grand Loop Road from West Thumb to Old Faithful.

Travel season: From early to mid-May through early Nov. This is one of the last roads in the park to open each year, so check with the National Park Service for the exact date.

Camping: No camping is available on this portion of the loop.

Services: Full services available at Old Faithful and at Grant Village near West Thumb. No cell service.

Nearby points of interest: Shoshone Lake, Lone Star Geyser.

For more information: Yellowstone National Park Headquarters, Old Faithful Ranger Station, Xanterra Reservations.

The Route

As you head west out of West Thumb, an overlook soon appears on your right. From it you get a panoramic view of Duck Lake, Yellowstone Lake, and the Absaroka Mountains beyond. Tiny **Duck Lake,** formed by a steam explosion 10,000 years ago, is a perfect spot from which to survey the countryside. On a sunny day, the steam rising from **West Thumb Geyser Basin** is an intriguing and beckoning sight.

Continue climbing, dipping, and winding through pine- and spruce-covered hills. Watch for animals, mostly elk and deer, which sometimes stand well-camouflaged by trees at the side of the road or graze in the small meadows. The fire that hit this section of the park, the 1988 North Fork fire, did less damage here than on other segments of the Grand Loop, although occasional clumps of burned trees line the roadside. At 3.7 miles, the Divide picnic area appears on the right. It signals the upcoming crossing of the Continental Divide that shortly follows. At about 4 miles, cross the imaginary line at 8,391 feet elevation. Water flowing east from here winds up in the Atlantic Ocean, while water flowing west goes to the Pacific.

Shoshone Point, to the left at about 8 miles, overlooks **Shoshone Lake,** about 3 miles to the southwest. This is the second-largest lake in the park, after

West Thumb to Old Faithful

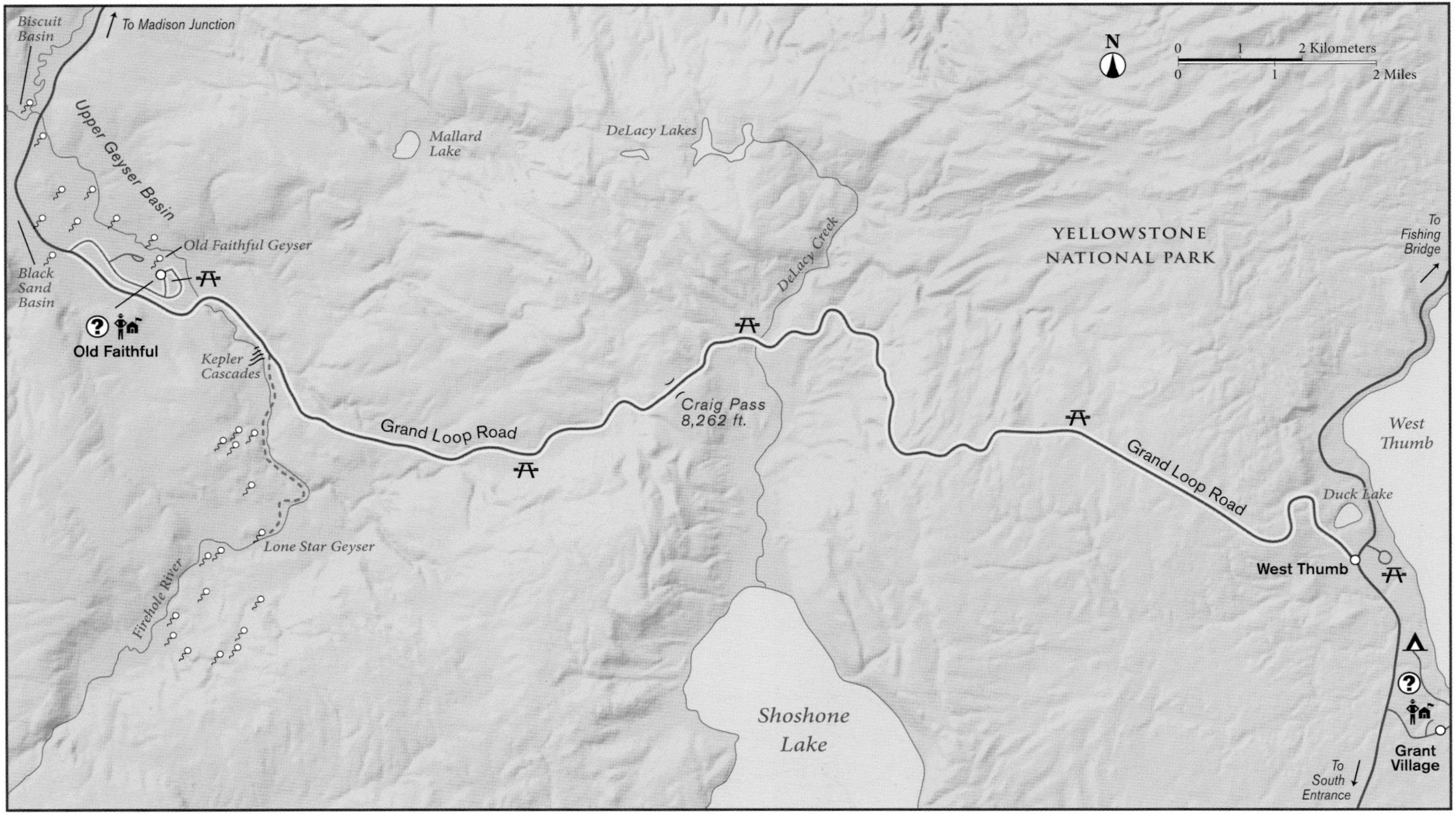

Water lilies bloom in late summer on tiny Isa Lake.

Yellowstone Lake. It probably has not escaped your notice that many bodies of water that would be described as "ponds" elsewhere are called lakes in Yellowstone. Only four park lakes really deserve the designation—Yellowstone, Shoshone, Lewis, and Heart, in order of diminishing size. Shoshone Lake covers 8,050 acres and measures 205 feet at its deepest point. Shoshone is the source of the Lewis River, which empties into the Pacific Ocean by way of the Snake and Columbia Rivers.

In 1914 Ed Trafton, a highwayman, held up 15 coaches of tourists in 1 day as they passed by on their tour of this part of the park. His booty came to almost $1,000 in cash and more in jewelry. Nicknamed the Merry Bandit, he reportedly allowed attractive young ladies to keep their jewelry if they would hide it in their stockings, which, to his delight, several did. But as is the case with so many modern and hapless bandits, three travelers took his photograph and one made a sketch, helping to hasten his capture and sentencing to a five-year sentence in Leavenworth. He had had a previous conviction for robbing his own mother-in-law.

Beyond Shoshone Point the road winds downward, toward **DeLacy Creek,** with another picnic area to the right at 8.4 miles. DeLacy Creek was named for Walter Washington DeLacy, a surveyor and engineer who led a group of prospectors through the area in 1863. He made the first map of Shoshone Lake and the park's geyser basins, which was published in 1865. His reports were dismissed by many as tall tales. **DeLacy Creek Trail,** which begins just beyond the creek, is the shortest route to Shoshone Lake at 3 miles long.

Continue on this hillside road. This is **Craig Pass,** not the steepest pass in the park, named for Ida Craig, the first lady to traverse this road built by Hiram Chittenden and his corps of engineers. At 9.8 miles stop at a second and most fascinating crossing of the **Continental Divide,** elevation 8,262 feet. A popular spot to take photographs, the divide here cuts across small **Isa Lake,** singular because it drains to both the Atlantic and Pacific oceans in a most peculiar fashion. The snowmelt pond has two outlets, one on either side of the road; the western outlet drains into Spring Creek, which flows east, while the eastern outlet empties into DeLacy Creek, which flows west. Isa Lake is also notable for the lush yellow water lilies that bloom here in mid- to late summer, a scene that echoes a fine Monet.

The Descent

As you descend the pass beyond Isa Lake, you can see a rock slide area that alternates from one side of the road to the other. Several turnouts provide chugging cars, sightseers, and polite drivers the opportunity to pull over and let others pass. The road curves toward the northwest, marking the turning point of the Grand Loop toward the north.

Scaup Lake (named for a type of duck), at about 13 miles on the right, is the approximate site of a 1908 stagecoach robbery. This bandit, more successful than Trafton at Shoshone Point, garnered close to $2,000 and was never caught. Fifteen coaches passed this way during the day of the robbery. He allowed the first seven to pass because cavalrymen accompanied the first several coaches of the day, but he robbed the next eight. Although warnings were sounded, communication and transportation were such in 1908 that officers couldn't get there in time to make an arrest. Altogether five separate stagecoach robbery incidents took place in the park, but they stopped abruptly when automobiles became the preferred means of travel.

The road is flanked by downed trees to the right and forest and dales to the left. At about 14.8 miles a sign points to the **Lone Star Geyser Trail** for hikers and bicyclists. This partially paved, relatively flat 2.4-mile trail closely follows the Firehole River. **Lone Star Geyser** spouts from a 12-foot-high cone of travertine in 45- to 50-foot eruptions about every 3 hours. The eruptions can last for up to 30 minutes and are followed by long, robust emissions of steam. Hikers can continue beyond the geyser to Shoshone Geyser Basin 7.5 miles away, but bicycles are not allowed on that section of trail. This hike makes a good all-day park adventure.

Kepler Cascades, a many-tiered fall, is the next roadside feature. At about 15 miles you will find a parking area on the left side of the road. A wooden bridge spans the **Firehole River** near the base of the cascades, and from it you have an impressive view of the falls and the small ravine through which the river tumbles.

Within a mile of the cascades you approach the Old Faithful and Upper Geyser Basin area, the most visited area of the park. The complex of cabins, lodges, stores, and employee housing comprises the second-largest community in the park, after Mammoth Hot Springs. Slow to 35 miles an hour and watch carefully for signs pointing to your destination. Soon, a pedestrian crossing will slow you even further to 15 miles an hour. At about 17 miles, reach the junction and turn right to enter the Old Faithful area, or go straight to continue on to Madison Junction. A right turn takes you to Old Faithful Inn, the lodge, and the geyser itself.

This road leads to three parking lots, all within easy walking distance of the geyser. The first lot serves Old Faithful Inn, a service station, and a Yellowstone General Store. The second and third provide parking for the visitor center and lodge, respectively, within easy walking distance for the sights and services of the area. If walking is a concern, park in the west (second) lot to be closer to the inn or visitor center, or the easternmost (third) parking lot to easily reach the lodge and cafeteria. Between the two are a service station, Yellowstone General Store, post office, Snow Lodge, and photo store. A clinic and ranger station also are in the area.

Old Faithful Lodge, built in 1928, includes a cafeteria, ice-cream store, gift shop, and large windows in both a sitting room and a restaurant that overlook Old Faithful. Arrange for rooms in the lodge and reservations for cabins at the information desk. Keep in mind that many people make reservations a year in advance.

Old Faithful Inn, constructed over the winter of 1903–04, was designed by Seattle architect Robert Reamer. This showplace of the park was one of the buildings of which he was most proud. Of the design he wrote, "I built it in keeping with the place where it stands. Nobody could improve upon that. To be at discord with the landscape would be almost a crime. To try to improve upon it would be impertinence." Seven stories high, the inn is thought to be the world's largest log structure, built of logs and stones collected in the park. Wandering through the lobby is a striking treat in itself. The fireplace alone is made of over 500 tons of stone. Stairways and balconies of glowing, burled pine logs overlook the sights, both inside and out. Old Faithful Inn is an American treasure.

When fire threatened the building in 1988, two happy circumstances combined to help save it. In the summer of 1987, a sprinkler system had been installed on the roof in case a fire ever came within licking distance. When the fire did come close the following year, firefighters were aided by the new system, which kept the inn wet and less susceptible to sparks and flames. The second fortuitous

Do you love rustic? Try a cabin at Old Faithful.

circumstance was a last-minute wind shift that turned the flames away when they came within 0.25 mile of the building and headed straight toward it. It is amazing to note that during that fiery summer, when about 30,000 firefighters struggled to control the blazes in the park, there were no human fatalities and a relatively small number of animal deaths.

The geyser basin here is so rich that this is an excellent place to stay for a day or two, if you can afford the time. Many rooms in the inn have views of Old Faithful, and the restaurant is excellent. Free tours of the inn are given every day at 9:30 and 11 a.m., and 2 and 3:30 p.m., from mid-May through late Sept.

Old Faithful, the showpiece of the park, erupted reliably 20 to 23 times a day for the first 120 years that its eruptions have been recorded, but it is slowing down slightly. It now erupts approximately every 90 minutes, or 16 to 17 times a day. Although neither the largest nor most regular geyser in the park, this endearing symbol of Yellowstone is impressive. Each eruption still lasts 2 to 5 minutes and spouts 3,700 to 8,400 gallons of water up to 130 feet into the air. The benches surrounding the geyser hint at the waiting time until the next eruption. If you arrive and the benches are empty, the geyser has just erupted. If a few people are sitting around, it is probably 30 to 40 minutes until the next blast. If crowds are sitting or milling about, you may have a 15- to 20-minute (or shorter) wait to see the next show. As a rule of thumb, the longer it takes for the geyser to erupt, the higher and greater the next eruption of water and steam.

The visitor center houses a Yellowstone Association bookstore and an auditorium that shows a short film, *Yellowstone, a Living Sculpture,* about the creative properties of geysers. Approximate times for geyser eruptions are posted in the visitor center and Old Faithful Inn. By all means, spend as much time as you can in this area. Enjoy not only Old Faithful, but also the boardwalk to follow throughout the geyser basin, where a majority of the world's geysers are found. A nice hillside climb to the east affords a wonderful viewpoint from which to watch the spectacle below.

You will find more information about the Upper Geyser Basin and Old Faithful in the next drive, "Old Faithful to Madison Junction."

18

Old Faithful to Madison Junction

General description: A 16-mile drive through the world's largest and most amazing region of geothermal activity, with mud pots, fumaroles, hot springs, and geysers scattered in abundance across the landscape. A short side drive leads through a dramatic canyon with one of the only places in the park where swimming is allowed.

Driving time: About 35 minutes, if you make no stops.

Special attractions: Old Faithful, Upper Geyser Basin, Black Sand Basin, Biscuit Basin, Midway Geyser Basin, Lower Geyser Basin, and National Park Mountain.

Location: West-central Yellowstone.

Drive route names & numbers: Grand Loop Road from Old Faithful to Madison Junction.

Travel season: Mid-May through early Nov, weather permitting.

Camping: At Madison only (277 sites), operated by Xanterra.

Services: Full services at Old Faithful. Cell service at Old Faithful, and partially along the drive to Madison.

Nearby points of interest: Upper Geyser Basin walks, Fairy Falls, Firehole Lake Drive, Three Senses Nature Trail, Fountain Flat Drive, Firehole Canyon Drive.

For more information: Yellowstone National Park Headquarters, Xanterra Reservations, Madison Junction Ranger Station, Old Faithful Visitor Center and Ranger Station.

The Route

Synonymous with Yellowstone National Park, **Old Faithful** is unquestionably the most famous geyser in the world. In more than 130 years of recordkeeping by park officials, Old Faithful's eruptions have never strayed far from its intrinsic schedule. The pattern of the eruptions is consistent. On an average of every 90 minutes, splashing precedes the actual eruption of water and steam by 3 to 20 minutes. When the geyser actually begins to spout, it can shoot to 106 to 184 feet within seconds. Although the plume of water doesn't maintain its maximum height for the entire blast, from 3,700 to 8,400 gallons of water are emitted every eruption.

Old Faithful is probably about 25,000 years old. By the turn of the last century, souvenir hunters had destroyed its large base of siliceous sinter (geyserite), taking samples as mementos. Since then, Congress has passed a law making it illegal to remove anything from any national park—plants, petrified wood, and even stones.

Old Faithful is not the tallest geyser in the park; that distinction belongs to seldom-seen **Steamboat Geyser** in Norris Geyser Basin. Nor is it the most

Old Faithful to Madison Junction

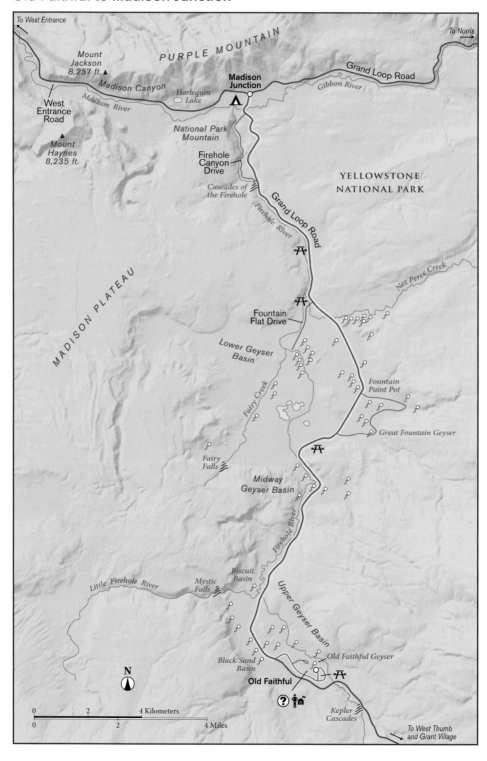

regular; **Riverside Geyser** here in Upper Geyser Basin holds that honor. Nonetheless, it is the most popular and the most asked-about feature in the park. Ask any park ranger what question he or she hears most frequently, and the answer inevitably is "What time does Old Faithful go off?" Other common inquiries include "Do they shut Old Faithful off at night?" and "Where is the person located who runs Old Faithful?" Occasionally, the lucky visitor will see Old Faithful erupt while nearby **Plume Geyser** simultaneously shoots in the background. Plume is one of more than 150 geysers found within 2 square miles of here—the highest concentration of geysers found anywhere in the world.

Geysers Galore

Paved trails, boardwalks, and paths lead a winding route through the geysers and pools of **Upper Geyser Basin.** This tour should not be missed. Obtain maps of the paths at the visitor center. Begin by climbing to **Observation Point,** a short hike to a high vantage point of both Old Faithful and Geyser Hill to the north. After watching Old Faithful from this height, continue along the descending path to **Solitary Geyser,** which erupts every 2 to 6 minutes, spurting 25 feet into the air for almost 2 minutes.

Rejoin the main trail system to see many of the features in this astounding area. **Morning Glory Pool** is one of the most famous geothermal features along this walk, despite damage by vandals that altered its vibrant color. **Riverside Geyser** erupts about every 7 hours, sending an angled 100-foot plume into the air across the Firehole River. **Grotto Geyser** has formed around old petrified tree trunks, resulting in a strange configuration of geyserite. Its eruptions can last anywhere from 1.5 hours up to 26 hours. **Grand Geyser,** the world's tallest predictable geyser, erupts every 7 to 15 hours. **Castle Geyser,** which has the largest cone in the park; **Beehive Geyser,** with unpredictable eruptions of up to 220 feet; and the frequently spouting Daisy group all are found on this walk. Schedules for the more regular geysers are posted in the visitor center.

Although many geysers do not erupt with regularity, you are likely to see something blow as you walk these paths. In the Upper Geyser Basin alone, more than 150 geysers and more than 600 hot springs and steam vents have been catalogued. Almost 25 percent of the world's known geysers are found within 2 miles of Old Faithful.

Often it is the unexpected that will stand out among your park memories. My favorite is the astounding **Artemisia Geyser,** which I happened upon just after it began its 20-minute show. Artemisia erupts from an underwater cone in a wide blue pool. It goes off about every 14 hours, predictable within 4 hours of its eruption time. As with many geysers, reportedly the "whole earth rumbles" before it erupts.

While you walk the paths of the Upper Geyser Basin, three cautions are in order. Many geysers spray water containing dissolved siliceous sinter, or silica. Be aware that this mist can coat glasses, binocular and camera lenses, and can be difficult to remove. Second, elk and bison that frequent this area (along with the occasional bear), still fall under the category of wild animal. Although they seem placid, observe them from a distance and treat them with respect. Finally as always, please stay on the paths. Frederic Remington, the great artist who is famous for his paintings of the West, once rode through here on horseback and later perceptively wrote that the ground was "very thin and hazardous, and to break through is to be boiled. One instinctively objects to that form of cooking."

When you are ready to leave the Old Faithful area, there is more to see. From the parking area, a right turn leads to the Grand Loop and Madison Junction. The road is well marked; to head north to Madison Junction, stay to the right. The left lane turns toward West Thumb and Grant Village. Once you've made the turn that will take you north, get in the left lane for the **Black Sand Basin,** almost directly across from the junction leading to Old Faithful. The name Black Sand refers to the granulated obsidian scattered here, formed when lava suddenly came into contact with ice, hardened into a glasslike substance, and then shattered. Spouter Geyser, Sunset Lake, Rainbow Pool, Cliff Geyser, Opalescent Pool, and Emerald Pool are located here. Cyanobacteria, which thrive in hot water, give the hot springs their varied hues, with different species growing at different temperatures.

Return to the Grand Loop and turn left (north). This stretch of road crosses and recrosses the Firehole River, one of two tributaries that form the Madison River at Madison Junction. If you didn't see the Daisy Geyser group while walking in the upper geyser basin, you can reach it by a hiking/biking trail to the right, at 1.5 miles. The Daisy group—Daisy, Splendid, and Comet Geysers—is surrounded by small pools, including Punchbowl Spring, found along this same walk.

At about 1.8 miles, **Biscuit Basin** on the left is the last geothermal feature of the Upper Geyser Basin. Biscuit Basin has a volatile volcanic background. On August 15, 1959, a major earthquake reaching 7.5 on the Richter scale convulsed this area, changing the patterns of many hot springs and geysers. The large white "biscuits" of geyserite that used to ring Sapphire Pool were crumbled or washed away by the changing patterns of the runoff of water. A 0.5-mile walk takes you around the basin. Notice how silica from geysers and pools saturates surrounding trees, slowly encasing them in stone. Trails from here lead to Summit Lake, Observation Point, and 70-foot Mystic Falls. The shortest route to 197-foot Fairy Falls, a 1.2-mile trek, begins at Biscuit Basin. The trail to Artemisia Geyser is directly

Yellowstone presents . . . Old Faithful, which is now "faithful" about every 90 minutes.

across the Grand Loop Road from the parking lot, although you can also reach it by hiking from the upper geyser basin.

Beyond Biscuit Basin, drive along the Firehole River, which runs through meadows and trees on the left. Many pullouts allow you to take pictures of animals or scenery without tying up traffic. Beyond Muleshoe Bend, an obvious curve in the road, another hiking trail on the left leads 2.5 miles past several fumaroles and hot springs to **Fairy Falls,** an easy day hike. Two trailheads go to the falls, one here and a longer one farther up the road, at the end of Fountain Flats drive.

Vapor rising to the west signifies **Midway Geyser Basin,** which has hot springs and bubbling pools in vivid color. As you draw near to the geyser basin, steaming water runs over a ledge and into the Firehole River. It comes from **Excelsior Geyser Crater,** a dormant geyser that has left a large pool, where we once saw a ranger patiently casting a line over and over, trying to catch two hats that had blown down the crater's embankment. The pool discharges almost 4,000 gallons of 199-degree-Fahrenheit water per minute into the Firehole River below, or an impressive 5.5 million gallons of hot water a day.

Another attraction at Midway Geyser Basin, **Grand Prismatic Spring,** at 370 feet long by 250 feet wide and 120 feet deep, is Yellowstone's largest hot spring. The colors of the pools at Midway are caused by different forms of algae and bacteria that thrive at temperatures of 160 degrees F and higher. Photography buffs should climb the short hiking trail to **Bluff Point** for the best view of Midway Geyser Basin.

A large picnic area is on the right less than 0.5 mile beyond Midway Geyser Basin. Watch the marshy flats and the wood's edge on the other side of the river for moose. The big animals sometimes step into the river looking for "moose moss" to munch. To the right at about 6.5 miles, vapor rises from the area of Firehole Lake Drive, site of **Great Fountain,** one of the park's most regular and impressive geysers. About the first of June, this 4-mile, two-lane loop road opens, coursing through sporadic meadows and trees, past hot pools, fumaroles, and geysers. Many people stop and wait for one or more of the geysers located here to erupt, going by the time approximations from the Old Faithful Visitor Center. Benches have been provided for those who want to keep watch. Great Fountain Geyser is a major attraction, erupting 100 to 200 feet every 8 to 12 hours, with a predictability range of about 4 hours. The process begins about 1 hour before the actual eruption, with water overflowing from the crater. The geyser erupts in cycles for about 60 minutes.

Near here, also, is **Octopus Spring,** the hot spring where *Thermus aquaticus* was first found. This tiny bacterium, an organism discovered by Dr. Thomas Brock of the University of Wisconsin, has become instrumental in DNA screening and

All cones are not for ice cream. Here is the cone of the Great Fountain geyser.

fingerprinting, and is used in detecting the AIDS virus. Scientists are just beginning to explore the potential of microorganisms living in the hot springs and other thermal areas of Yellowstone. These life forms, invisible to the naked eye, are being studied for their scientific properties and potential medical and other practical purposes. Just as Lewis and Clark on their journey "discovered" or identified 178 plant and 122 animal species that had not been recognized before east of the Mississippi, modern-day explorers here are identifying and cataloging hyperthermophiles, microbes and other organisms that thrive at high temperatures. The implications of this new research could lead to a greater understanding of our origins, as well as give valuable new tools to the fields of medicine, energy, and even our own existence under extreme circumstances. An important policy has been put in place guaranteeing that any profits derived from these studies benefit the National Park Service, as well as the scientists, researchers, companies or corporations who will undoubtedly prosper. This is one more example of Yellowstone as a gigantic, pristine laboratory that those who have gone before have had the wisdom to preserve.

Other geysers share the basin with Great Fountain. **White Dome Geyser,** rising from a 30-foot sinter cone, erupts about every 12 to 24 minutes and is probably one of the oldest geysers in the park. The National Park Service has erected blackboards by many of the geysers to advise of their next estimated time of eruption. Firehole Lake, about 3 miles into Firehole Lake Drive, discharges about 3,500 gallons per minute of simmering water into Tangled Creek, which then empties into Hot Lake across the road. The river braids throughout this area, collecting geyser runoff as it flows. **Three Senses Nature Trail,** specially built for the visually impaired, offers a chance to touch, smell, and hear the "world" of the geyser. The trail is enjoyable for everyone.

Firehole Lake Drive returns to the Grand Loop across the road from the parking lot of **Fountain Paint Pot.** If you have skipped Firehole Lake Drive, Fountain Paint Pot is about 7.5 miles from the Old Faithful junction. A perennial favorite with visitors to the park, the Fountain Paint Pot area showcases all four geothermal features found in Yellowstone—colorful pools, fumaroles, geysers, and mud pots. A boardwalk begins at the northern end of the parking lot. This nature trail is always fun, because geysers here are so plentiful that something is always spouting. The "paint pots" themselves are mud pots that gurgle and spurt but never erupt because there is not enough ground moisture to make an actual pool. Surrounding claylike soil remains thick and bubbling. The colors of the paint pots depend on the oxidation stage of iron dissolved in the mud. Favorites in this basin, besides the colorful paint pots, are frequently erupting **Clepsydra Geyser** and nearby **Spasm Geyser,** which often spout at the same time.

The next side trip after leaving Fountain Paint Pot and continuing north on the Grand Loop is Fountain Flat Drive to the left. It leads a mile through a field to where a footpath leads another 2 miles to several trailheads and a picnic area near the shore of Goose Lake. Imperial Geyser, Fairy Falls, and Spray Geyser can all be reached from the picnic area. Elk and bison congregate in the fields to graze in the evenings along Fountain Flat Drive. Buffalo frequent these meadows in winter, using their muzzles as shovels to brush away snow and get at the grass underneath. Hot springs and fumaroles in the field help keep the massive animals warm. With a look back at Fountain Paint Pot and the outcroppings of rising vapor, it is not hard to imagine the sense of mystery and magic early travelers placed on this landscape.

Beyond Fountain Flat Drive a roadside marker on the left tells of "Chief Joseph's Trail of Tears." Chief Joseph was the leader of a band of 800 Nez Perce Indians who crossed Yellowstone in 1877 while fleeing the US Army after the Battle of the Big Hole. Their 1,300-mile flight began in Idaho and ended 20 miles south of the Canadian border with the Battle of the Bear's Paw.

The river beyond here, somewhat camouflaged by trees, is another good place to look for moose, which are always fun to see. Huge, gawky, and shy, moose are not as unintelligent as they look. One bull moose along this stretch of river climbed out of the water and hid when a man with a camera tried fording the river. When the intruder turned back to the far shore, the moose, which had been peeking from behind the trees, plodded back into the water. Because of their cautiousness, moose are the least seldom seen large animal in the park. You are very fortunate if you spot one.

The Firehole River is wide and swift here. Turnouts and picnic areas line the road as it descends toward Madison Junction, and the river disappears behind the hills to the west.

Cross the Gibbon River as it rushes to join the Firehole to form the world-famous fly-fishing stream, the Madison.

Half a mile before you reach Madison Junction, the entrance road to Firehole Canyon juts to the left. Although this 2-mile, one-way road will force you to retrace your steps a little, don't miss the drive into the marvelous canyon just behind the hills. From the Grand Loop there is no hint that this small but dramatic river canyon is here.

Firehole Canyon Drive, an old Indian route, begins by the river and canyon bottom. Soon, perpendicular sheets of rock rise 800 feet on the west side of the river, revealing crosscuts of ancient rhyolite lava flows. Park next to the interpretive sign about halfway through the drive that tells about the formation of the rock walls, and then cross the road to view the 40-foot **Firehole Falls** tumbling from the ridge. Farther along you come to a warm spring, the one place in the park where swimming is acceptable. Two bathhouses have been constructed for the adventurous, and steps descending to the river make this a fun, accessible stop

The water burbles up in Firehole Spring, Firehole Lake Drive.

on a hot summer day. The swimming hole occasionally closes because of high or swift water, but it is well posted. Beyond the swimming hole the drive quickly rejoins the Grand Loop.

Retrace 1.7 miles of the Grand Loop to the Firehole Canyon entrance. The mountain you see to the left of the road is **National Park Mountain,** supposed birthplace of the national park concept. When members of the Washburn-Langford-Doane party camped near here on the final night of their adventure in 1871, they supposedly discussed what should happen to this area of so many marvels. The concept of a national park was born, and their ensuing reports to the powers that were, along with their lobbying efforts, led to the Hayden surveying excursion, which in turn led to the dedication of Yellowstone National Park.

Madison Visitor Center, on the left immediately before Madison Junction, has a picnic area, restrooms, and a Yellowstone Association bookstore. The stone-and-log building of the visitor center, originally a small museum, dates back to 1929 and is registered as a National Historic Landmark. A nice path leads behind the visitor center to the confluence of the Firehole and Gibbon Rivers. Madison Junction campground is immediately to the left after turning west at the junction. If you continue on the Grand Loop, Norris Geyser Basin is 14 miles and 30 minutes away.

19

Madison Junction to Norris

General description: A 14-mile drive that climbs past geothermal areas, waterfalls, scenic forest, and meadow to fascinating Norris Geyser Basin.

Driving time: About 30 minutes.

Special attractions: Terrace Spring, Tuff Cliffs, Gibbon Falls, Beryl Spring, Gibbon Meadows, Elk Park, and Norris Geyser Basin.

Location: West-central Yellowstone.

Drive route names & numbers: Grand Loop Road from Madison to Norris.

Travel season: Mid-Apr through early Nov, weather permitting.

Camping: Madison Junction (277 sites) and Norris (116 sites), National Park Service campgrounds, first-come, first-served basis.

Services: Other than camping, no services are available on this segment of the drive. The closest services to Madison are in West Yellowstone; the closest to Norris are in Canyon Village.

Nearby points of interest: Artist Paint Pots Trail, Monument Geyser Basin.

For more information: Yellowstone National Park Headquarters, Madison Ranger Station, Norris Ranger Station.

The Route

As you leave **Madison Junction,** elevation 6,806 feet, the road begins to climb immediately. Although rarely steep, the climb continues all the way to Norris, by my odometer about 13.2 miles away. This is one of the first routes to open in spring, allowing people in Gardiner to cut 100 miles off a trip to West Yellowstone. A trail to the left at 0.2 mile leads to the top of **Purple Mountain,** where a wide vista rewards the ardent hiker. In spring bison follow this road to lower ground, where grass is more readily available. This road is widely used as a snowmobiling route in winter, and the groomed track allows bison easy access to the western valleys of the park.

Round a bend within the first mile and notice the steam rising on the left. A turnout provides parking for a small thermal area, delicate **Terrace Spring,** which is laced with colorful hot springs, fumaroles, and trickles of streams. From the boardwalk here you also have a pleasant view of the valley and hills to the south.

Tuff Cliffs rise to the left of the road at 1.5 miles, towering above a picnic area in a small meadow. Formed by volcanic ash carrying rock fragments so hot they welded together, the light-colored tuff exposed in the cliffs is easily eroded by wind and rain. Rock slides here are common. To the right of the road, burned areas reveal the slope of the hills to the south. Wildflowers flourish throughout the

Madison Junction to Norris

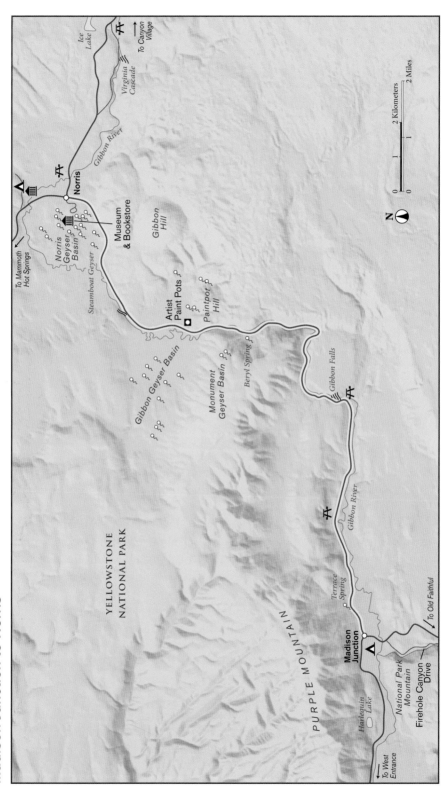

summer in the mineral-rich soil left by the fires. Regeneration of the forest is evident here. Seedlings, saplings, and taller lodgepole pines race to the sun.

The road chases the Gibbon River for most of the next 10 miles. At about 3 miles the forest closes in, as you approach the rhyolite and welded ash of **Gibbon Canyon.** The road climbs past forest and rock outcrops on the left, with the river flowing past on the right. A short road leads down an embankment to the Gibbon River, a nice place for a picnic or fishing. Proceed north to a new parking area, a true accomplishment of engineering, for an overlook of **Gibbon Falls,** which tumbles 84 feet over the rim of the Yellowstone caldera. The farther you walk along the rimside trail, the more impressive the view of the falls.

Charred hilltops make this stretch of road vulnerable to mud and rock slides; drive with your eyes open. Beyond Gibbon Falls the river, high and swift in spring, hugs the road on the right. As you drive farther into the canyon, the rocky mountainsides seem to weep, even in late August, as water trickles down the walls.

Cross the river several times in the next few miles. At about 8 miles **Beryl Spring** on the left, one of the hottest springs in the park, actually emerges from the ground boiling, as its temperature remains about 200 degrees Fahrenheit. Named for the blue-green gemstone, the hissing spring empties into the Gibbon River. Watch for hot springs in the river, indicated by steam rising sporadically as you drive along. One of the smaller bison herds in the park, always fun to watch, is sometimes found here.

Artist Paint Pots Trail

At the beginning of this expanse of meadow, at a little over 9 miles, you come to a side trail worth taking, one of my favorite short hikes in the park. A turnout to the right allows parking for a half-mile walk to **Artist Paint Pots.** A broadening of the path here has led to many more visitors discovering this treasure every year. I'm debating whether or not this improved path has helped or hurt this attraction, which used to be a quiet walk in the woods, but the paint pots are easier to see with the new boardwalks, and probably less damage is done to the surrounding area. The easy trail leads to an off-the-beaten-track group of hot springs, fumaroles, and paint pots. (Mud pots become paint pots when minerals, algae, and bacteria tint the mud/clay mixture.) The walk is fairly level until the end of the trail, where a series of stairs and platforms lead to a terrific overview of the thermal area. The thermal features lie in a private setting that quietly assaults the senses— the smell of moist earth, the sight of delicate wildflowers, the sound of bubbling springs, and if you're lucky, the feel of sunlight. Away from the road it is easy to hear morning birdsong, as well as an occasional plane overhead. Steam spouts from the hill next to the gleaming pools and bubbling pots of the area.

This area is one of the few places in Yellowstone where ferns grow, because of the moisture in the glen. Notice that many of the surrounding trees have been killed by absorbing the mineral-laden hot water. As you make your way along the trail, look for a fairly new small spring at a bend just as you turn right to head uphill. This little bubbler appeared in 1989, a reminder that this earth is constantly changing. The slightly acidic water maintains a temperature of about 193 degrees Fahrenheit; by comparison, hot bathwater is about 102 to 104 degrees Fahrenheit, and very hot coffee that is still drinkable would be about 138 degrees Fahrenheit. From this point boardwalk stairs ascend the hill, allowing you to get a close-up view of simmering mud pots. After taking in the overview from the top, continue the loop and retrace your steps to the parking lot. This little side trip makes you wonder how many thermal features exist in the park away from the Grand Loop, and reminds you how little of Yellowstone, only 2 percent, can be seen from the road.

Just beyond Artist Paint Pots on the left is **Gibbon Meadows,** which has another picnic area and trail. For the hearty hiker, this 1-mile trail on the west side of the road leads up a steep incline to **Monument Geyser Basin.** All that's left of the geysers are the sinter cones, standing sentry at the top of the hill. Gibbon Meadows is a good place in the evening to watch grazing elk or bison. In the river beyond Gibbon Meadows, you may see the "chocolate pots," caused by bubbling hot springs that deposit iron and siliceous sinter formations.

Although the road has slightly leveled off, beyond 10.5 miles it climbs again toward Norris. **Elk Park,** shortly beyond Gibbon Meadows, is appropriately named. Beyond 12 miles begin to watch for fields of steam to the northwest. These are the lower planes of the Norris Geyser Basin, a sprawling and varied collection of geothermal features. The drive ends at Norris Junction.

Norris Geyser Basin

Norris Geyser Basin, to the left, is a perennial favorite of park visitors. It was named for Philetus W. Norris, the second superintendent of the park. A lively character who affected the clothing and style of Buffalo Bill Cody, he both loved and protected the park. He steeped himself in its environment and history and wrote extensively of Yellowstone, educating the public and Congress. He is also appreciated for building the first roads here, making it possible for visitors to tour in the early years.

Norris Geyser Basin is the hottest bed of thermal activity in the park. Its proximity to the magma chamber, the underground molten material, makes it possibly

Aptly-named Artist Paint Pots Trail presents beautiful, colorful surprises.

the hottest thermal area in the world. Very dynamic, infinitely changeable, it is also the oldest. Its hot springs have been active for more than 115,000 years. Ongoing seismic activity causes constant changes in water pressure and underground channels. Here hot springs can flash into geysers. Each time you visit Norris, it is likely to be different.

From the parking lot the faint odor of sulfur greets you. A paved walk leads to a Yellowstone Association bookstore—located in a log cabin to the left—and beyond that a small museum and the information center. Stop at the museum for the most comprehensive explanation of thermal features found in the park and to pick up an interpretive brochure of the area. Other exhibits include information about the Yellowstone caldera, and the cavalry's tour of duty in the park in the 19th century. Ranger-led walks, given several times a day, impart extensive information; check the schedule at the information center. Here you will also find estimated geyser eruption times, information on the junior ranger program, and free brochures (multilingual) on biking, birds, hiking, fishing, flowers, geology, and history of the area.

Two very different geothermal basins surround the information center. To the north is **Porcelain Basin,** and to the south is **Back Basin.** You won't want to miss either. Begin at the overlook of Porcelain Basin, where the broad view reveals an eerie landscape of white, chalky, steamy terrain. The wonder of geological and biological forces in progress is all around. Small plants grow in the most amazing places, out of rocks or rivulets of water, while grass grows out of, for want of a more scientific term, black muck. The paths and boardwalks curving through Porcelain Basin pass gurgling hot springs and spouting geysers. A good portion of the paths are flat and, although not labeled as such, seem wheelchair accessible. Because this is the most active and changeable area in Yellowstone, it is especially important to remain on the trails at all times.

The Porcelain Basin is obviously named for its pearly color. Sinter, a form of dissolved limestone, comes to the earth's surface by way of all the springs, pots, fumaroles, and geysers of Porcelain Basin. The sinter, carried by the hot water, is deposited as the steam cools or moisture returns to the earth. Porcelain Basin is one of the fastest-changing places in Yellowstone, because constant deposits of the siliceous sinter, also called geyserite, flow across the landscape, clogging vents along the way. Water then bursts through weaker spots elsewhere where cracks and fissures allow it to reach the surface. The sinter is so prevalent that as you walk, clothes and shoes pick it up, leaving your feet and legs covered with milky white powder. At times it sounds as if the whole ground is bubbling up in this incredibly alive area. Arsenic and iron give many of the pools their orangish color, and algae and bacteria tint the others.

Haunting Porcelain Basin makes up half of the Norris Geyser Basin.

After visiting Porcelain Basin follow the map in the 50-cent brochure of the area and walk to Back Basin via the wooded path that passes by Minute Geyser and Palpitator Spring. Several small steam vents come seemingly from nowhere, and the smell of pine combined with sulfur wafts through the air. Sounds of the breeze stirring the pines, muted footsteps, and the occasional murmur of a vent make this an exceedingly peaceful, if short, walk. This path, thick with trees both live and fallen, emerges at the back loop of Back Basin.

Back Basin, home of a majority of the world's acidic geysers, holds several popular thermal features. **Steamboat,** the tallest geyser in the world, erupts anywhere from every 4 days to every 50 years. In a major eruption erratic Steamboat shoots to more than twice the height of Old Faithful, but more frequently it erupts 10 to 70 feet into the air. A major eruption can loose over a million gallons of water.

On May 23, 2005, Steamboat erupted at 2:41 p.m. Water shot 250 feet or more into the air, and the highway, more than 0.25 mile away, was so wet that passing cars had to turn on their windshield wipers. At this writing, it has not erupted in the past several years.

Echinus Geyser, which a few years ago erupted very predictably, has also quieted, but you might be lucky enough to see it in action. When sunlight hits the spray just right, Echinus resembles a shower of diamonds. Benches placed fairly close to the pool give geyser gazers a unique vantage point, unprotected from Echinus's mist. The entire Back Basin Trail is approximately 1.5 miles, round-trip. It passes Pearl Geyser, Porkchop Geyser (which in different phases has acted as a fumarole, a hot spring, a geyser, and currently a hot spring), and Emerald Spring.

As you leave Norris, elevation 7,484 feet, turn left (north) to visit Mammoth or head straight across the junction for the 12-mile drive to Canyon Village. Drive carefully, as elk frequent the woods surrounding the geyser basins and the campgrounds.

20

Norris to Mammoth Hot Springs

General description: A 21-mile drive through high meadows and forests, by many small lakes, waterfalls, and fumaroles. Stop at dramatic Golden Gate Canyon for a wonderful overview before moving on to the travertine terraces of Mammoth Hot Springs.

Driving time: 40 to 45 minutes.

Special attractions: Museum of the National Park Ranger, Twin Lakes, Roaring Mountain, Mount Holmes, Swan Lake Flats, Rustic Falls, Golden Gate Canyon, the Hoodoos, and Mammoth Hot Springs.

Location: Northwestern Yellowstone.

Drive route names & numbers: Grand Loop Road from Norris to Mammoth.

Travel season: Mid-Apr through early Nov, weather permitting. This is one of the first routes opened in the spring and the last closed in the fall.

Camping: This is prime camping territory. Norris (116 sites), Indian Creek (74 sites), and Mammoth (85 sites), National Park Service campgrounds, first-come, first-served basis.

Services: Full services at Mammoth Hot Springs, including medical clinic, post office, and Yellowstone National Park Headquarters.

Nearby points of interest: Sheepeater Cliffs, Bunsen Peak Road, Osprey Falls, Upper Terrace Loop Drive.

For more information: Yellowstone National Park Headquarters, Norris Ranger Station, Xanterra Reservations.

The Route

The route begins as you leave the Norris Geyser Basin and head north. An overlook to the left allows a look back at the ghostly landscape of fumaroles and springs with their steam rising from the white baked earth.

About 1.25 miles from Norris, the **Museum of the National Park Ranger** is on the right in a small log cabin, originally a cavalry outpost. Built in 1908, the cabin replaced an earlier structure built in 1897 when the cavalry first came to protect the park. This small museum tells the history of the guardians of the park, from early soldiers to National Park Service rangers, who, from 1916 to the present, have become specialists as historians, educators, geologists, environmentalists, and more. The film *An American Legacy* shows in the small auditorium here.

Cross the Gibbon River and drive beyond the Norris Campground (one of the nicest in the park) to begin the climb toward Mammoth Hot Springs. A pair of small lakes, **Nuphar** and **Nymph,** named for varieties of water lilies once found on the water, decorate the landscape to the left. Look for **Frying Pan Spring** at about

Norris to Mammoth Hot Springs

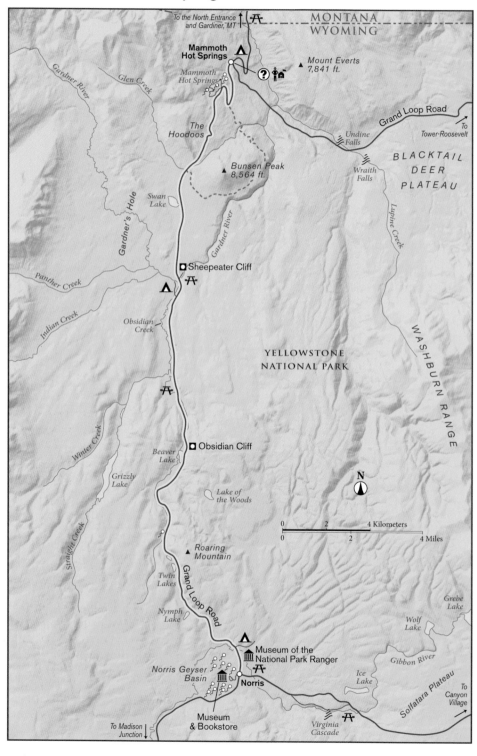

To the North Entrance
and Gardiner, MT

MONTANA
WYOMING

**Mammoth
Hot Springs**

▲ Mount Everts
7,841 ft.

Mammoth
Hot Springs

Gardner River

Glen Creek

The
Hoodoos

Grand Loop Road

To
Tower-Roosevelt

Undine
Falls

BLACKTAIL
DEER
PLATEAU

▲ Bunsen Peak
8,564 ft.

Wraith
Falls

Swan
Lake

Gardner River

Lupine Creek

Gardner's Hole

Panther Creek

□ Sheepeater Cliff

Indian Creek

Obsidian
Creek

YELLOWSTONE
NATIONAL PARK

WASHBURN RANGE

Winter Creek

Beaver
Lake

□ Obsidian Cliff

Grizzly
Lake

Lake of
the Woods

N

Straight Creek

0   2   4 Kilometers
0   2   4 Miles

▲ Roaring
Mountain

Grebe
Lake

Twin
Lakes

Grand Loop Road

Nymph
Lake

Wolf
Lake

Gibbon River

Museum of the
National Park Ranger

Ice
Lake

Norris Geyser
Basin

Norris

Solfatara Plateau

To
Canyon
Village

To Madison
Junction

Museum
& Bookstore

Virginia
Cascade

2.5 miles, named both for its sound, which imitates water being dripped on a hot griddle, and the spattering effect of the hot acidic water as it reaches the pond's surface. The marshy willow flats beyond the spring are potential moose habitat, and a likely place to see elk as well.

Forest and hills close in on both sides of the road as the uphill trip continues. **South Twin Lake** and **North Twin Lake** to the left, separated by only a thin strip of land, are interesting because, as Hiram Chittenden once noted, they "never simultaneously exhibit the same colors." The lakes also straddle a divide, and experts can't agree as to whether they drain to the north or south.

Trails & Tales of Early Travelers

Roaring Mountain, on the right about 5 miles from Norris, was once just that—a roaring mountain. The hill was named in 1885, when the noise from the fumarole was loud enough to be heard about 4 miles away. Reports confirm that its rumbling and hissing could be heard from Obsidian Cliff to the north. Over time, the roar waxed and waned and waxed again until about 1920, at which point it quieted considerably. Seismic activity in the area could at any time turn the volume up once more. Today, however, Roaring Mountain merely murmurs, and one's imagination alone can re-create the din of a hundred years ago. Even the current hiss is nearly drowned out by the babbling brook that wanders nearby. The name Whispering Mountain might be apt. The ashen, barren hillside, once covered with lodgepole pines, now bakes in acid sulfate strong enough to bleach and crumble the surrounding earth. **Lemonade Pool,** by the roadside, is named both for its color and its degree of acidity.

Obsidian Creek travels on the left beside the road, leading toward **Obsidian Cliff.** Watch for steamy spots in the creek, indicating where hot springs empty into it. At about 7.5 miles, **Beaver Lake,** to the left, holds the remnants of several beaver dams from years ago. Now overgrown with grasses and hampered by little water, this was once a popular trapping spot, before trapping and hunting in the park became illegal. Today, the picnic area here is still an inviting place to stop. One mile beyond, at about 8.5 miles, 200-foot-high Obsidian Cliff is one of the largest obsidian deposits in North America. Obsidian is rhyolite lava that for some reason cooled so suddenly that crystals had no time to form. As a result, the rhyolite almost flashed to glass—in this case, clear black glass. Although the cliff is now covered with moss and lichen, a careful look reveals the shiny material that was often crafted by Native Americans into arrowheads and other tools. In fact, if you look really carefully, swirling flow banding—the last movements of the magma before it cooled—is still evident. An interpretive sign reminds you not to remove any of the stone from the cliff or the park. It is illegal.

Roaring Mountain has been reduced to a whisper.

Beyond the cliff, meandering Obsidian Creek widens and begins braiding and lollygagging its way through a long meadow. An interpretive sign to the left of the road tells of the two fires that swept through this section of the forest in 1988. Watch for brilliantly hued mountain bluebirds, which make their homes in dead trees. Moose and elk also roam the area. As you pass from forest to meadow, **Mount Holmes** rises 10,336 feet on the left. It was named for William Henry Holmes, a member of the Hayden Survey and the first geologist to write about the park. An artist as well as mapmaker, Holmes once directed the National Gallery of Art in Washington, D.C.

At about 9.5 miles, shortly after you exit the canyon and enter the meadow, **Apollinaris Spring** and picnic area are on the left. The spring fills with cold mineral water, which was once sipped by park guests. Early concessionaires sold pricey bottled water for sightseers to carry with them on their tours, but someone discovered the mineral water of Apollinaris, and visitors believed they could do better for free. Because of the possibility of contamination, it is a practice that is definitely no longer recommended.

At about 10.5 miles, an exhibit to the left offers information about the moose population of Yellowstone. The area, **Willow Park,** is marshy, willow-laden terrain that makes the perfect hiding place and dining room for the largest member of the deer family. A moose's long legs allow it to wade in marshes and creeks to feed on vegetation growing underwater, or to move through high snow, or to trot along at the pace of a horse in a canter. While feeding in the marshes or streams, moose can keep their heads submerged for up to 3 minutes. Unlike bison and elk, moose travel alone, except for mothers with their babies. Once between Canyon and Norris, I saw a cow moose cleverly walk into the road to stop traffic while her calf crossed to the other side. No motorist dared challenge her.

Next you approach a meadow from which several trails lead into the backcountry. Turnouts all along this route allow anglers a chance to fish along wandering Obsidian and Indian Creeks, and at Swan Lake Flat to the north. Cross Indian Creek, so named because the Bannock Trail once paralleled the creek; Indian Creek Campground, popular with hikers and fishers, is set back to the left of the road.

The Only Known Tribe to Inhabit the Park

After the road crosses the creek, a short side road to the east leads to a view of **Sheepeater Cliffs,** named for the one Indian tribe that lived in Yellowstone year-round. In their native tongue, the Sheepeater Indians were known as Takuarikas, meaning "those who eat sheep." Because bighorn sheep were plentiful here, the Sheepeaters were not nomadic, which differentiated them from the "bison eaters," who had to travel to hunt. When trappers began traveling through Yellowstone in the mid-1800s, they once reportedly took five Sheepeater guides along with them to the geyser basins less than 14 miles away, which the Indians had never before seen and which left them in amazement. A branch of the Shoshones, the Sheepeaters lived here until 1872, when the national park was created, at which point Chief Washakie invited them to join his Shoshone tribe at the Wind River Reservation in northwestern Wyoming. For anyone who has ever visited here in winter, it is incredible to imagine living a year-round life here in the shadow of the cliffs, which rise in hardened columns of lava flow basalt.

About 16 miles from Norris, the meadow known as **Swan Lake Flats** comes into view on the left. Swan Lake itself is only 3 feet deep, but the famous Yellowstone trumpeter swans do land and swim here. A turnout to the left has an interpretive sign identifying the peaks of the Gallatin Range to the west. They are beautiful from this vantage point. This whole area is known as **Gardner's Hole,** named for Johnson Gardner, a famous old mountain man and rascal. The term hole was used by early trappers to describe a high plateau surrounded by mountains. Open, sagebrush-covered fields on both sides of the road attract Yellowstone's most famous residents, its wildlife. In spring, on the meadow below Bunsen Peak, bison take advantage of early warmed earth as the snow melts on the high plain; in fall, elk congregate here. Commonly, one bull elk grazes morning and evening with a harem of about a dozen females. When last I drove through here, people lined the road, peering through binoculars, watching a bear so far away that it looked no bigger than a pencil point.

To the north just after you cross Glen Creek, a tributary of the Gardner River, **Bunsen Peak Road** on the right offers a good tour for hikers and cyclists. The 9-mile-long gravel road follows the ledge of 800-foot-deep **Sheepeater Canyon,** affording a beautiful view of **Osprey Falls.** In fact, for the ardent hiker, a trail leads over the rim of the canyon to descend 800 feet to the base of the falls. The Bunsen Peak Road rejoins the Grand Loop just below the one-way Upper Terrace Drive at Mammoth.

The Golden Gate Pass

Beyond Swan Flats the road begins a short ascent across the northern edge of the Yellowstone Plateau to the **Golden Gate Pass.** The pass is a surprising change in terrain between Gardner's Hole and what looks like a scene from a 1950s Arizona postcard. Yellowstone's Golden Gate has rocky cliffs rising to the west above the deep canyon to the east. The pass is named both for the yellow color of the rocks, caused by lichen and moss growing on the canyon walls, and the fact that this was the first real navigable gateway to the higher plateau for visitors entering the park through the Roosevelt Arch in Gardiner.

The road through the Golden Gate was originally built in 1887 by the US Army Corps of Engineers, led by Daniel Kingman. Kingman also designed the Grand Loop Road as a route that would take park visitors by many of the most memorable features of the park. Before this road was built, the route to the Yellowstone Plateau lay over Snow Pass to the west, a route so steep that wagons and carriages heading south frequently, but accidentally, dumped luggage and provisions on the road as they climbed. Stop at the pullout to look back at the roadway and wonder at the engineering feat that allows concrete to seemingly hang on the canyon wall to bolster the road. This stop offers a view of **Rustic Falls,** which descends in terraces in a 47-foot drop to the river below.

As you pull away from the falls, notice the alternating swaths of trees on the nearby hillside. Lines of burned forest are flanked by lines of trees untouched by fire; the capricious nature of the 1988 burn is evident in this scene on the northern slope of Bunsen Peak. A little beyond Rustic Falls, the **Silver Gate** and the **Hoodoos,** odd and obvious boulder configurations to the left of the road, remind one of a moonscape from an old B movie. The large travertine boulders, silvery

A pullout at the top of the Golden Gate allows a view of ethereal Rustic Falls.

in color, were cast downhill in an ancient rockslide. Here, the road—good 1940s Hollywood terrain—has once again changed too quickly for travelers to orient themselves. The word *hoodoo*, a common geologic appellation, is African in origin, meaning a voodoo figure signifying bad luck. A very short one-way road cuts about 0.1 mile from north to south through the Hoodoos, but don't try to make the turn onto it if you are traveling south to north.

Beyond the Hoodoos the route steeply descends and winds through Douglas fir and aspen forest toward the **Mammoth Hot Springs Terraces.** Occasional small ice ponds appear to the right as the canyon yields to more gentle slopes. A roadside interpretive sign explains the benefits to nature from uneven forest wildfire. After a burn the forest becomes interspersed with meadows, attracting a larger variety of wildlife to the area.

Hot springs are the most common geothermal feature in the park, and the accumulation and variety of springs found at **Mammoth** are wonderfully impressive. The terraces are actually ancient mounds of travertine, dissolved limestone also known as geyserite, which is carried to the surface by water seeping through underground channels. Here in Mammoth it is deposited as travertine at the rate of about 2,000 pounds a day. This ancient process has sculpted terraces of intricate and delicate beauty that cover an entire hillside.

A little over 19 miles from Norris, turn left onto **Mammoth Terrace Drive,** a one-way 1.6-mile loop that makes its way through the **Upper Terrace.** Too narrow for campers or buses, the drive takes you by features such as **Canary Spring,** where sulfur-producing bacteria color the water; intriguing **Orange Spring Mound,** where springs atop its cone have actively deposited travertine since at least 1871; **White Elephant Back Terrace,** named for its shape; and the now inactive **Angel Terrace.** The loop opens in late May or early June, depending on snow accumulation. A parking lot along the drive affords an overlook of the Lower Terraces, as well as the opportunity to hike to them on **Mammoth Terrace Trail.** From the overlook you can also enjoy a view of the community below, old Fort Yellowstone and environs; except for the automobiles, the scene has changed little in nearly a century. More information about the village of Mammoth is found in the description of Scenic Route 12, "Mammoth Hot Springs to Tower-Roosevelt." Welcome this loop drive, as the Lower Terraces offer extensive opportunities to stretch your legs.

After you leave the Upper Terrace, the Grand Loop road descends through scrubby terrain toward the **Lower Terraces** and what is nearly the lowest elevation in the park. A view to the east shows the high steel bridge on the route leading to Tower-Roosevelt. Watch for elk, which frequently graze or soak in the sun on the hills close to the road. Two parking lots are available for you to stop and explore the Lower Terraces. The first provides easy access to springs at the top

A prism of colors can be found in Orange Spring Mound in the Upper Terrace of Mammoth.

of the terraces, and the second is at the lowest part of the configuration of hot springs. At either place, grab a brochure with map provided by the Yellowstone Association—buy it for 50 cents, or use it for no charge and return it—and follow the path through the ever-changing terraces and pools. As always, stay on the boardwalks, because the ground around the thermal features is delicate and unpredictable. Dr. A.C. Peel, a mineralogist, described this area in 1871: "We were totally unprepared to find them, the grand mammoth hot springs and terraces, so beautiful and extensive. Before us lay a high white hill composed of calcareous sediment, deposited from numerous hot springs. The whole mass looked like some grand cascade that had been suddenly arrested in its descent and frozen."

The terraces never appear exactly the same, day to day. Springs appear and disappear as vents become clogged with travertine. This hill is growing, with travertine deposits adding 8 inches to 2 feet a year. However, as the self-guided tour brochure says, the mountain is literally turning itself inside out by dissolving the underground limestone in pools of hot water and depositing them on the surface.

Minerva Spring is the grandest feature of the terraces. Named for the Roman goddess of wisdom and the arts, Minerva covers a huge portion of the hill. In spring it is surrounded by imposing amounts of steam, and snow-covered peaks rise in the background. Other features of the Lower Terraces include 37-foot-high **Liberty Cap,** a travertine deposit uniquely shaped like the caps popularized during the French Revolution. Several geyserite deposits resemble outdoor stalactites and were formed much the same way. **Palette Spring** and **Opal and Jupiter Terraces** are active features continuing the water flow that forms the terraces. Allow about 2 hours to walk the entire trail system. This path is moderately difficult, with an elevation change of close to 300 feet.

As you leave Mammoth Hot Springs, continue on to explore Mammoth, the oldest established community in Yellowstone, or travel more of the Grand Loop. The Albright Visitor Center is always worth a stop, as are the other attractions described in the Gardiner to Mammoth and the Mammoth to Tower-Roosevelt drives. Whichever direction you take, travel with anticipation. More treats are in store.

GRAND TETON
NATIONAL PARK

Overview

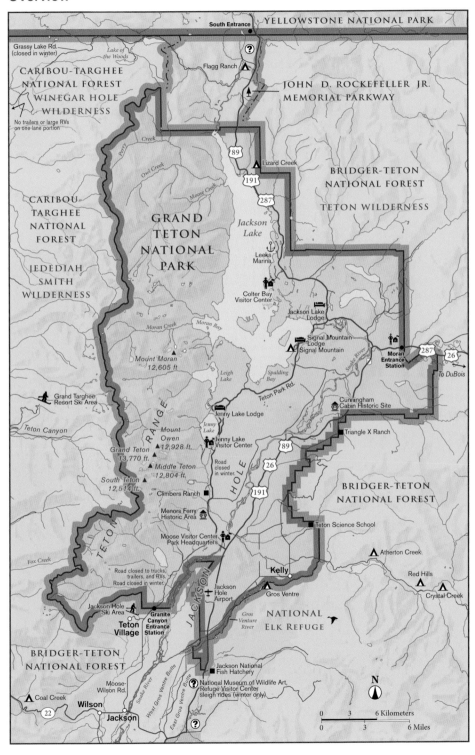

GRAND TETON NATIONAL PARK

The Grand Tetons, the high craggy peaks majestically rising 7,000 feet above the floor of Jackson Hole, are enduring symbols of the American West. The mountains dominate the park that bears their name and assault your senses with their grandeur.

Unlike Yellowstone, where rare intriguing features appear one after the other, in Grand Teton National Park the mountains are the attraction. With no foothills to interfere with their soaring height, the Tetons jut from the base of the valley in dramatic and astonishing splendor. Opportunities for photography and outdoor activities abound. The creation of 310,000-acre Grand Teton National Park was the result of a large battle between those who wanted to conserve the area and those who wanted to profit from it. Today Jackson Hole uneasily accommodates both, although tensions remain.

Topography

The Tetons are a relatively small mountain range by Rocky Mountain standards. Only 40 miles long by about 15 miles wide, this imposing stone wall was formed by uplift and erosion along a major fault line. About 10 million years ago, a split occurred along the fault, thrusting the western block of granite upward while allowing the eastern block to sink, creating the stunning mountains and the valley known as Jackson Hole. The process continues today. The mountains are still rising and the valley is sinking as seismic activity continues to disturb land along the fault. Most quakes in the area are too small to feel, although occasionally larger tremors grab the attention of residents and tourists, and the potential for a massive earthquake is ever present.

The Snake River runs through the valley, and a string of glacial lakes decorates the base of the mountains. The unparalleled combination of craggy pinnacles, crisp mountain air, crystalline waters, sagebrush- and wildflower-covered fields, and abundant wildlife would be a paradise if not for the nearly 8-month-long winters. Some argue that this is paradise anyway.

The Tetons are the youngest range in the Rocky Mountain chain. The Rockies, probably 70 to 80 million years old, predate the Tetons by more than 50 million years. Although the valley has filled with gravel and sediment over the eons, it is still dropping at about four times the rate of the rising mountains. The wild and rugged profile of the peaks was carved by the last ice age, 10,000 to 12,000 years

It's a beautiful day in the neighborhood.

ago. Very large, closely spaced glaciers covered the mountains, and the valley floor was covered by a continuous thick sheet of moving ice, a piedmont glacier. As glaciers slipped from and honed the mountain peaks, the piedmont glacier extended almost to where US 89 runs now, paving the way, as it were, for flat, sage-covered fields. Glaciers from the mountains formed basins and left moraines as the ice melted about 10,000 years ago. The basins now form the series of beautiful lakes at the foot of the mountains that on a clear day reflect the peaks in glorious symmetry. About a dozen small glaciers remain today, but they are powerless to further sculpt the mountains. Although they are still visible on several peaks, they are too small to have a visible effect on the shape of things.

Explorers & Settlers

Evidence shows that native hunters have peopled the area since the end of the last ice age, about 10,000 years ago. As early as the 16th or 17th century, Indians probably hunted the valley regularly in summer; the winters were too severe for habitation. Among the earliest cultures here were probably the Sheepeaters, an isolated and peaceful band of Indians who lived in family groups rather than tribes. Blackfeet, Crow, Shoshone, Bannock, and Gros Ventre tribes also visited the region.

When mountain men arrived, signs of Indian trails and hunts imprinted the valley. From early written and oral records, the peaks clearly astounded visitors from the beginning.

John Colter, who had left the returning Lewis and Clark expedition to explore the region with trappers, probably made his way through here during the winter of 1807–08, a daunting journey at best. He spent the winter wandering the mountains and valleys on foot, making notes and descriptions of what he found in his lengthy travels. His information opened the way for fur trappers and traders. Indeed, the opening of the West was accelerated by a whim of fashion—the desire for beaver pelts to make hats. In 1829 David Jackson and William Sublette, two of the owners of the Rocky Mountain Fur Company, met at Jackson Lake near the Tetons, a meeting that probably resulted in the valley and lake being named. Trappers quickly began referring to "Jackson's Hole," but eventually the "s" was dropped in favor of the modern usage.

From the 1840s, when "beaver fever" ended, until the 1870s or early 1880s, few came to the area. It was so remote, in fact, that it provided perfect protection for a group of horse thieves led by Harvey Gleason, who was also known as William "Teton" Jackson. He and his gang became adept at stealing horses from states and territories to the west and driving them to Jackson Hole for rebranding. When the new brands healed, the horses were moved to South Dakota or elsewhere in Wyoming and sold. This band of creative bandits would then steal horses from the east, sometimes the very horses they had previously sold, drive them back through Jackson Hole, and sell them in the west. Nearly 300 men were reportedly involved in the operation. They had many run-ins with authorities, as well as many escapes. Stories of Gleason and his men add to the Wild West aura of Jackson Hole.

Homesteaders and former trappers began moving to Jackson Hole in 1884. The earliest route used, Teton Pass, was very difficult to traverse, so settlement was slow. People often carried their goods by hand over the pass from Idaho. When wagons did try to make the trek, their wheels would have to be locked by large logs in order to keep them from turning while going downhill. The first road over the pass wasn't built until 1905, and one can only imagine how treacherous the journey was. Homesteaders found it too cold to farm here, and the growing season was too short, but it was possible to grow hay and raise cattle. Even today, jackleg fences, also known as buck-and-rail fences, divide the landscape, a reminder of the early settlers.

As early as 1915 people spoke of making the Teton Range a part of the National Park System, when Stephen Mather, head the National Park Service, and Horace Albright, superintendent of Yellowstone, were touring the area. Their first thought was to make the mountain range a part of Yellowstone National Park, but opposition from politicians in both Wyoming and Idaho thwarted the idea. Local residents wanted no road construction or extra people in the region, preferring to remain isolated. However, when ranchers in Idaho attempted to gain water rights for irrigation and when building continued, it became clear to many in Jackson that the Teton area was in danger of changing drastically. Many residents rethought their opposition to the Tetons becoming a national park.

Rockefeller's Foresight

In 1924, on a visit to Yellowstone with his three sons—Laurance, Nelson, and John—John D. Rockefeller Jr. was escorted to the southern part of the park by Horace Albright, who was still pursuing, albeit surreptitiously, the national park idea. Although Albright had been warned by his superiors not to lobby Rockefeller for anything, he steered his visitors just far enough south that they could marvel at the magnificent Teton Range. Albright's furtive inspiration was successful, and Rockefeller, ignited by what he saw, devoted the next 30 years to preserving the pristine beauty of the region.

When Grand Teton National Park was first set aside in 1929, it encompassed only the mountain range; none of the valley was included. Rockefeller, however, had a grander vision. Knowing that his efforts for preservation would be fought by developers and ranchers in the area who wanted to profit from the land's resources, Rockefeller formed the Snake River Land Company, a local coalition in which he was a silent partner. Over the years the company quietly bought up private land whenever it was offered for sale. It was not widely known at the time that Rockefeller was involved in the ploy. Paying about $39 an acre, "the Snakes," as the land company was called by its enemies, ultimately purchased 33,562 acres of private land for a total of about $1.4 million.

In 1933 Rockefeller and the Snake River Land Company offered to donate their acreage to the US government as a national monument. Years of argument over the idea ensued, with preservationists pushing the plan, and ranchers and developers angrily opposing it. After a lengthy battle, which lasted more than a decade and generated more paper for the Department of the Interior than any other US conflict over land, the tussle looked as if it would conclude. In 1943 President Franklin Roosevelt signed an executive order declaring the area between Yellowstone and the town of Jackson a national monument. Of course, this only fanned the flames of controversy. The state of Wyoming challenged the legality of the order, but the federal court refused to be involved. Congress ultimately rescinded the president's order, and the dispute wasn't resolved until 1949, when Rockefeller helped focus Congress by threatening to put the land up for public sale. In September 1950, Congress expanded Grand Teton National Park.

Wildflowers proliferate throughout the summer.

Although development of the area obviously continues today, park visitors owe a debt to all who had the foresight to try to preserve this land for wildlife and recreation. The Tetons provide unparalleled space and beauty for outdoor enjoyment, luring both vacationers and residents. Trails for hiking, biking, and horseback riding; rivers and lakes for fishing, boating, and whitewater rafting; and awe-inspiring mountains for skiing, camping, and rock-climbing—all grant sanctuary from everyday preoccupations.

The scenic routes in the park form a large ellipse. The road that passes closest to the mountains is called the Inner Loop Road. The Outer Loop Road passes closer to the eastern side of the valley, offering a different but still magnificent perspective. Unlike the Grand Loop in Yellowstone, this route is easy to drive in one day. Then you can decide whether to spend the rest of your vacation time rafting, resting, fishing, hiking, or shopping in nearby Jackson. Whatever you decide, Grand Teton National Park could turn out to be one of the most spectacular vacation destinations of your life.

21

John D. Rockefeller Jr. Memorial Parkway

General description: A 6.8-mile drive connecting Yellowstone National Park to Grand Teton National Park.

Driving time: 10 to 15 minutes.

Special attractions: Flagg Ranch Resort, camping, scenery, Bridger-Teton National Forest, and Teton Wilderness.

Location: Northwestern Wyoming.

Drive route names & numbers: John D. Rockefeller Jr. Memorial Parkway; (US 89/287).

Travel season: Year-round on the Outer Loop Road, from Jackson to Moran to Flagg Ranch. Entrance to Yellowstone Park is closed during the winter beyond Flagg Ranch.

Camping: Flagg Ranch, operated by the ranch, reservations required (175 sites).

Services: Full services at Flagg Ranch. No reliable cell service.

Nearby points of interest: Hot springs, Huckleberry Mountain, Grassy Lake Reclamation Road.

For more information: Flagg Ranch Resort, Grand Teton Lodge Company, National Park Service at Yellowstone or Moran, Bridger-Teton National Forest.

The Route

Used as an entryway to either Yellowstone or the Tetons, this short drive begins at the second-most traveled gateway to Yellowstone National Park: the South Entrance. (West Yellowstone is the busiest.) The 6.8-mile route to Grand Teton National Park is bordered by thick lodgepole pines, the Snake River, creeks, campgrounds, and rugged backcountry. Depending on the traffic, this drive can be a quick jaunt or a slow crawl. A Burma Shave-like sign gives a good warning.

> WE SAW WILDLIFE
> FROM AFAR
> UNTIL WE HIT THEM
> WITH OUR CAR.
> SLOW DOWN, AND ENJOY THE RIDE.

The **John D. Rockefeller Jr. Memorial Parkway,** designated in 1972, honors the man most responsible for the conservation of the land encompassing the Teton Mountain Range. In a fascinating display of political acumen and tenacity, Rockefeller and the local Snake River Land Company worked to buy and preserve 33,562 acres here, which they donated to expand the park. The parkway itself

John D. Rockefeller Jr. Memorial Parkway

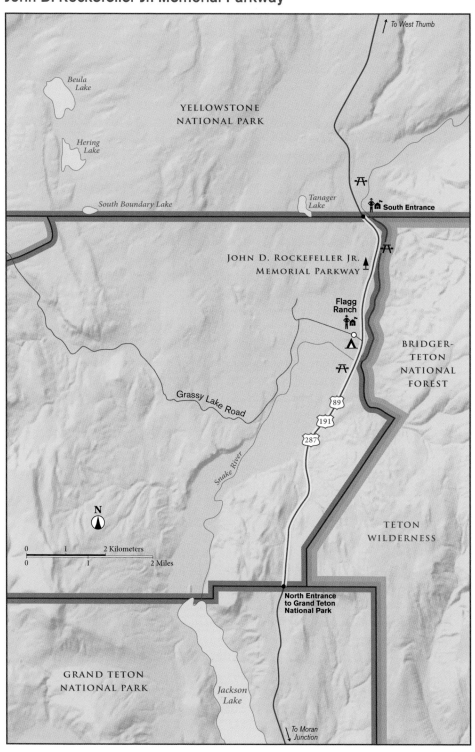

To West Thumb

Beula Lake

YELLOWSTONE
NATIONAL PARK

Hering Lake

South Boundary Lake

Tanager Lake

South Entrance

JOHN D. ROCKEFELLER JR.
MEMORIAL PARKWAY

Flagg Ranch

BRIDGER-
TETON
NATIONAL
FOREST

Grassy Lake Road

89
191
287

Snake River

N

0   1   2 Kilometers
0   1   2 Miles

TETON
WILDERNESS

North Entrance
to Grand Teton
National Park

GRAND TETON
NATIONAL PARK

Jackson Lake

To Moran
Junction

consists of 23,770 acres, or 37 square miles between the parks that are now protected against development.

The road follows the **Snake River,** which was probably named not for its serpentine shape but for the Shoshone, or "Snake," Indians who lived near it. To the left (east) of the parkway are the **Bridger-Teton National Forest** and **Teton Wilderness.** In this pine-pervaded corridor, a spate of charred trees stands as a reminder of the 1988 Yellowstone fires.

Shortly after exiting Yellowstone, look across the meadow to the east to see steam rising about 0.5 mile away from the Huckleberry Hot Springs. An easy walk, especially at the end of summer when the Snake River is low and easy to cross, takes you to a grotto and a pleasant soak. More hot springs simmer another 0.5 mile beyond the first ones, on Polecat Creek. As you venture farther, you get a beautiful view of the north end of the Tetons.

About 2 miles from Yellowstone's southern exit, to the right (west) of the road, is **Flagg Ranch Resort.** Since the roads entering Yellowstone from the south and the east were the last to be built, in 1892 a soldier station to protect the park was established along the west bank of the Snake River at a place mistakenly thought to be in Yellowstone. This army post eventually was moved 2 miles to the north to the correct border, but a service area gradually developed around the old site. Flagg Ranch, named for the American flag the army flew at the site, now offers lodging, camping, supplies, gas, food, and RV hookups. You can also make arrangements here for horseback riding, float trips, and fishing expeditions. The new concessionaire for the ranch, the Grand Teton Lodge Company, also runs Jackson Lake Lodge, Colter Bay, and Jenny Lake Lodge. Upgrading of lodging, cabins, and the addition of a coffee shop enhance services available on the Rockefeller Parkway and the northern end of the park. The nearby ranger and information station provides updates and answers for questions, and you can enjoy evening campfire programs offered at the Flagg Ranch amphitheater.

Grassy Lake Road, to the west near the Flagg Ranch turnoff, leads to the trailhead for a short hike back to Huckleberry and Polecat Hot Springs, heated by buried, but still cooling, lava. Grassy Lake Road itself continues to Ashton, 45 miles to the west, but you should attempt the drive only in dry summer months. Several people have wound up in trouble by following this road that appears on their GPS systems as a reasonable route. Their GPS systems are wrong. I once tried Grassy Lake Road in July with three children in the car and, seeing no other cars the whole way, quickly questioned my sanity. To this day, I wonder whether I was actually on the road, which seemed to disappear at the summit of Calf Creek Hill, or just working my way by car through the wilderness. Rocky and bumpy, Grassy Lake Road is not for RVs or trailers. The road is open in winter as a snowmobile route, and probably a spectacular one.

Cabins at Flagg Ranch are a bit more upscale than those in Yellowstone.

The parkway follows the path of the Snake River, which has its headwaters just outside the southeastern section of Yellowstone, in the **Bridger-Teton National Forest.** The river enters Jackson Lake about 4 miles beyond Flagg Ranch, then continues writhing through Wyoming and Idaho, forming a good portion of Idaho's western border, until it meets the Columbia River on its way to the Pacific—a 1,038-mile journey.

Below Flagg Ranch an unmarked road leads eastward to the Sheffield Creek Trailhead, the Bridger-Teton National Forest, and the Teton Wilderness area. For the adventurous, a 5-mile hike east on the **Sheffield Creek Trail** leads to the **Huckleberry Mountain Lookout,** at an elevation of 9,615 feet. Assume, however, that any topographical feature named "Huckleberry" might just as aptly be named "Grizzly," as the fruit is one of the mighty bears' favorite snacks.

The first national forest in the country, the Bridger-Teton (established in 1891) surrounds Jackson Hole on three sides and covers 3.4 million acres, making it the second largest national forest outside of Alaska. Timber harvesting, hunting, and oil, mineral, and gas exploration are all allowed in national forests, as is recreation. Camping, swimming, hiking, fishing, horseback riding, climbing, wildlife viewing, sightseeing, floating, boating, skiing, and snowmobiling are all popular and permissible pursuits. The Teton Wilderness was once home to dinosaurs, as evidenced by fossilized footprints found here.

Sheffield picnic area to the west at about 3 miles offers a chance to get out and enjoy the scenery, but many more opportunities present themselves in the next 40 miles. Dime Creek turnout to the east at 3.7 miles is notable because the creek passes near Nickel Creek and Quarter Creek. The story is probably rich.

Before you enter Grand Teton National Park, **Steamboat Mountain** rises on the right to a mere 7,872 feet, not high by Rocky Mountain standards. The peak was reportedly named for an active steam vent. At about 6.8 miles, cross into Grand Teton National Park. The entrance is marked by a stone pillar but no ranger station. Staffed entrances can be found to the southeast at Moran, and to the south at both Moose and Granite Canyon. Get out your camera, relax, and enjoy this special place.

22

Dubois, WY, to Moran Junction

General description: A 55-mile trip, beginning in high scrubby desert, through Wind River Valley badlands, climbing to high Togwotee (TOH-gah-dee) Pass, and descending into Jackson Hole, approaching the Grand Tetons from the east.

Driving time: 1 hour and 15 minutes.

Special attractions: Dubois Museum, National Bighorn Sheep Interpretive Center, Bridger-Teton National Forest, Shoshone National Forest, Teton and Washakie National Wilderness, Absaroka Mountain Range, and Wind River Range.

Location: Northwestern Wyoming.

Drive route names & numbers: Part of the Wyoming Centennial Scenic Byway, US 287/26.

Travel season: Year-round, but summer through early fall is the most reliable travel time. The pass receives heavy snow.

Camping: Several camping areas near the highway, including Hatchet (9 sites), Brooks Lake (13 sites), Pinnacles (primitive backcountry), Falls (54 sites), and nearby Horse Creek (9 sites), and Turpin Meadows (18 sites).

Services: Full services in Dubois. Lodging, food, and gas at Cowboy Village on Togwotee near the top of the pass, and occasionally along the way. Cell service is spotty along this route.

Nearby points of interest: Jackson Hole Mountain Resort, Brooks Lake, Brooks Lake Creek Falls, Washakie Needles, Turpin Meadow Recreation Area.

For more information: Dubois Chamber of Commerce; Bridger-Teton National Forest, Jackson, Wyoming; Shoshone National Forest, Dubois, Wyoming.

The Route

Tiny **Dubois** (DOO-boyce)—reported population 962, elevation 6,917 feet— huddles next to the Wind River in the broad Wind River Valley. When the first post office was established here in 1886, the postmaster refused the town's original name of Never Sweat, Wyoming, believing it to lack dignity. Citizens accepted the suggested appellation, Dubois, for a Senator Dubois from Idaho, coincidentally on the Senate Postal Committee at the time, the funding source for the post office. A typical small western town with the regulation number of saloons, wooden boardwalks, western art concerns, and motels, Dubois is notable for its relatively mild winter climate. The sign that greets you as you enter town states WELCOME TO DUBOIS, WYOMING, VALLEY OF THE WARM WINDS.

The **Wind River,** actually the northern channel of the Bighorn River, is named for the temperate chinook winds along its course. In winter they blow so constantly that snow does not stay on the ground very long. While much of the

Dubois, WY, to Moran Junction

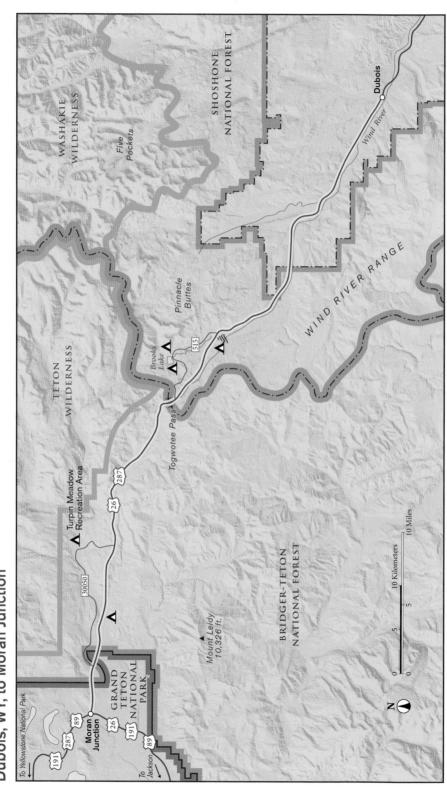

surrounding area is a winter playground, the population of Dubois escapes many of the extremes of winter weather.

Dubois has a heritage in ranching and timber, but tourism looms as a major part of its future. In 1987 lumber companies pulled out of the area, and the sawmill, the town's major employer, closed due to over-harvesting of usable timber from the nearby Shoshone and Bridger-Teton National Forests. However, the rising popularity of winter activities, the draw of nearby Jackson, and the natural beauty of the land have lured newcomers, many of whom have built second homes in the area. Winter visitors like to snowmobile, dogsled, and cross-country ski in the vicinity's recreational land. A nine-hole golf course and an incongruous espresso bar in the center of town attest to the growing popularity of this isolated location.

Local History, Local Historian

At the Dubois Chamber of Commerce you can pick up a self-guided tour map of area historic structures, including tie-hack cabins and logging flumes. Ponder the quirky log staircase in the center of town that retreats into a hand-dug cave, once used as a jail and, for a time, a bar.

For good conversation, stop at **Welty's General Store** on the main street and talk to Frank A. Welty III, grandson of the gentleman who founded the store, circa 1889. Frank spins a good tale of how the store came to be in possession of one of Butch Cassidy's pistols, and he can explain why, if Dubois lacks adequate snowfall, the weather in the rest of the country is affected. Welty's General Store is on the National Register of Historic Places.

Near the west end of town on the left (south) side of the highway, the citizens of Dubois built the **National Bighorn Sheep Interpretive Center** to provide information on this indigenous animal. The center features exhibits and interactive displays of bighorn and Dall sheep, and of the Sheepeater Indians of the Wind River Range. Here you can book tours of Whiskey Mountain, the sheep's winter range. The center is open from Memorial Day through Labor Day weekend, 9 a.m. to 8 p.m. Winter hours are subject to change.

Next door to the Interpretive Center, the **Dubois Museum** concentrates on the natural and human history of the area, with exhibits of timbering and pioneer artifacts. A display of fine Shoshone beadwork and painting on leather graced the main room when I last visited. Several vintage buildings, including a bunkhouse, an old schoolhouse, and a 1920s service station, have been relocated to the museum from nearby towns or ranches. This small museum—open every day from 9 a.m. to 6 p.m. in summer, and Tues to Sat 10 a.m. to 4 p.m. in winter—is worth your time. Another enterprise, the **Headwaters Arts and Conference**

A cattle drive halts traffic on the road from Dubois to Moran. Mount Moran rises in the background.

Center, promotes and exhibits local and regional artists. Dubois is clearly a town involved in both its history and its future.

For a good side trip, a well-marked turnoff leads to the National Fish Hatchery and the bighorn sheep wintering range about 4 miles from the east end of town. The land of the wintering range was carved by ancient glaciers, and glacial lakes and several small glaciers remain. You can hike to the largest glacial snowfields found in the contiguous US from a trailhead at the end of this road. Careful observers find Indian petroglyphs, ancient carvings on rocks, along the walls of hills on this route.

As you begin your trip from Dubois, a National Forest Ranger Information Center 0.25 mile from town allows an opportunity to obtain maps and ask questions, particularly about the forested lands through which this road passes. A scenic overlook to the north, about a mile from the town's western edge, offers a sweeping view of the river valley and surrounding mountain peaks. The drive to the overlook is steep and narrow, not recommended for RVs. Between Dubois and Togwotee Pass, the road courses through the colorful, eroded badlands of the **Eocene Wind River Formation.** To the right of the road, hills, rather than peaks, lie behind the valley's fields, and to the southwest, stratified rock outcroppings slope off the Wind River Range. Jackleg fences confine the horses, cattle, and sheep that populate the valley, and the river's course nurtures cottonwoods, willows, and wildflowers. From the very beginning of this drive, the striated hills and land formations catch your eye and command attention. The scenery is picturesque in a western sort of way—all fences and horses, ridges and mountains, corrals and sagebrush-covered buttes to the south; to the north, buttes and amazing red rock form badlands reminiscent of Sedona, Arizona, or southern Utah.

The road begins to climb shortly after leaving Dubois. The Du Noir public access area to the right (east), where the Du Noir River Valley joins the Wind River Valley, leads to the Shoshone National Forest and Bridger-Teton Wilderness. **Ramshorn Peak,** horizontal layers of volcanic conglomerate and ash, rises on the northern horizon.

About 9 miles beyond Dubois, the old Union Pass Road to the south meets US 287/26. A historical roadside marker tells the story of the Astorians, explorers for John Jacob Astor, who, in 1811, used the pass while assessing the area for its fur-trapping potential. This road led early Indians, trappers, assorted prospectors, and hunters southwest over the Wind River Range toward Jackson Hole. John Colter, an explorer from Lewis and Clark's entourage, was probably the first Caucasian to view and write about this land in about 1807, while looking for trapping and trading locations. Jim Bridger used the route on his way west. Ferdinand Hayden and his geographical expedition also crossed the pass in 1871 while mapping and surveying the area. **Union Pass,** elevation 9,210 feet on the Continental Divide, is thought by some to have been named in 1860 by Captain William F. Raynolds of the US Army Corps of Engineers in a moment of patriotism. Supposedly he thought the pass was in the center of the continent. Others believe the name is because the pass unites the Atlantic and Pacific watersheds. In fact, this point marks a division in the waters leading to the country's great rivers: **Jakey's Fork** ultimately empties into the Missouri/Mississippi, **Fish Creek** finds the Snake River on its way to the Columbia, and **Roaring Fork** winds up in the Colorado, via the Green River. However the name came about, a gravel road carries you to the top of the pass and beyond, if you want to go. On the back (western) side of the pass, the road becomes extremely rough, so travel slowly and with caution.

The ascent on US 287/26 to Togwotee Pass begins on a good three-lane highway. The road rises and falls for a few miles, gradually gaining elevation. Colorful clay stones and tuffaceous sandstones to the north date from about 49 million years ago. Their softness and vulnerability to erosion make them subject to landslides, but at this point they are not immediately by the road.

The border of the **Shoshone National Forest,** 2.4 million acres of mountain forest, more than half of which is wilderness, marks the beginning of the **Centennial Scenic Byway.** The river falls away as the road continues its gradual climb.

Road 532 to the left (south) passes Sheridan Creek and leads to **Warm Springs Creek,** hidden in the high peaks of the Wind River Range. The difference between a warm spring and a hot spring, naturally, is the temperature of the water. Most hydrothermal features labeled "warm springs" maintain year-round temperatures of about 82 to 88 degrees Fahrenheit. If they register over 90 degrees Fahrenheit, they will be called hot.

Shortly after you enter the national forest, about 18 miles from Dubois, the **Tie Hack Memorial** to the left of the road tells the history of an interesting group of people you have probably never thought about, but who contributed greatly to the economy of this area. Although the hill that holds the memorial can be very windy, climb to the historic marker to read about the Scandinavians who labored in the forests for the railroad, making cross-ties by hand for the tracks. A rowdy lot who fit right in with the suspiciously uncivilized manners of the Old West, these men (and allegedly a few women) were "hardworking, hard drinking, hard fighting," the marker says. The tie hacks were paid an astounding dime per tie, and on a good day could produce about 30 ties. Modern tools and methods replaced the tie hacks after World War II, and slowly the area's economy changed to logging and ranching, and then to tourism. The walkway to the top of the hill—lined by ties, of course—leads to a bas-relief erected in 1946.

Want to Hide Away?

Back on the highway, you continue to climb toward Togwotee Pass. This is more of a mountain drive, and the spires of **Pinnacle Buttes** come into view. To the right at about mile marker 3, the well-maintained 5-mile gravel road, Forest Road 515, leads to good-size alpine **Brooks Lake,** situated between thickly pined forest and green meadow. A popular fishing spot in pristine and dramatic surroundings, the lake sports rainbow, brook, cutthroat, and German brown trout, all common catches. Hiking trails, often crossing from forest to tundra, lead far back into the Teton and Washakie wilderness areas to other alpine lakes. The 585,000-acre **Teton Wilderness** stretches to Yellowstone Park, more than 20 miles to the north. This is prime grizzly bear country, surrounded as it is by remote forest, so observe all precautions while hiking. **Brooks Lake Lodge,** a lodgepole lakeside classic built in 1922, is backed by the breathtaking Pinnacle Buttes and **Breccia Cliffs** towering over 11,000 feet above. The lodge's great hall displays big-game trophies from the area. This spectacularly inviting place requires a three-night minimum stay and is expensive, but accommodations include meals and activities such as horseback riding, canoeing, fishing, and access to the spa. In winter the fee includes use of cross-country skis. Reserve your accommodations far in advance in any season.

Backtrack to the highway to continue to **Togwotee Pass,** climbing to an elevation of 9,658 feet. Togwotee was the name of a medicine man of the Sheepeater tribe, a subchief under Chief Washakie (Wah-SHAH-kee), who guided Captain William Jones and the US Army Corps of Engineers through this territory in 1873. The Sheepeaters, a branch of the Shoshones named for the mainstay of their diet, lived all four seasons in the high country in and around Yellowstone. Their name differentiated them from the neighboring Plains Indians, the "buffalo eaters." The Sheepeaters were peaceful Indians who used dogs for packing and for guarding their horses, and who reportedly, wearing their snowshoes, could run and jump between cliffs, a feat to contemplate as you look at the surrounding topography.

The **Absaroka cliffs** ahead and to the right are remnants of volcanic activity about 46 million years ago. Breccia is hardened lava and white ash cemented together with angular stone fragments broken and thrown from volcanic eruption. The present configurations of the cliffs come from eons of erosion by wind and water, although in geologic time the formations are new. The large areas of exposed rock are interspersed with mountain meadows and swaths of unbroken forests. To the left, flat-topped **Lava Mountain,** composed of black basalt dating 500,000 years into the past, rises to a height of 10,452 feet.

Falls Campground is found to the left, a little more than 0.25 mile after you return to the highway from the Brooks Lake turnoff. Take the turnoff to the falls, about 0.25 mile down a dirt road, and park your car. A short, easy trail along a ridge leads to **Brooks Lake Creek Falls,** tumbling into a gorge from an erosion-resistant ledge.

On the road again, to coin a phrase, this definite mountain road does not go through steep canyons, but land rises on both sides of the highway where the road was carved. The winter snow through this pass is so heavy that young trees bend out of the sides of the snow-plowed road in winter. The highway is two-lane toward the top of the pass, the speed limit slows to 50 miles an hour, and although the road curves around, it is not terrifically winding. Notice the orange snow poles at the shoulders. These not only measure how high the snow piles, but they also act as a guide to snowplowers who keep the pass open. In summer, if they are up, they indicate the depth of the winter. Crossing this pass in mid-April, I found the snow was so deep that the steep-grade signs were covered, making it impossible to read them. I thought of the happy truckers trying to get from one side to the other, and the challenge that circumstance presented.

After a steep ascent to the top of the pass, you trade the Shoshone National Forest for the Bridger-Teton. At the summit, 5 miles beyond Brook Creek Falls, a dirt road to the left leads to small, scenic **Wind River Lake,** with an inviting picnic ground. An information board and comfort station are conveniences for travelers. Signs that say OPEN RANGE indicate cattle ranging unhindered by fence up here in

Take in a panoramic view from the Togwotee Overlook.

the summer, so drive with caution. For a while the highway is surrounded by sloping hills, giving the rolling-hills feeling of New England. Occasional fields of willows hint that this might be good moose territory. Also watch these high open meadows for bears searching for summer treats. Grizzly bears particularly like to roam here.

From the top of Togwotee Pass, the road makes a gradual but continual descent through pine forest and high marsh and meadows, and crosses the Continental Divide. To the left (south) **Vista View** turnout gives a wonderful panorama of the mountains. To the right, between mile markers 21 and 20, a road leads to the starting point for a hike to **Holmes Cave,** about 4 miles back on a moderate trail. The hike affords beautiful views of the breccia cliffs to the north, and on clear days the Tetons to the south.

At about mile marker 16, you glimpse your first view of the magnificent **Teton Range.** On a sunny spring day when the peaks are snow-covered, the Tetons look like echoes of the clouds mounting the sky, dim but prominent on the horizon. Togwotee scenic overlook 9 miles west of the pass's summit affords one of the best views of the entire range. The astounding, spectacular view of the mountains makes this one of my favorite places in the country. From this spot, interpretive signs promote the National Forest System, the 3.4 million acres of the Bridger-Teton Forest in particular.

Beyond mile marker 16, to the south of the road, the **University of Wyoming** has installed a forest management demonstration area, a 0.25 mile boardwalk through the woods that shows management techniques and their results. Views of the Tetons are seen along the trail. This pleasant and informative walk is worth the time, but beware of mosquitoes if the weather has been rainy.

Continue your drive through Blackrock Canyon to commercial **Cowboy Village** in the small village of **Togwotee.** All services are available here, summer and winter. Lush forests of tall lodgepoles, Engelmann spruce, and whitebark pine fill the surrounding slopes. Descending the western side of the pass, come to the Turpin Meadows turnoff to the right (north) of the highway. This loop takes you on a rough, steep, curving gravel road to the valley bottom, where dude ranches and recreation areas come together. **Turpin Meadows** campground is a popular resting point. The road meets US 287/26 about 11 miles to the west of here.

Beyond mile marker 9 the terrain flattens out to meadows and stands of aspen and willow. **Blackrock Creek** to the south of the road leads to the **Blackrock Ranger Station,** another place to seek maps and information. Nearby is **Hatchet Campground,** the last camping spot on this highway before arriving at Teton National Park. Beyond the campground, the route picks up the jumble of the Buffalo Fork of the Snake River to the north, which finds its way to Moran Junction.

By mile marker 8 you leave the national forest and come to a wildlife habitat sign on the right side of the road. The interpretive sign talks about the thriving environment supporting the diverse wildlife of the area, and the benefits of occasional fire, which forces regenerative shoots from the willows and aspens.

From this point on, the Tetons are always in view. Ranchettes, dude ranches, and homes begin to show up on the landscape. **Grand Teton RV Park** offers a place for your home away from home. You can often see deer, moose, and elk by the side of the road. The end of the pass is about 5.5 miles from Moran Junction. The terrain for the rest of the drive is a hodgepodge of hills, mountains, fields, sagebrush, and willow flats.

At about mile marker 3, Buffalo Valley Road to the north connects with the Turpin Meadow Road, which looped from above Togwotee village. This is dude ranch territory, offering lodging, horseback riding, camping, and hiking to any with the inclination. Jackleg fences claim patches of sage-covered land.

At mile marker 2 you enter an unfenced boundary of Grand Teton National Park. Much of the Outer Loop Road, which extends south to Jackson from Moran Junction, is land donated to the public by John D. Rockefeller Jr.'s Snake River Land Company. **Buffalo Fork,** now on the south side of the road, leads beyond Moran Junction into the park. You frequently see moose, river otters, trumpeter swans, and other wildlife from an overlook of the slow, lazy, wide river.

It's difficult to pick a favorite view, or to take a bad picture.

At the bottom of this gradual descent, you arrive at **Moran Junction,** entrance to the park, elevation 6,742 feet. A post office is located near the park's border, a chance to mail all the postcards you've been collecting and meaning to send. The road leading into the park is an extension of the John D. Rockefeller Jr. Memorial Parkway. If you enter the park, you go straight to Jackson Lake Dam, and north to Yellowstone or south to Moose Junction, for the inner road of the Tetons. Turn left at Moran Junction to head to Jackson, the ultimate western tourist town, via the outer road of the park.

23

Pinedale, WY, to Jackson, WY

General description: About a 75-mile tour through pleasant high desert with good mountain vistas, through the narrow Hoback River Canyon to its junction with the Snake River, which leads north to Jackson and the beginning of the Grand Teton National Park drives.

Driving time: 1 hour and 15 minutes.

Special attractions: Museum of the Mountain Man, Trapper Point Vista, Hoback River Canyon, Snake River, hiking, fishing, camping, horseback riding, and most any outdoor pastime you can think of—including skiing at White Pine, 10 miles from Pinedale, or Snow King, a ski resort in the town of Jackson.

Location: Northwestern Wyoming.

Drive route names & numbers: Beginning on US 191, part of the Wyoming Centennial Scenic Byway, picking up US 189/191.

Travel season: Year-round, but summer through early fall is the most reliable time to travel.

Camping: Two campgrounds on Fremont Lake, Lower (52 sites) and Upper (5 sites, primitive); and one on Half Moon Lake (16 sites) outside Pinedale. Kozy (8 sites) and Granite Recreation Area Campground (52 sites) at the head of Hoback Canyon, and Hoback Campground (14 sites) in Hoback Canyon. All are Forest Service campgrounds.

Services: Full services in Pinedale, Hoback Junction, and Jackson; food, gas, and sparse lodging in Bondurant. Be aware that there is no cell service for much of this drive.

Nearby points of interest: Fremont and Half Moon Lakes, Half Moon and Soda Lake Wildlife Habitat Management Areas, Old Fort Bonneville, DeSmet Monument, Green River Basin, Bridger Wilderness Area, Bridger-Teton National Forest, Granite Recreation Area and hot springs. In winter, skiing at either Snow King or Teton Mountain Ski Resort.

For more information: Pinedale Chamber of Commerce; Museum of the Mountain Man; Pinedale Ranger District; Bridger-Teton National Forest, Jackson; Jackson Chamber of Commerce.

The Route

At an elevation of 7,175 feet, **Pinedale,** WY, sits in high, sagebrush-covered desert near the northern end of the Green River Valley. This almost one-street town (population about 1,412), with exquisite mountain vistas, supports an exceptional museum, a pleasant town park, several art galleries, lots of motels, and a passel of good restaurants. Because Pinedale is so close to Jackson, where good food is the norm, it is difficult to get a bad meal here. As the sign says as you enter town from the south: Welcome to Pinedale, all the civilization you need. Walk through town and browse through the local shops. Check out the saloon on the main

Pinedale, WY, to Jackson, WY

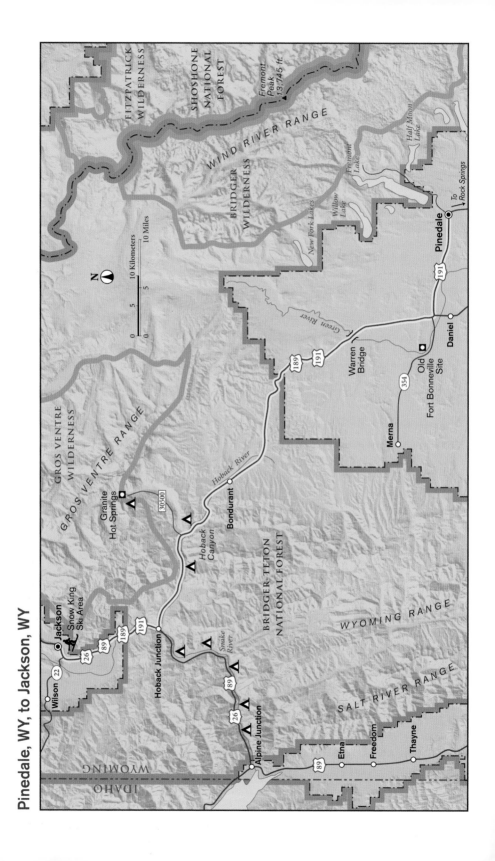

street sporting a sign stating Pinedale thinking service. Such a place is not without charm.

History is vividly alive here, rooted in tales of trappers, explorers, Indians, and early ranchers. **Rendezvous Days** is a major event, held annually since 1936 on the second Sunday in July. It celebrates and re-creates the fur- and bead-trading of the fur companies, mountain men, and Native Americans, with a pageant, parade, music, Old West skits, arts and crafts, shootouts, a rodeo, and a genuine buffalo barbecue. This area was the nucleus of the fur trade in the Rockies by the 1830s. From 1833 until 1840, mountain men and Native Americans gathered annually on the banks of the Green River to trade. Although trappers and Native Americans led nomadic lives, cattle ranchers and settlers were drawn to the area by the hay-growing potential of the Green River Valley. Serious settlement began around 1878. Like many other towns in western Wyoming, Pinedale began its life as a ranch that doubled as a post office. As the community grew, town fathers encouraged growth by granting lots to each person who promised to build on them and remain here.

Today, the area abounds in all the western opportunities for recreation. Nearby streams and lakes offer excellent fishing for brook, brown, cutthroat, rainbow, golden, and mackinaw trout, as well as grayling and whitefish. Float trips on stretches of the Green River are common summer activities, as are canoeing and kayaking. The **Soda Lake Wildlife Habitat Management Area** is an official Audubon site. Check with the local Forest Service office for maps of hiking and cross-country ski trails.

Before leaving Pinedale, take a side trip from the northeastern end of town to view or play along the banks of two of the many glacial lakes in the area. Glacial lakes form when retreating glaciers deposit rubble and boulders in a river's path, creating a natural dam. In this case, these lakes provide beautiful fishing, boating, and camping opportunities. Fremont and Half Moon Lakes were created when the Pinedale glacier covered this area about 70,000 to 15,000 years ago, not long in geological time. To get to the lakes, turn east on Fremont Lake Road, which carries you 3 miles to a turnoff to **Fremont Lake,** sporting more than 22 miles of shoreline and a depth of 600 feet, at the base of the Wind River Mountains. Fremont can hide a lot of fish, most notably mackinaw trout weighing up to 40 pounds. Fremont Lake, at 12 miles long and 0.5 mile wide, is Wyoming's second-largest natural lake, after Yellowstone Lake. Boat rides and rentals are available at **Lakeside Lodge Resort and Marina,** where there is also a nice sandy beach. **Fremont Lake Campground,** open from late May to mid-September, is 7 miles northeast of Pinedale along Fremont's eastern shore. From here you may take a boat to **Upper Fremont Lake Campground** at the northern end of the lake. Upper Fremont Lake Campground is described as "rustic" (read primitive), with no facilities offered.

To reach **Half Moon Lake,** return to Fremont Lake Road and continue northeast through the **Half Moon Wildlife Habitat Management Area** to a well-marked turnoff 7 miles farther. Trails from the campground on the northwest shore of Half Moon Lake lead far back into the Bridger Wilderness. It also offers trails leading into the wilderness. This is a backpacker's paradise. The Pinedale Ranger District office, located in town (see Appendix A), provides maps of hiking trails and further information.

At the beginning of Fremont Lake Road, near town, you'll find the **Museum of the Mountain Man,** an impressive small museum, built in homage to the early residents of the area. Mountain men were not only trappers but important guides and explorers. Their geographic and natural knowledge of the area, second only to that of the Native Americans, helped open the gateways to the West. The museum was begun on a shoestring, with donations of artifacts, letters, and photographs from local families, found in their homes and attics. The community worked to raise money from donations and grants to build the museum, which now houses exhibits of the mountain men, explorers, settlers, Native Americans, and wildlife, focusing on how the interrelationships among these cultures has produced western life as it is today. On the main floor, fur-trade and Plains Indian artifacts include Jim Bridger's rifles, baskets, beaver hats, knives, clothing, felting, and a collection of correspondence from Mountain Men. An outstanding children's corner contains stuffed animals of indigenous wildlife, or "museum buddies," which children may carry around in the museum. The life of 18th-century children, both Native American and European, is explained in easy-to-understand exhibits. The computer game, "The Oregon Trail," tempts adults, who have been seen edging out their children for a chance to play. The basement of the museum contains exhibits of Sublette County history. If you have the opportunity, stop by to see what a little time and community effort can do. A good book and gift shop inside and picnic tables outside invite you (and about 15,000 other summer visitors) to relax and enjoy the surroundings. The entrance fee is $5 for adults, $4 for seniors, $3 for children under twelve, and free for those under six. The exhibits are definitely worth the price.

As you drive from Pinedale to Hoback Junction, take time to read the many historic markers along the route. The Astorians, groups sent out by John Jacob Astor in search of fur trade locations, passed through here, leaving their mark on history. Fur companies and trappers held the Green River Rendezvous in this area often between 1833 and 1840. Many of these early travelers kept journals, filled with colorful incidents and insights into the past. Their descriptions of their way of life are invaluable to understanding our heritage.

Before you leave town, a small, inviting park at the west end of town offers picnic benches, a playground, and a short river walk for a respite from car travel. The fitness walk along the brook offers a little exercise at a leisurely pace.

Head west out of Pinedale on US 189/191 toward Daniel. Gasoline prices in Pinedale are a little less than in Hoback Junction and Jackson, so there is no great advantage to tanking up here, although you may save a penny or two. Houses become infrequent as the route begins, and sagebrush and bunch grass desert dominates the view. Near mile marker 103 along Duck Creek, a riparian viewing area explains the intertwining relationships of the habitat's wildlife, including brown trout, caddis-fly nymphs, yellow warblers, flycatchers, beaver, mallards, sandhill cranes, long-billed curlews, and human beings.

The Trappers & Early Gatherings

At **Trapper Point Vista,** mile marker 105, a historical sign points to the upper Green River Basin. This spot affords an overlook of the valley and a **Green River Rendezvous** site. As your eyes scan the valley, imagine more than 300 trappers and 2,000 Native Americans with their white buffalo-hide tepees coming together here. The trappers, who lived a solitary life much of the year, looked forward to the party that was the rendezvous. Eating, drinking, gambling, and general carousing were the order of the day. On the second day of the get-together, the fur trading companies would raise their gigantic tents and barter for furs with supplies from St. Louis. Beaver pelts, gathered for a full year by the trappers, would garner $5 to $8 worth of goods, a hefty amount in the early 1800s. Trading could go on for up to a month as mountain men and Native Americans would make their way here from all over the mountain states. The rendezvous began in 1825 as a means for trappers and Native Americans to receive supplies without having to carry their furs all the way back to St. Louis. In addition, the fur companies avoided the extra expense of maintaining year-round trading posts. Famous trappers such as Jedediah Smith, Kit Carson, and Jim Bridger all gathered here.

Wild stories from the rendezvous abound. As the men lingered on, drinking would lead to heavier gambling, and as the beaver pelts ran out, stakes switched to whatever was assessed to be of value—horses, women, tools, weapons, and in one reported case, a trapper's scalp. The last rendezvous was held here in 1840. By then, overtrapping and the new fashion of silk hats caused the beaver pelts to diminish in value. It is amazing to note that an item of apparel—the beaver pelt top hat—was so closely linked to the encroaching settlement of half a continent.

To the right (north) of the highway, the **Wind River Range** dominates the view, with **Mount Sacagawea** and **Jackson and Fremont Peaks** rising, seemingly side by side. Mount Sacagawea, 13,569 feet, is surpassed by Fremont's 13,745 feet. Almost directly behind Sacagawea is **Gannett Peak,** the highest point in Wyoming at 13,804 feet. The Wind River Range has forty peaks of over 13,000 feet, making it one of the tallest mountain ranges in the country.

The Wind River Range includes Sacajawea and Fremont Peaks.

About 10 miles west of Pinedale, at the junction with US 189, the route divides. A side trip could take you left (south on 189) to **Daniel** to view a monument to Father Pierre Jean DeSmet, who performed the first Catholic Mass in the state of Wyoming during the 1840 rendezvous near Daniel. Father DeSmet came in response to inquiries from some of the Flathead tribe who had heard of his religion from the Iroquois. The mass, recited in both French and English, was translated for the attending Flatheads and Shoshones. To see the **DeSmet Monument,** go about 3.5 miles south of Daniel and turn left on Route 188, graveled DeSmet Road. Go 2.5 miles east to the monument. An overlook on a ridge shows you the site of the rendezvous, near the grassy cottonwood-lined banks of Horse Creek. Mass is still said here each year during Rendezvous Days in Pinedale.

Return to the junction of US 189/191 and WY 354. A left turn on WY 354 would take you to **Old Fort Bonneville,** built in 1832 as a fur trade center and run by Captain Benjamin Bonneville. Because of the winter snow, cold, and inaccessibility, the fort quickly became known in the area as "Fort Nonsense." It was occupied for only 1 year.

As you continue north on US 189/191, the road becomes slightly hilly as it passes by geologic features with names like **Forty Rod Flat, Kitchen Flat,** and my favorite, **Apex Ditch.** Keep your eyes peeled for pronghorn, frequently found here at night. Along this section of the drive, the road crosses red-gray mudstone and sandstone, with a lot of sagebrush growing and not much else. In that way, this area has changed little in the past 150 years.

At the Warren Bridge, cross the **Green River,** the principal tributary to the Colorado. The Green River was not only significant to trappers for their rendezvous, but it also provided an important landmark for emigrants on the Oregon and Overland Trails. Probably named for its green color, it had been known by many other names before the standardization of maps. Early on, named by Spanish explorers, it was sometimes known as the Rio del Norte, or "River of the North," or the Spanish River. Indian tribes had referred to it as the Poor River, because of the quality of the soil along its banks, or the Prairie Hen River. Wilson Price Hunt and his party of Astorians, trappers exploring for John Jacob Astor's Pacific Fur Company, were probably among the first non-natives to see this river. The name Green River began to come into general use about 1833, probably referring to the "refreshing appearance of the broad river, with its timbered shores and green wooden islands, in contrast to its dry sandy plains" as John C. Frémont, western explorer, reported.

The road takes you past **Aspen Ridge, Hay Gulch,** and nearby **Cow Gulch.** The whole vast expanse of this valley is higher than 7,000 feet. In the late spring, if snow is still on the ground, the orange-red of the willows contrasts with the white of the snow, the pale green of the sage, the deep blue-green of the mountains, and the clear pale blue of the sky, painting an elegant bit of scenery. Gradually, as the road curves westward, lodgepole pines and aspen slip into the landscape, deepening the hue to a lush forest green. Near the southern end of the Gros Ventre Mountain Range, where snow often lingers on the peaks into late August, lodgepole dominate the slopes to the west, while aspen command the eastern slopes.

Beyond mile marker 127, a pullout marks the spot of an Astorian campsite of 1811. The Astorians passed this way just 5 years after Lewis and Clark made their initial exploration across the continent. Beyond this point the road turns west, crossing a small pass known as the Rim, elevation 7,921 feet. The Rim is a drainage divide where the Hoback River empties into the Snake River on the west side, and the east side drainages flow into the Green River. The road from here parallels the old overland stage route taken by early travelers. The **Bridger-Teton National Forest** surrounds the remainder of the drive, although for a while it keeps its distance from the road. A span of winding road offers a view of a nice open valley with little gulches, gullies, and draws, with colorful names such as **Rim Draw** and **Raspberry Ridge.** Hundreds of small creeks cut into minor canyons and trickle down from nearby rising peaks. The two-lane road, speed limit 65 miles an hour, follows small rivers that nurture willow bogs. Wherever willows grow at this altitude, look for moose. Occasionally you'll get lucky enough to see one, but you don't want to be unlucky enough to collide with one.

Along this drive, the beauty of the nearby **Wyoming Range** can be breathtaking. As you descend toward Hoback Canyon, the road crosses and recrosses the river. As the many creeks meld with the river and grow larger and flow faster, you might say that the creek is "picking up stream." It doubles, then triples in size, as it leads to **Bondurant** (elevation 6,588 feet), a very small town of over 200 people. Guest ranches, a trading post, and cabins offer amenities here. Bondurant is named for its first settlers, Sarah Ellen and Benjamin Franklin Bondurant, who figured out how to earn a living by providing easterners with western fantasies. Thus began one of the first dude ranches of the area, operating as early as 1904. Near here at a rendezvous in 1835, the Reverend Samuel Parker was giving what is believed to be the first Protestant sermon hereabouts to a group of mountain men, including Kit Carson and Jim Bridger, when a herd of bison crossed within eyesight of the trappers, who quickly grabbed their rifles and jumped on their horses. The opportunity for fresh meat competed with food for the soul. The soul lost.

Hoback Canyon

Beyond mile marker 145 the valley narrows as you approach **Hoback Canyon.** John Hoback, a trapper from Kentucky, came west with the Missouri fur trappers in 1809. Wanting to return to St. Louis, he and his companions sidetracked through Wyoming to avoid conflicts with Native Americans on the Missouri River. When Wilson Price Hunt and the Astorians, heading west, crossed their path, Hoback and his two companions were hired as guides. They led Hunt's party back through this canyon to the Snake River and over Teton Pass into what is now Idaho. Hoback and his friends remained in Idaho to trap until they were eventually killed by the Native Americans they had initially sought to avoid. Hunt named the canyon and river in honor of his guide.

Travel through the canyon was dangerous for early explorers and settlers, as trails were high and narrow on the ridge, and the drop steep. Horses often lost their footing and tumbled 200 feet into the canyon. You can read about the area and time in Washington Irving's story "Astoria."

The Hoback River gains width and speed through the canyon and repeatedly crosses the path of the road. Beyond mile marker 150, two camping areas offer sites to those who want to stop and relax. **Kozy Campground** is to the right (north) of the road, with picnic spots by the river. By mile marker 152, find the **Granite Recreation Area Campground** 10 miles to the right (north) on a dirt road, FR 30500. In this red-rocked gulch, hot springs await those who make the trip. The rugged road leads to scenic views of the **Gros Ventre Range** and a

Every bend in the road brings something new.

50-foot waterfall. Near the campground are a picnic area and hot springs pool, constructed in 1933 by the Civilian Conservation Corps. The pool temperature varies between 93 and 112 degrees Fahrenheit, and is open from 10 a.m. to 8 p.m. during the summer, 10 a.m. to 5 p.m. during the winter, but closed in the autumn and spring. During summer, 4-wheel-drive vehicles are recommended. Although the road is not plowed in winter, it is popular with snowmobilers and cross-country skiers. A concessionaire for the Forest Service collects a fee for pool use.

Farther west on US 189/191, **Hoback Campground** to the left also has picnic tables. Camping anywhere in this area yields the restful sounds of the river nestled between river-carved cliffs and pine-laden canyon walls. US 189/191 also provides views of the many dramatic and beautiful gorges throughout the canyon. About 5 miles before you reach Hoback Junction, a pullout to the north highlights a bighorn sheep lookout spot. The sheep are not always in sight, but the roadside marker explains how fire is beneficial to the survival of the bighorns.

Rolling hills begin to replace canyon walls, and the view opens up of a slightly broader valley. By mile marker 160 you are approaching civilization and the inevitable sprawl that will lead you to the town of Jackson.

Descend into **Hoback Junction,** a small town that is the junction of road and river, where the Hoback meets the Snake. At the junction, turn right (north) on

US 26/89/189/191. Twenty years ago this route was barely populated; now it's an extension of Jackson, 12 miles to the north.

The Snake River cuts a beautiful narrow swath through the north end of the Snake River Canyon. Cottonwoods again line the river. As you near Jackson, the valley opens to what is the beginning of the area known as **"Jackson's Hole,"** a high, wide valley surrounded by mountains. Cultivated green fields with horses give way to subdivided housing developments. Whitewater rafting outfitters and other tourist shops line the road as you get closer to town. What was once a pristine paradise has become a web of tourist exploitation, but you will have a good time, in spite of it all. Jackson Hole is one of the most beautiful places in the country, and there is a reason why hordes flock each summer to this playground. Information on the town of Jackson is included in Scenic Route 28, "Jackson Lake Junction to Jackson, WY." Head east on US 189/89 at the junction to Wilson on WY 22 and hightail it to town.

24

Bear Lake, UT, to Jackson, WY

General description: Beginning by a beautiful aqua lake, a 155-mile drive through three states and their small towns, along pioneer routes that carry you through forest, canyon, and vale to the Snake River Canyon and Jackson.

Driving time: About 3 hours, with no stops.

Special attractions: Bear Lake and its fresh raspberry milkshakes, a Mormon pioneer trail, Paris Tabernacle, Montpelier Canyon, and great fishing in the Star Valley, Snake River Canyon, and Bridger-Teton rivers and streams.

Location: The Northeast corner of Utah, the southeast corner of Idaho, through northwest Wyoming.

Drive route names & numbers: US 89 to WY 26/US 89 to US 189/191. The Oregon Trail/Bear Lake Scenic Byway.

Travel season: Year-round, with the Snake River Canyon occasionally closed by snow.

Camping: All along the route—KOA in Garden City and Montpelier, plentiful around

the Bear Lake area, North Beach (36 sites), East Bear Lake (47 sites), and many more at the southern end of the lake. US Forest Service campgrounds in Montpelier Canyon (15 sites), Idaho; all along the Salt River, and in the Snake River Canyon, Cottonwood (for large groups of up to 40 people), and Wolf Creek (20 sites), among others.

Services: All services available along the entire route. Cell service is generally good.

Nearby points of interest: Bear Lake State Park, Rendezvous Beach State Recreation Area, Minnetonka Cave, Bear Lake National Wildlife Refuge, Pioneer Oregon and California Trails, the Lander Cutoff to the Oregon Trail, Periodic Spring, Palisades Reservoir.

For more information: Garden City, Greater Bear Lake Area, and Star Valley Chambers of Commerce; Bear Lake National Wildlife Refuge; Montpelier Ranger District; Caribou-Targhee National Forest Service; National Oregon/California Trail Center; Grey's River Ranger Station.

The Route

This three-state route is great for people who fly to Salt Lake City and rent a car, and who want to take the scenic route to Jackson rather than the faster route through Idaho Falls. The road that leads from Salt Lake to Bear Lake is in itself a wonderful scenic route. (From Salt Lake, head north on I-15/84 to the Brigham City exit, number 362. Go east on US 89 for about 54 miles through Logan to Bear Lake.) Actually, one would be hard-pressed to find an area of Utah that is not incredibly beautiful. Whichever way you arrive at Bear Lake, alluring scenery and an interesting trip lie ahead.

Begin your journey in **Garden City,** Utah, population 562, a small, rather 1950-ish resort town, the kind that boasts many ice-cream stands, all serving

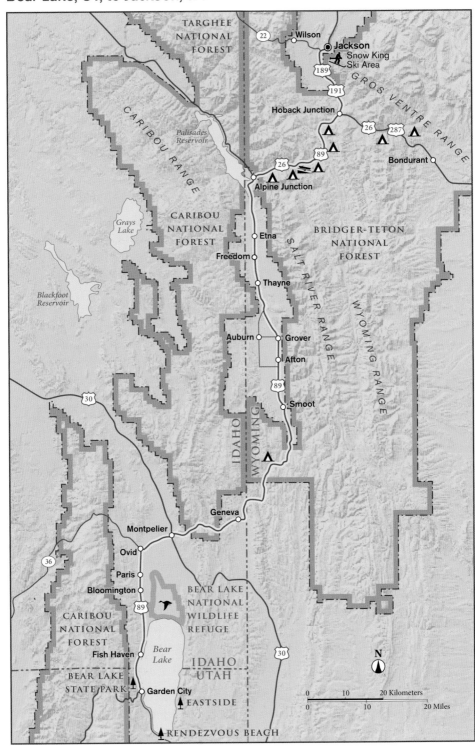

popular fresh raspberry ice-cream milkshakes. If you're there during the summer, especially in early August during the **Raspberry Festival,** don't miss this local passion. The festival offers craft fairs, helicopter rides, a parade, rodeo, local entertainment, and fireworks, as well as too many raspberry shakes, if you're willing. Sweetshops, shake shops, fudge shops, drive-ins, and real estate offices seem to make up the local economy here. You get the picture. Garden City (city is a misnomer) hasn't changed much over the last few decades, and that's a good thing for summer visitors. Slow, pleasant, and beautiful are apt descriptors.

Bear Lake Basin

The **Bear Lake** area has held an attraction for people for a long time. Ute, Bannock, and Shoshone Indians traveled through and camped here for centuries, and in 1819, when Donald "Fats" Mackenzie, Canadian trapper, saw this body of water, he dubbed it Black Bear Lake because of the preponderance of the animals in the area. It became an important fur trade center. Two mountain men rendezvous, in 1827 and 1828, brought fur trappers, Indians, explorers, traders, and scalawags together to gather, trade, and celebrate. In the 1840s Thomas "Pegleg" Smith, a former trapper and mountain man, built a trading post here to provide Mormon settlers and other emigrants with supplies. The **Bear Lake Basin** has been slowly, very slowly, populating ever since.

The lake, a great place for all water sports, is not overrun, even in summer. Bear Lake, half in Utah and half in Idaho, attracts players from both states and beyond. More a retreat than a resort, Bear Lake has four state-run parks that offer opportunities for camping, picnicking, swimming, and sailing: **Rendezvous Beach, Bear Lake Marina, Eastside State Park,** and **North Beach State Park.** A couple of small resort towns south of Garden City make the whole area worth exploring for fun and recreation. The **Pickleville Playhouse** and **Bear Lake BBQ and Shakes** (with great barbecued ribs) both deserve a stop. Condos and motels are beginning to crop up, though, and it is probably a matter of time before the lake rim is developed. At this writing, Bear Lake maintains a little midcentury rustic charm.

The beautiful natural freshwater lake itself, formed by fault subsidence that continues deepening the lake on the eastern side, measures 20 miles long and about 8 miles wide. Some people believe that the distinctive almost turquoise hue comes from limestone suspended in the water, while others, including some geologists, find no evidence for that and instead hold that the apparent color is a combined effect of the green plants on the lakebed and the reflection of the blue sky. At an elevation of almost 6,000 feet, this high-mountain splendor offers a unique place to begin your drive. We began our trip on an early morning at the end of August, when the lake was crystal blue and still.

The water in Bear Lake really is Caribbean blue.

Leaving town, you pass the **Bear Lake State Recreation Center,** where boating, picnicking, and camping sites are available, and boats are offered to rent. It is not far to the first of many interpretive signs that tell how travelers meaning to settle the West crossed to the north of here on the Oregon Trail. When these emigrants from the East hit the Rocky Mountain front, many efforts were made to find the most passable route west. Some were successful, many were not, but when an explorer did find a relatively tolerable way, the route quickly turned into popular trails and finally roadways. In many places wagon tracks and ruts can still be seen on routes in and out of the Bear Basin, almost a century and a half after they were made.

Land of Small Towns

Just 2 miles beyond Garden City you reach Idaho on the **Oregon Trail Bear Lake Scenic Byway.** Pass through tiny **Fish Haven,** population 139, or stop at the visitor bureau for information about camping, fishing, and other recreational activities around the lake. Fish Haven is the first of many small towns that dot this corridor.

Fish Haven Creek Road to the west takes you to **Minnetonka Cave,** as does FR 411 from St. Charles, 4 miles away. The better road, from Fish Haven, leads about 10 miles to the largest limestone cave in the state. A geologic splendor of travertine formations created about 320 million years ago, Minnetonka Cave boasts breathtaking tunnels that delve more than 2,000 feet into the hillside. The cave's nine rooms take about 1.5 hours to explore, and a jacket is a good idea, as the temperature is a pretty steady 40 degrees Fahrenheit. For spelunkers and plain old curious tourists, it is worth looking into. Tours are offered daily, June through Labor Day, every half hour from 10 a.m. to 5:30 p.m.

As you continue north, farmhouses, horses, tractors, bales of hay, and groves of trees replace condos. **St. Charles,** population 156, 4 miles from Fish Haven, was the birthplace in March 1867 of Gutzon Borglum, accomplished painter, designer, and sculptor of Mount Rushmore. His marble bust of Abraham Lincoln resides in the Capitol Rotunda in Washington.

Towns along this sleepy byway reflect the influence of the Mormon pioneers who settled the area and defined the culture. Signs tell of church followers sent by Brigham Young to settle here. The first building constructed in St. Charles was a combination school and church, a testimony to Mormon values.

At the north end of Bear Lake, a well-marked turnoff at Turnpike Road leads to **North Beach** (4 miles) and **East Beach** (11 miles), two state parks where campsites are plentiful. The same turnoff takes you to **Bear Lake Hot Springs** (6 miles) and the **Bear Lake National Wildlife Refuge** to the north. The refuge consists of over 18,000 acres of marsh, water, and grasslands that provide safe nesting areas for a variety of waterfowl, including ducks, sandhill cranes, snowy egrets, pelicans, herons, and Canada geese. Walking trails lead to areas where you can view the birds and other wildlife. Take along good binoculars and your camera.

Beyond St. Charles you leave the northern tip of the lake and pass through **Bloomington,** population 251. Pioneer cabins and outbuildings dot the fields all the way to Paris, about a mile down the road. **Paris,** which boasts that it was the first settlement in the Bear Lake vicinity, was founded in 1863 when a wagon train brought more than 30 families of Mormon colonizers to this site. These first settlers and the more than 700 who arrived the following year believed they were in Utah, until an 1872 boundary survey showed that this was part of the Idaho Territory. When Bear Lake County was created in 1875, Paris became the county seat.

This small town, population about 576, has a remarkable architectural legacy, distinguished by the Mormon tabernacle that was designed by Don Carlos Young, son of Brigham Young. The Romanesque revival-style church built between 1884 and 1889 was constructed of red sandstone carted by horse and ox teams from a canyon 18 miles away, to the east of Bear Lake. The stone, which was stockpiled and stored for years until the building plan was completed and money raised, was then cut and carved by local stonemasons. The inside of the tabernacle was built by James Collings, a shipbuilder, which explains why the

sanctuary resembles an upside-down ship hull. A 629-pipe organ was added in 1929. The **Paris Tabernacle,** completed for $50,000, was a labor of love for many members of the community, some of whom worked on the church before they built their own homesteads. The **Paris Hotel,** the old **Pendry Drug** building, and the **Bear Lake County Courthouse** also show character and flair of design, in a town where proximity to larger cities with comparable architecture is nonexistent.

As you drive north from Paris, another road to the wildlife refuge appears to the right about 3 miles out of town. Dingle Swamp parallels the road, and an access for sportsmen is to the right. Beyond mile marker 19 the road curves toward **Ovid,** so tiny that you must not sneeze or you'll miss it. An old pioneer church, still standing but probably not used, stands near the turn to the east. The names of settlements here tell much about the people who founded the communities: Bern, Ovid, Montpelier, Geneva, Georgetown, Paris. From Ovid travel about 7 miles to **Montpelier,** with a population of 2,785, the largest town in the Bear Lake area.

As you enter town, bear statues and bear benches show off the obvious town mascot. Bears are everywhere. One claim to fame in Montpelier is the bank robbery of 1896, when one Butch Cassidy and a few of his Wild Bunch made off with more than $16,500 in gold, silver, and cash (over $400,000 today). The story goes that a deputy sheriff hopped on a nearby bicycle to chase the men on horseback, trying to pursue them up steep Montpelier Canyon (the road on which you will continue your journey). Despite his brave but hapless chase, none of the money was recovered. Of all the members of Butch's Hole-in-the-Wall gang, only one—Bob Meeks—was apprehended. Meeks was sentenced to 35 years in the state prison in Boise, from which he twice escaped. He was then committed to an insane asylum, from which he also escaped, this time to his brother's home in Fort Bridger, Wyoming, where he spent his remaining days.

A couple of interesting museums, located in the same building, offer local history in Montpelier. The **Rails and Trails Museum** presents fascinating information about the mountain man rendezvous that took place in the region in the early 1800s, as well as exhibits on the Oregon Trail, the Indian history of the Bear Basin, and early settlers. As you take a left turn in the center of town to follow US 89, head to the **National Oregon/California Trail Center,** an interactive museum that depicts pioneer life and achievements. The center offers a dramatic re-creation of the pioneers' journey from Missouri to Clover Creek—the original name of Montpelier Creek—a nearby encampment site. Both museums are open Memorial Day through Labor Day.

Tour guides willingly lead you through the Mormon Tabernacle in Paris.

Montpelier Canyon

Upon your right turn to follow US 89, you immediately enter the hills of **Montpelier Canyon.** A sign indicates that cattle may be roaming on the road, so drive with appropriate care. You are entering the **Caribou-Targhee National Forest.** Willow and wild roses mark the brook bed, and the road follows intermittent Montpelier Creek as it cuts through yellow rock. Sunflowers and other wildflowers grow in profusion. At about 3.5 miles, **Montpelier Campground** and picnic site offer a stop near the river. The climb to the top of the pass is quick through this short, 13.7-mile-long canyon. Within about 9 scenic miles you reach the Geneva summit, elevation 6,923 feet. The view of surrounding mountains toward the east—layers and layers of mountains—is a beautiful sight, even on an overcast day.

Descend from this height through aspen stands that give way to sagebrush and scrub, to reach **Geneva,** another small farm town, the last one before reaching the junction with ID 61, where veering to the left keeps you on the right path. As you drive north through this broad farming valley, look to the east for the farm where the owners have both humor and imagination. Painted monsters lurk along the highway, crafted of old farm implements and machinery. I hope these treasures remain.

After crossing and recrossing **Thomas Fork Creek,** the road heads east at about mile marker 44 and leaves Idaho behind for Wyoming. Follow US 89 as it winds through **Salt Creek Canyon** beside the tiny stream, through willow rushes and marshy places. The creek gains strength, moving through bright red siltstone and shale, and the road begins to climb through the **Gannett Hills.** A US Forest Service campground to the left is the first of many you'll find along this route, and frequent turnouts are available for admiring the view or contemplating your next activity. At the top of the rise, just beyond a sign that says open stock on road, we saw about 400 sheep grazing dangerously close to the highway.

At a turnout at the top of the **Salt River Pass,** elevation 7,630 feet, a historical marker points out the **Lander Cutoff,** a shortcut from the Oregon Trail that hastened the trip west. This route took 7 days off the journey and afforded travelers the benefit of water, wood, and forage for their stock. Named for the superintendent who engineered and oversaw the construction of the road, Frederick W. Lander, the Lander Cutoff was used from about 1857 until 1910, but the advent of rail routes diminished its use. The last wagons were seen crossing here in 1912. From this vantage point, imagine crossing these mountains by foot or in wagons, leading family or stock.

Salt River Pass was an important route to early settlers in this part of Wyoming.

The Starved Valley

Continue to the bottom of the pass, through green rolling mountains grounded by red rock, to reach the **Star Valley.** One version of how the valley got its name says that an early settler called it "the star of all valleys." Another, more likely version, claims that after the severe winter of 1889 people called the place Starvation Valley, which was shortened to Starve Valley. The winter was so bitterly cold and long that over 2 days and nights in March about 40 inches of snow fell, and many cattle were lost.

The sign that greets you as you leave the canyon says welcome to the Star Valley. Home of Rulon Gardner—olympic super heavyweight greco-roman champion, 2000, a thoughtful tribute for a native son. At the beginning of the valley the scene is one of aspen- and fir-covered hills, and occasional remnants of pioneer cabins that speak of local history. Flanked by the Salt River Range to the east and the Webster Range of Idaho to the west, this valley is closely tied, both culturally and geographically, to Utah and Idaho.

Most, if not all, of these towns were settled by Mormons who came here to farm. Many were settled by men with their families fleeing the Idaho laws against polygamy. Wyoming officials either looked the other way, as this still barely populated state wanted and needed settlers, or Wyoming sheriffs and constables had more pressing problems in the very wild West than the conformation of a man's family. At any rate, the influence of the Mormon Church is very strong along this whole corridor.

As in the area around Bear Lake, the Star Valley shelters many very small towns, where local ranches and small businesses provide a living. It's been said that the valley is home to 7,000 people and 20,000 cattle. The road to Smoot, population 100, leads to **Afton** (population 1,950, elevation 6,134 feet), the first town since Montpelier to offer full services. Afton is a growing town, the largest in the Star Valley. For that reason, gas prices here are a little lower than in Jackson, so this is a good place to fill up, as is Thayne, a few miles beyond.

The elk antler arch in Afton, the "largest in the world," spans the road about halfway through town. Containing 3,011 elk antlers and weighing about 15 tons, the arch gives you fair notice that you are in the Wild West.

A good side trip, particularly if you are passing through in August or September, is **Periodic Spring,** east of Afton in the Salt River Range. Periodic Spring, also called Intermittent Spring, the largest of three natural springs in the world that naturally turn off and on, interrupts its water flow from anywhere between 3 and 30 minutes and then gushes again for about an equal amount of time. A cave behind the spring creates a siphon that temporarily halts the flow. Shoshone Indians believed this to be a sacred place controlled by powerful medicine men. To get to Periodic Spring, turn east on Swift Creek Road after you pass through the antler arch and travel about 4 miles. A 0.75-mile hiking trail leads to the spring.

So many outdoor activities are possible here; stop to have a little fun. To the east of the road the immense **Bridger National Forest** offers hiking and backcountry camping. The Forest Service Ranger Station in Afton dispenses information about nearby campgrounds and fishing spots, and countless access roads for sportsmen lie along the Salt River.

Continue driving through **Grover** (population 120, elevation 6,167 feet) or take a left turn in the middle of town toward **Auburn,** population 599, where the Auburn fish hatchery, a popular place to visit, protects about 50,000 trout. Note that the fish population is about 1,000 times the town population. To get to the hatchery, make a left turn on County Road 134, a well-marked side road, to drive about 10 miles to the west. The hatchery is open in summer from 8 a.m. to 5 p.m.

A few miles beyond Grover you reach **Thayne** (population 407, elevation 5,950 feet), a sportsman's paradise because of its proximity to the Salt River. The Salt, named for its saline springs and salty deposits along its banks, parallels US 89 all the way to the northern end of the valley. More fishing, hunting, and camping access areas are found along here. A fresh-fruit stand in Thayne is always one of our favorite stops, as is **Star Valley Cheese,** a local restaurant and well-known cheese factory that serves plain good food—malts, burgers, and shakes.

Freedom, the next wide spot in the road, was supposedly named by Mormon settler Arthur Clark, who moved here from Idaho for the freedom from the polygamy laws he had escaped. This theme echoes throughout the valley. Pass through Etna (population 200) to approach **Alpine** (population 714, elevation 5,700 feet), basically a collection of motels, condos, and visitor centers.

About a mile before Alpine, a roadside sign depicting a pair of binoculars identifies the **Grey's River Wildlife Management Area,** where you have a chance, especially in winter, to observe hundreds of elk that are fed here. Park to watch the animals at close range from your car. **Palisades Reservoir,** to the west, a 16,100-acre lake, presents another chance to catch (and probably release) the local trout. The Grey's River Ranger Station in Alpine offers information about all camping and sporting here at the confluence of Grey's River, the Salt, and the Snake. Beyond Alpine, you approach the junction of US 26 and US 89. At the junction, 0.5 mile north of town, head east to enter the **Snake River Canyon** for the final portion of your drive.

On a sunny day the Snake River, the largest tributary of the Columbia, is bright blue-green, reminiscent of the water at the beginning of this drive, Bear Lake. The river has carved through an escarpment of granite, separating the Snake River Range to the west from the Wyoming Range to the east. Shortly after you enter the canyon in winter, a flashing light announces when the road to Jackson is impassable because of snow or ice. Should this happen, the alternate route to Jackson, over Teton Pass, would more than likely also be closed, explaining the need for all those motels in Alpine.

Huge old cottonwoods line the entrance to the canyon. Wildlife—moose, elk, deer, osprey, eagles, and the occasional bear—frequent the area. The **Caribou-Targhee National Forest** encompasses the river drive, and canyon walls millions of years old rise above. Several Forest Service campgrounds are available along the way, many named for the whitewater runs in the river below, but be warned that they usually fill up early in the day. Plan ahead and arrive in time to stake your claim.

The road through the canyon snakes away from the riverbed to high above, and scenic turnouts are plentiful. Watch as kayakers, rafters, and other adventurers make their way south on the white water. Numerous commercial rafting outfits in Jackson will offer you the opportunity for your own adventure, once you hit town.

Travel may be slow as you make your way through the beautiful serpentine canyon. As you approach Hoback Junction near mile marker 141, a bridge carries you across the river to a flashing red light and a little civilization. Rising away from the Snake River, US 89 becomes US 189. Stay on this road for Grand Teton National Park. At this point you are 13 miles from Jackson Hole. The drive from Hoback Junction to Jackson is described in Scenic Route 23, "Pinedale, WY, to Jackson, WY." Turn to page 213 and enjoy the ride!

25

West Yellowstone, MT, to Jackson, WY

General description: A three-state drive past two popular lake recreation areas that takes you across the Continental Divide, through high forest, then descends to a broad farming valley along the back side of the beautiful Teton Range on the Teton Scenic Byway. The first 40 miles of this route has several interesting and scenic side drives or alternate routes. Whether starting from West Yellowstone or US Highway 87, Montana, the drive is about 125 miles.

Driving time: 2 to 2.5 hours, depending on traffic.

Special attractions: Henry's Lake State Park, Island Park Recreation Area, Caribou-Targhee National Forest, Harriman State Park and Wildlife Refuge, Teton Range, and Teton Pass. Boating, fishing, hiking, and other outdoor sports opportunities abound along the entire route.

Location: South-central Montana, southeastern Idaho, and northwestern Wyoming.

Drive route names & numbers: Begin either in West Yellowstone on US 20 or in southern Montana on MT 87, which connects to US 20 (if you are traveling from Ennis to Jackson, rather than from Ennis to Yellowstone)—to ID 32, ID 33, and WY 22.

Travel season: Year-round. However, late fall through early spring the snow could be flying. Be sure to check on road

conditions. For highway road conditions see Appendix A.

Camping: Ample camping is available in West Yellowstone at the many private campgrounds and RV parks. Henry's Lake (50 sites), Harriman State Park West End Campground (19 sites), Box Canyon (17 sites), Big Springs (15 sites), Buttermilk (52 sites), Buffalo (105 sites), Grandview (5 sites). Campgrounds are scattered all along Henry's Fork River; Driggs, Victor, Pine Creek (10 sites), Upper Coffee Pot (14 sites), Mike Harris Campground (12 sites), Trail Creek (10 sites), Flatrock (38 sites), McCrae (28 sites), Riverside (55 sites), and around the Jackson area.

Services: Full services in West Yellowstone, Montana; Ashton, Tetonia, Driggs, and Victor, Idaho; Wilson and Jackson, Wyoming. Partial services at Mack's Inn and Island Park, Idaho. Cell service in West Yellowstone and along most of the drive.

Nearby points of interest: Hebgen Lake, Yellowstone National Park, Caldera Park Lookout, Mesa Falls Scenic Byway and Falls, Grand Targhee Resort, and Jedediah Smith Wilderness.

For more information: West Yellowstone, Jackson, Teton Valley Chamber of Commerce; Harriman State Park, Island Park Ranger District; Caribou-Targhee National Forest; Grand Targhee Resort.

The Route

You can begin this three-state drive in **West Yellowstone** and follow US 20 west and south; or, if you are coming from Ennis, MT, take the cutoff before you reach West Yellowstone, from US 287 to MT 87, an 8-mile connection to US 20. If

West Yellowstone, MT, to Jackson, WY

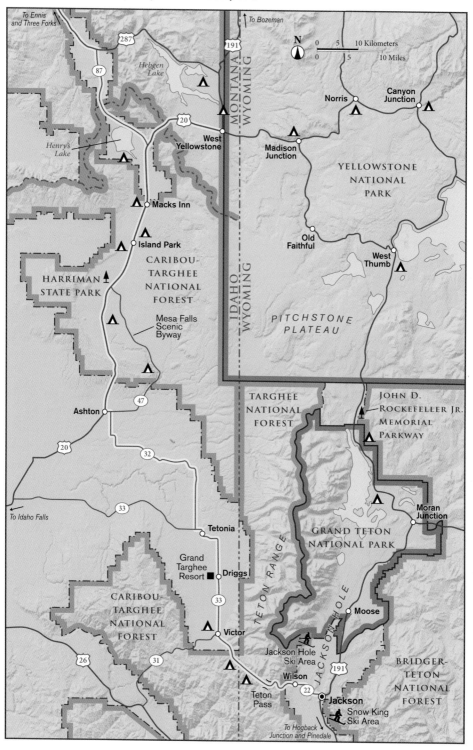

To Ennis and Three Forks
To Bozeman
287
191
87
Hebgen Lake
MONTANA
WYOMING
N
0   5   10 Kilometers
0   5   10 Miles
Norris
Canyon Junction
20
West Yellowstone
Madison Junction
YELLOWSTONE NATIONAL PARK
Henry's Lake
Macks Inn
Island Park
CARIBOU-TARGHEE NATIONAL FOREST
Old Faithful
West Thumb
HARRIMAN STATE PARK
IDAHO
WYOMING
Mesa Falls Scenic Byway
PITCHSTONE PLATEAU
47
Ashton
20
32
TARGHEE NATIONAL FOREST
JOHN D. ROCKEFELLER JR. MEMORIAL PARKWAY
33
To Idaho Falls
Moran Junction
Tetonia
GRAND TETON NATIONAL PARK
Grand Targhee Resort
Driggs
CARIBOU-TARGHEE NATIONAL FOREST
33
TETON RANGE
26
31
Victor
JACKSON HOLE
Moose
Jackson Hole Ski Area
Wilson
191
BRIDGER-TETON NATIONAL FOREST
Teton Pass
22
Jackson
Snow King Ski Area
To Hogback Junction and Pinedale

traveling directly to Jackson from Ennis, the cutoff on MT 87 provides an 18-mile stretch of good road and saves about 30 miles of backtracking from West Yellowstone. Regardless of the starting point, the drive to Jackson, Wyoming, passes from Montana through southeastern Idaho across the southern end of the awe-inspiring Teton Range, and down into the lush valley known as Jackson Hole.

If your starting point is West Yellowstone, follow the signs to pick up US 20 two blocks north of the exit from the park. The route goes about 10 miles through thickly forested Targhee Pass and crosses the Continental Divide before meeting up with MT 87. Continue south on US 20 and through Idaho for the bulk of the route.

From Ennis, head south on US 287. If you want to take a side trip to Quake Lake, the area and route are described in Scenic Route 3, "Three Forks, MT, to the West Entrance." Turn right (south) onto MT 87 and cross the Madison River as it dashes from its headwaters in Yellowstone. Within 0.5 mile, an interpretive sign tells of the naming of Raynolds Pass, and a fishing access hints of the sporting territory surrounding this route. Scenic mountains to the left and the marshy Missouri Flats to the right should alert wildlife watchers to the possibility of moose sightings. Travel 9 miles to the Continental Divide at the Idaho border, and another 9 miles to the junction with US 20.

Into Idaho

Across the Idaho border, the road skirts the north shore of **Henry's Lake,** a good-size lake (around 8 square miles) and a popular all-around recreation area, named for Andrew Henry, who led a group of trappers here from the east in 1810. They built cabins on what is now known as Henry's Fork of the Snake River. John Hoback, another mountain man whose name landmarks the Teton territory, was a member of that party. (See "Pinedale, WY, to Jackson, WY," Scenic Route 23.) Henry's Lake offers camping on a first-come, first-served basis, as well as boating, fishing, and other western diversions and serious avocations. Fishing is especially notable here, as the lake is shallow and harbors brook, cutthroat, and other trout.

As you leave the lake, at the junction with US 20, turn right and head south with all the travelers coming from West Yellowstone, and be on the lookout for wildlife. While I was driving through here one May, a large bull moose in the field to the right was stepping gingerly through the mud, successfully avoiding snow patches. The sight echoes each time I come to this point in the road.

This route was once traveled by Father Pierre-Jean DeSmet, famous for his work with and conversion of Indians from many tribes. He traveled here from St. Louis in 1839 at the request of members of the Flathead and Nez Perce tribes, who wanted a "black robe" to minister to their people. A roadside marker tells a little of his story.

Once on US 20, it's 41 miles to Ashton, Idaho, and the Teton Scenic Byway. Beyond mile marker 397, gas stations, lodges, and cafes sporadically appear. Caribou-Targhee National Forest, which shadows the western borders of Yellowstone and Grand Teton National Parks, spills over into this section of Idaho. Around mile marker 394, as the road begins to incline, a lodgepole pine reclamation area extends south for the next 30 miles. Roadside signs burned into wooden slabs give dates of tree plantings, graphically showing how long it takes to reclaim a forest.

Campgrounds abound on this stretch of the road. Big Spring (15 sites, fee), Upper Coffee Pot (14 sites, fee), Flatrock (38 sites, fee), Buttermilk (52 sites, fee), McCrae (23 sites, fee), Riverside (55 sites, fee), Box Canyon (17 sites, fee), and Buffalo (105 sites, fee) all accommodate avid campers along the next 20 or so miles of the journey.

For the adventurous who enjoy canyon scenery, **Black Canyon Loop Road** (FR 59 to FR 66), to the left as you enter the forest, is approximately a 35-mile scenic drive on a gravel road. FR 59 loops back to **Mack's Inn,** a resort lodge by Henry's Fork of the Snake River, only about 2 miles down the highway from the beginning of the drive. The Black Canyon loop (FR 66) continues on about 9 miles from the junction with Big Spring, but requires backtracking when it meets FR 71. This route is popular with birders. The road gives access to many good hiking trails and fishing spots.

Outdoor Playground

If you stay on FR 59 rather than turning onto the Black Canyon Loop, a shorter 10-mile drive leads to **Big Springs,** one of the largest natural springs in the country. The river from the springs also comes out at Mack's Inn. Big Springs contributes 120 million gallons of temperate (52 degrees Fahrenheit) spring water per day to Henry's Fork. If you have a canoe, raft, or inner tube, the boat launch at Big Springs is a great place to put in and float back to Mack's Inn, about a 3-hour trip or less, depending on the laconic progress of the water. Fishing, hiking, and boating—all popular summer pastimes—replace the snowmobiling crowds who flock here in winter.

From Mack's Inn it's about 5 miles on US 20 to tiny **Island Park,** population 159, and more of this extended recreation area. The community may be small, but on many holidays it has the second-largest population in the state, after Boise. The 7,000-acre **Island Park Reservoir** is ideal for fishing and boating in summer and snowmobiling and ice fishing in winter. Tourists traveling through the area should be forewarned of heavy traffic possibilities around Memorial Day, the Fourth of July, and Labor Day. The surrounding lakes and national forests lure the adventurous into the open countryside through much of the year.

This high plateau continues through the **Caribou-Targhee National Forest,** 1.7 million acres of prime forest, hiking trails, and fishing streams including **Henry's Fork,** with its abundant supply of trout. About 8 miles from Island Park, a turnoff on the right (west) side of the road leads to an interpretive sign and detailed map of the **Harriman State Park and Wildlife Refuge.** The state park began as a 10,700-acre cattle ranch and retreat. It was originally owned by several railroad executives, including Edward H. Harriman, father of former ambassador Averell Harriman. The elder Harriman eventually bought out the others, and his family became sole owner of the property. They deeded it to the state of Idaho in 1977, stipulating that it be maintained as a wildlife preserve. Harriman State Park has grown to over 16,000 acres of refuge for moose, deer, elk, eagles, hawks, owls, and more. Trumpeter swans remain year-round in water warmed by hot springs emptying into the river. Catch-and-release fly fishing is allowed in the refuge on Henry's Fork as it rambles through the ranchland, but this is a day-use-only area, so no camping is allowed in the park. Local commercial outfitters offer horseback rides into the area, and 20 miles of trails contain possibilities for hiking and mountain biking through the refuge. To reach the main entrance, drive beyond the pullout, turn right onto Green Canyon Road, and travel southwest about 3 miles.

Three-quarters of a mile south of the Harriman State Park pullout, another wonderful side drive presents itself for those not in a hurry. Accessible only in summer, **Mesa Falls Scenic Byway** is a 45-mile alternate route to Ashton. If you have the time, take a left off US 20 onto ID 47/FR 294 and proceed on a newly paved road that takes you by **Upper and Lower Mesa Falls,** about 14 miles from the beginning of the route. The two waterfalls on Henry's Fork pass through a narrow gorge, where the upper falls plunge 114 feet and the lower falls drop 65 feet. About 1.3 million years ago, a volcanic eruption left a layer of ash hundreds of feet deep, which over time compressed into the **Mesa Falls Tuff,** over which the upper falls flows. A mile south of the upper falls you'll find the **Grandview Overlook** of the lower falls. Nearby **Grandview Campground** (5 sites, free) makes this a peaceful place to stop and pitch a tent. Of course, the campsites go to the first to arrive. After viewing the falls, those who enjoy scenic back roads can drive the remaining 29 miles on ID 47 to Ashton or, if they prefer, backtrack to US 20 to continue south. Back on US 87, the road to the **Harriman State Park West End Campground** (19 sites, free) is just beyond Osborne Bridge over Henry's Fork. Turn west on Green Canyon road and drive 9.5 miles to reach this lightly used camping site with great fishing access.

Cross **Osborne Bridge** shortly after returning to US 20. About 2 miles beyond Osborne Bridge, to the right before mile marker 376, a historical marker points the way to a tall forest vantage point, the **Caldera Park Lookout.** A caldera is a volcanic crater that has collapsed back in on itself, leaving a ring of hills or mountains at the rim. Geologists discovered the caldera, one of the world's largest, in a 1939 expedition. The forest lookout, a 72-foot tower once used to spot fires, now affords a good view of this 2-million-year-old formation. The caldera lies very close to the boundaries of Yellowstone, where volcanic action also created much of the topography. To get to the lookout, take FR 168 (Antelope Flat Road) about 6 miles west. It turns into FR 120 and in about another 5 miles climbs **Bishop Mountain** (7,810 feet) to reach the lookout tower.

Continue south on US 20 as the road begins to descend, leaving Caribou-Targhee National Forest and heading into the Teton Valley. Cross the bridge over the Ashton Reservoir for your first glimpse of the west side of the Tetons, the youngest mountain range in the Rockies. The mountains actually lie just across the Wyoming border and are the prime showpiece of that state.

As you enter the valley, watch for the highway sign (or the root beer diner) marking the junction with ID 47/32, the route that leads through **Ashton.** At US 20's junction with ID 47, turn left (east) and drive through the town of Ashton, a conglomeration of motels, log cabins, little cafes, train tracks, and grain elevators. Gas here is more expensive than in Driggs, about 40 miles away, but less expensive than on the other side of the mountains, so either town is a good place to tank up before you head over the pass. As you come to the end of the downtown area of Ashton, watch for ID 32 heading south. This T-intersection leads to ID 33, Tetonia, Driggs, and beyond through the Teton Pass to Jackson, Wyoming. Welcome to the Teton Scenic Byway.

Famous Potatoes, Famous Mountains

Turn right (south) on ID 32. The beginning of this segment of the drive travels through farmland on two-lane roads, reminiscent of roads and land conformations throughout southeastern Missouri near the Ozarks. However, where the Tetons dominate the landscape, the resemblance to the Midwest ends. This open valley outside of Ashton inspired the motto emblazoned on Idaho's license plates, Famous Potatoes. Over 11,000 acres that yield about 10 tons of seed potatoes per acre give Ashton its claim to fame. For about the next 30 miles of this drive, evidence of plentiful potato crops decorates the landscape in the form of potato cellars nestled into the earth.

An alternate route across the mountains, one for the more adventurous, should be taken only in dry weather late in summer by those with 4-wheel-drive vehicles. FR 261, the Ashton-Flagg Ranch road, called Grassy Lake Road from the other side, makes a left (eastern) turn from ID 32 about a mile from the junction with ID 47. Within 14 miles from this turnoff, the road turns from a paved, two-lane route into a dirt logging road that almost disappears at the drive's summit. This route through the **Teton National Forest,** though beautiful much of the way, is not a shortcut, as travel is slow and winding on the elusive gravel path.

ID 32 passes through broad farmland. Tin and sod roofs call attention to the unique presence of the potato sheds. Long irrigation pipes, grain elevators, and ranch houses declare the mainstay of the valley's residents. Students here take long work breaks to help out at harvest time—often from late September all the way through October, depending on the size of the crop. At about mile marker 23 the road turns decidedly east, meandering around hilly terrain and through grassy ravines, before it finally hits its southerly route. Small stands of aspen and patches of wildflowers adorn the fields near the farmhouses. Large plantings of mustard-colored alfalfa bloom in July, painting the meadows yellow and bright.

From this point in the drive the mountains loom large, imposing on the landscape. Although Native Americans had passed through this valley for centuries, non-native people, the trappers, first viewed the Tetons from this western valley. In his *Journal of a Trapper,* Osborne Russell said the Native Americans had named the peaks "Hoary-Headed Fathers," undoubtedly because of the snow on their summits. French-speaking trappers and explorers, perhaps as early as 1819, called the mountains les trois tétons, "the three breasts," because of their appearance. Rising above the horizon, the mighty granite mountains served as a compass to all who saw them. Wilson Price Hunt, crossing Union Pass from the east near Dubois, named them the "pilots' knobs" because of their use as guideposts. However, the euphonious, image-invoking name Tetons adhered, appearing most often in early writings and on rough maps.

Beyond mile marker 20 the road again turns east, to head to Drummond, only 60 miles from Jackson. It is easy to miss the tiny towns of France, Lamont, and Felt as the road swoops and curves through the rolling farmland. Silos in fields, stands of young aspen, cultivated land, and wildflowers brighten the roadside. Pass through here at the end of June and the valley floor is green and alive while mountains ahead are still capped with snow. Although this countryside is inviting in summer, only the hearty can withstand the winter. The flat fields have few features to stop the deep snow from drifting in the heavy wind.

The junction with ID 33 is 3 miles beyond Felt. Turn left (east) to continue to Driggs and Victor. Five miles beyond the junction, the minuscule town of **Tetonia** consists of a few small houses, a post office, a gas station with relatively reasonable prices, and the attractive **Teton Mountain View Inn.**

A historical marker beyond mile marker 134 (the mile markers change at the junction with ID 33) tells of John Colter's early travels through here. Colter, one of the most interesting of the early mountain men, asked for Meriwether Lewis's permission to leave the Lewis and Clark expedition on their return trip in 1806.

Two trappers scouting for beaver had asked Colter to join them. Permission was granted, and after spending a nearly impossible winter with the two in the wilderness, he headed back to St. Louis alone. On his way, Manuel Lisa, who was establishing fur-trading posts along the Missouri River, persuaded him to stay to search for trapping sites and to forge trade relations with the Native Americans. He spent the winter of 1808 exploring northwestern Wyoming on foot, walking through parts of Yellowstone and the Tetons, even traveling to the Cody area and back—an incredible journey. Colter was attacked more than once by Blackfeet Indians; once he escaped naked and traveled more than 250 miles to find sanctuary at Fort Lisa.

This area is the **Teton Valley** (elevation 6,000 feet), flanked by impressive mountains. The **Big Hole Mountains** to the southwest are approximately 2.5 billion years old, whereas the youthful **Tetons** are about 9 to 10 million years old. Historical marker 315, on ID 33 next to the Trouts Ranch outside of Driggs, details the formation of the mountains.

The Back Side of the Mountains

Driggs, Idaho, population 1,100, is the largest town in the basin. It was settled by brothers Benjamin and Don Carlos Driggs in the mid 1800s.With a Super 8 and Best Western motel and a Chevron station with a Burger King inside, Driggs is taking a dubious step toward civilization. The gas station pumps out cowboy music along with fuel. Gas prices here are reasonable, a little less expensive than in Ashton, which makes it a good place to refuel.

As you enter Driggs, if you enjoy history and antiques, make a stop at the **Teton Valley Museum,** to the east of the road, near the fairgrounds. Highlights of this special place include a stone unearthed by local farmer William Beard and his son, sometime between 1931 and 1933, that was reported to be carved and signed by John Coulter in 1808. While not authenticated, the stone carving seems to be from the time that Coulter would have been in this part of the valley, and most believe the claim to be valid. The museum also contains a wonderful memorial room that gives testament to the military men who have lived in the valley and served their country through several wars. A modest fee helps support the museum's mission.

Development on the western side of the Tetons has spread northwest to Driggs, and the price of land along this corridor increases yearly. The **Stomping Grounds Cafe and Coffee** adds a little extra western atmosphere to the place, and Driggs is a good stopping point if you're not quite going to make it to Jackson. The last best recreation spot in Driggs, the authentic **Spud Drive-In Theater,** offers first-run movies and appropriately greasy popcorn all summer long. The

The Spud Drive-In Theater in Driggs, Idaho, remains a popular summer attraction.

Spuds is the hottest, albeit the only, ticket in town, and it operates 7 days a week. I am always relieved to make this drive and find The Spud still in operation.

Grand Targhee Resort, east of Driggs, is making a name for itself as an alternative to skiing or vacationing in Jackson. Turn off to Grand Targhee south of Driggs, near mile marker 141. The resort itself, 12 miles to the east, lies in Wyoming, but the only way to reach it and the neighboring town of Alta, Wyoming, is through Idaho. Grand Targhee has become a good ski destination in its own right, with both downhill and cross-country trails. A peaceful summer resort as well, Grand Targhee offers hiking, downhill biking, horseback riding, and just relaxing. Several summer music festivals resound through the hills in summer, including a good bluegrass gathering in early August. To get to Grand Targhee, where prices are reasonable and competitive, or Alta, turn left on Buxton Road and left again on FR 15. The route is well marked. Beyond Alta, the road again forks left (northeast). This road, FR 025, leads to the resort.

The Teton Valley was once known as **Pierre's Hole,** named for fur trapper Pierre Trevantiagon, an Iroquois who worked for the Hudson Bay Company. Pierre, one of the first to trap here, was killed in Montana by Blackfeet Indians in 1827. During the height of the beaver fur craze, between 1820 and 1840, traders and trappers stayed in the valley in summer, and several even camped here during the harsh winters. In 1832 Pierre's Hole was the designated site of the mountain man rendezvous, a nearly monthlong party held annually for trappers, fur traders, and Native Americans who met, bartered for wares and supplies, drank, and swapped stories. This rowdy festivity was eagerly anticipated by the men and few women who spent most of the year in relative isolation.

As you travel south of Driggs, the traffic as well as the pace picks up. The terrain subtly changes from fields and farmland to creeks, cottonwood stands, ridges, and canyons. The **Teton Basin** to the right (west) of the road is a marshy haven for waterfowl, foxes, coyotes, and the occasional wandering moose. Several sportsmen's accesses to the many creeks in the area provide for hunters and anglers alike. Ask in any of these small towns to find out where to purchase fishing or hunting licenses. Local sellers or the Idaho Fish and Wildlife department dispenses information on current fees.

About 8 miles beyond Driggs, near the southern end of the Teton Valley, **Victor,** population 840 at last count, has restaurants, an antique shop or two, galleries, and bed-and-breakfast inns cropping up on the landscape like daisies in spring. The town is named for a mail carrier, George Victor Sherwood, who courageously carried the mail by horseback over Teton Pass during the days of hostile Native American attacks.

Beyond Victor you begin the last leg of this journey. The road curves east toward Teton Pass for the 24 miles to Jackson, or the **Teton Village Mountain Resort** area. At mile marker 151 the road crosses Trail Creek and begins to climb the pass, gradually at first. Jackleg, or buck-and-rail fences, mark off segments of ownership. Wildflowers and a deer crossing sign announce the beginning of wilder terrain. You re-enter Caribou-Targhee National Forest, which was left behind somewhere around Harriman State Park over 1 hour ago.

Near Moose Creek, **Mike Harris Campground** is to the right of the road. Watch for ungulates in this territory, which looks suspiciously moose-friendly. Horseback riding is available along this route, so it's a good idea to be alert for anything with four hooves. Aspen and wildflowers grow on the graveled hillside to the left, while hills to the right are pine-covered. Other campgrounds in the area, Trail Creek, and Pine Creek provide great places to stop and enjoy the surroundings.

Teton Pass

By mile marker 155 the grade of the road steepens and ID 33 becomes WY 22— WYOMING, LIKE NO PLACE ELSE ON EARTH, as the sign says. This pass intermittently closes during the winter. While crossing the pass, you'll notice the tall, skinny orange poles at the side of the road. They not only measure the height of

The mountains rise from the valley floor, as seen from the far side.

the snow, but also show snowplow drivers the parameters of the road after a blizzard. If a light is flashing at the beginning of the pass, the pass is closed. Travelers in winter frequently must choose among turning around to take a long alternate route to Jackson, forgetting their ski trip altogether, or skiing at Grand Targhee on this side of the pass (not a bad alternative). Call (800) TARGHEE for the weather on the pass or road conditions.

In summer wild asters spread across the hillsides of the pass in violet profusion. To the left (north) of the road, the **Jedediah Smith Wilderness** covers almost the 45-mile-length of the mountain range. Jedediah Strong Smith was a mountain man, notable for the literate journal he kept, which provided colorful information of the trapping life in the 1820s and 1830s. With his partners David Jackson and William Sublette, he purchased the profitable Rocky Mountain Fur Company. Smith was reportedly the first Caucasian to cross Teton Pass from the east, and he recognized its significance as a route for trappers, traders, and settlers. After spending years exploring and leading parties of men across the West from Wyoming to California and back again, Smith was killed in 1831 on the Santa Fe Trail by Comanches.

WY 22 continues its steep climb across **Teton Pass.** Although there are few convenient stopping places until you reach the summit of the road (elevation

8,429 feet), the view westward of the valley and foothills is a beautiful sight. The granite mountain is covered in stones of pink and yellow gneiss and schists, and untimely patches of snow are scattered along the pass in late June.

While making this crossing in late May, a carload of adolescents in front of us pulled over, took out their snowboards, and carried them to the summit of the mountain (elev. 9,270 feet). After a laborious climb of about 15 to 20 minutes, they mounted their boards and carved their way down the slope of the mountain into the vale on the eastern slope. These robust young souls, prepared for anything, had their bikes strapped to the back of their car and were headed for the outdoor playground of Jackson Hole.

A scenic pullout just beyond the summit, indicated by a sign with a picture of binoculars, gives a wonderful view of the valley below to the east. The descent from the pass is steep for about 5.5 miles. The 10 percent grade of the road necessitates runaway-truck ramps at the side of the road. These ramps allow vehicles with brake failure to leave the road to coast up a sand-filled incline. It is not the upward slope that stops runaway cars and trucks, but rather the weight of the vehicle that causes it to sink into the sand. The ramps have saved more than one motorist a harrowing ride to the bottom of the pass.

Cabins and homes, buck-and-rail fences, and posts strung with barbed wire indicate that you have reached the community of **Wilson,** Wyoming, population 1,467 at last count. This small outpost of Jackson was founded by Elijah Nicholas Wilson. He first viewed the valley as a boy while in the company of the Shoshones. Supposedly, Chief Washakie of the Shoshones tried to honor his own mother whose son had died. In a dream she saw a young white boy taking his place. When Washakie came across Nick Wilson in 1856 in Utah, and Wilson spoke the Shoshone language, the chief offered him a pinto pony if he would travel with his party to Wyoming. The boy and his family agreed. Although Wilson returned to his family within 2 years, he never forgot this beautiful section of Wyoming. As an adult with a family of his own, he traveled with his brother Sylvester through Teton Pass to homestead in the southern end of Jackson's Hole. In 1895 he established the town of Wilson. The area's green summer belies the short growing season of the valley.

At almost any time of year, traffic between Wilson and Jackson is plentiful and slow. Just beyond Wilson, at mile marker 5, a left turn at the first light, the junction with WY 390, will take you to the Jackson Hole ski resort of **Teton Village.** If you're not starting your tour of the area here, cross the bridge over the Snake River and continue 6 miles to town. At the next junction with a light, where WY 22 meets US 89, turn left with all the traffic that's heading into Jackson—Old West town, tourist center, and starting point for a great vacation in Jackson Hole and Grand Teton National Park.

Wilson, WY, to Moose, WY

General description: Although this 16-mile drive is not entirely in Grand Teton National Park, it leads to the newest entrance to the park, the Granite Canyon entrance. The road travels about 7 miles through developed land around Jackson to the Granite Canyon entrance and beyond, through 9 miles of verdant hillsides, stands of aspens, and running brooks. If the two-lane road, partially unpaved, were better, increased traffic would destroy its charm. This drive is not recommended for people in a hurry, or those driving large motor homes or RVs.

Driving time: 45 minutes to 1 hour, or more, if you stop. Note the time allotted for a short drive. Driving is, and should be, slow.

Special attractions: Teton Village Mountain Resort, a country lane, the Laurance S. Rockefeller Preserve with hiking trails to Phelps Lake, The Murie Center, and a fair chance to see a moose at dusk or dawn at the Sawmill Ponds.

Location: South of Grand Teton National Park, northwestern Wyoming.

Drive route names & numbers: Moose-Wilson Road (locally known as Teton Village Road), WY 390.

Travel season: Year-round on the pavement to a little over a mile beyond Teton Village. Travel beyond the Granite Canyon entrance to Moose from late May to Oct or early Nov, depending on weather.

Camping: A commercial campground is located along the road about a mile from the junction of WY 22 and WY 390.

Services: Full services at Teton Village, at Dornan's just beyond the Moose Visitor Center, food and gasoline available in Wilson, restaurants along the way and at Teton Village. Cell service good for most of the drive.

Nearby points of interest: Jackson, Snake River access, Jackson Hole Mountain Resort (Teton Village), tram to the top of Rendezvous Mountain, Death Canyon and Granite Canyon hiking trails, hiking to Phelps Lake, Laurance S. Rockefeller Preserve.

For more information: Teton Village ski area (Jackson Hole Mountain Resort), Jackson Hole Chamber of Commerce, Grand Teton National Park.

The Route

This is a good starting point for people staying at the ski area who want to make a complete tour of the park. Begin in **Wilson** (population 1,467, elevation 6,160 feet), the town at the southern base of the Tetons. Turn left (north) from WY 22 at the junction with WY 390, indicated by a stoplight. The Teton Village ski area (also known as the Jackson Hole Mountain Resort) is 6.5 miles away. Within 0.25 mile of the stoplight, a Snake River access point to the right provides parking and boat access for rafters and anglers. Within the next mile, Teton Village KOA

Wilson, WY, to Moose, WY

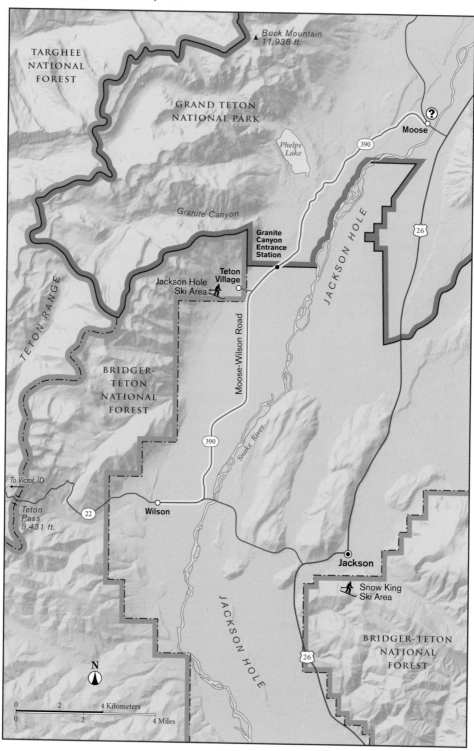

TARGHEE
NATIONAL
FOREST

Buck Mountain
11,938 ft.

GRAND TETON
NATIONAL PARK

Phelps
Lake

Granite Canyon

Moose

390

26

JACKSON HOLE

Granite
Canyon
Entrance
Station

Teton
Village

Jackson Hole
Ski Area

TETON RANGE

BRIDGER-
TETON
NATIONAL
FOREST

Moose-Wilson Road

390

Snake River

To Victor, ID

Teton
Pass
8,431 ft.

22

Wilson

Jackson

Snow King
Ski Area

JACKSON HOLE

BRIDGER-TETON
NATIONAL
FOREST

26

N

0   2   4 Kilometers
0   2   4 Miles

campground is located to the right of the road. The drive begins in semi-rural Wilson and continues along a jumble of old and new homes and condos, several good restaurants, a golf course, tennis courts, and a bike or multi-use trail that extends into the park—all the earmarks of developing land in transition.

Hike, Bike, Jump, Ride, or Ski

At about 6.5 miles you come to the left turn for **Teton Village, Jackson Hole Mountain Resort,** one of the best and most challenging ski areas in the West. The average snowfall here is 38 feet, and about half of the ski runs are expert. The ski hill has a vertical drop of 4,139 feet, making it one of the longest in the country. There are still plenty of trails for beginners and intermediates, however, and usually enough powder snow to keep all levels of skiers and snowboarders happy. The village offers shops, restaurants, a hostel and 11 hotels, bike and horse rentals, a golf course, and climbing wall. **The Mangy Moose,** a local staple, has good food and a lively saloon on weekends. Many fine restaurants in the village offer good food and a great time.

Entertainment flourishes at Teton Village. The **Grand Teton Music Festival** features both the symphony and guest artists, and **Alive @ Five lectures** and presentations occur weekly. Concerts and the art and antique show are only a few of the summer offerings. The new downhill mountain bike park lures those looking for an extra biking thrill. Six trails for varying levels of biking skills extend from the Teewinot chair lift, and a bungee trampoline guarantees that no one need be bored or hide indoors during a stay here. For a real treat, take the 100 passenger aerial tram to the summit of **Rendezvous Mountain** (elevation 10,450 feet). The ride costs $25 for adults, $20 for seniors, $19 for young adults (ages 13 to 17), and $12 for juniors (ages 6 to 12); free for children 5 and under. From the summit view an exceptional 360-degree panorama of the mountains and valley that make up Jackson Hole. The daring can even paraglide from the summit, in tandem with a professional.

After exploring Teton Village, return to the Moose-Wilson Road (WY 390) and continue north about a mile to cross into the park at the **Granite Canyon** entrance. The park's boundaries were formed over a long period of time through continuing land acquisitions from area ranches. Unlike in most other national parks, private landholdings exist within the Grand Teton park's borders. Several private ranches that have been kept within families for more than half a century still operate here, although this accounts for less than 1 percent of the park's land.

Moose-Wilson Road curves west and then juts north. Within a mile the surface changes from pavement to gravel, and the winding, narrow, bumpy nature of

Good old-fashioned trail rides begin at Teton Village.

the road prohibits access for trailers, RVs, and trucks. In 2 miles pavement again takes over, but the narrow road remains off-limits to larger vehicles. The two-lane route requires slow going as it enters a corridor lined with picturesque buck-and-rail fences and stands of aspens, firs, and pines forming a natural arch above. When travelers speed through here it intimidates both nature lovers and nature, so please drive slowly on this road and enjoy the surroundings.

Wildflowers bloom by the road and in nearby meadows. Slow to 25 miles an hour to cross a small bridge over Lake Creek, draining from Phelps Lake. The road winds gently around the foothills, as **Granite Canyon Ridge** rises to the left. At about 7.5 miles, a parking lot on the left is for hiking on the **Granite Canyon Trail,** one of several popular trails that form a web across the backcountry. In midsummer the area is lush with grasses and flowers. You cross a narrow wooden bridge over a burbling stream that flows from willow marshes to the north. Small hills that overlook the road through here make perfect spots where less hardy hikers may watch the sunrise or listen to the birdsong permeating the air on otherwise still mornings, or enjoy a wine and cheese picnic in the evening.

Engaging with an Intelligence

Much of the property that surrounds you here belonged to the JY Ranch, owned and enjoyed for decades by the Rockefeller family. In 2007 the land was deeded to the park, an action that had been announced by Laurance Rockefeller in 2001. To accomplish this transition, Mr. Rockefeller wanted to oversee the removal of the homes and buildings that had been part of the JY Ranch, to return the land to wilderness. This generous action added a total of 1,106 acres to Grand Teton National Park. Large log gates on the southern side of the road lead to the **Laurance S. Rockefeller Preserve.** This newest center in the park, finished in 2008, is dedicated to the idea that we can and must live in a sustainable stewardship with nature. As Mr. Rockefeller so eloquently said, "Nature quiets the mind by engaging with an intelligence larger than our own." The preserve center focuses on that intelligence. The small, unimposing building shows the potential of an environmentally green living and learning space that leaves a gentle footprint on the landscape. It comprises a resource center, exhibits, and a wonderful "Sound Room," where the soft sounds of nature permeate the acoustically designed area. The preserve, which offers daily "chats," sunrise and evening strolls, as well as occasional guest speakers, is the starting point for several trails of differing lengths and challenge levels. The longest is a 7-mile hike that circumnavigates **Phelps Lake.** Often our heroes are people from the past, and we don't clearly see our contemporaries. Laurance S. Rockefeller has become a hero of mine. When you leave the preserve, you take away thought-provoking ideas, as well as a special peace.

After your visit to the LSR Preserve, return to the Moose-Wilson Road to continue your trip north. At a little over 11 miles, a road to the left leads to the **Death Canyon Trailhead.** The canyon got its name in 1899 when a member of a surveying team was lost and died here. The dramatic canyon walls rise 3,000 feet above the canyon floor. To reach the trailhead, take the one-lane rugged road less than 1 mile to the parking area. A sign on this spur warns of rough road ahead, meaning the turnoff is not recommended for low-clearance vehicles. This hiking trail leads as far as 37 miles to the northwest to Driggs, Idaho. For the less zealous, in about 1 mile on the trail you reach Phelps Lake overlook; the short trek makes a good hike with a picnic spot at the end.

As you continue on Moose-Wilson Road, about 0.5 mile beyond the Death Canyon Trail turnoff, willow marshes to the right are a good place to watch for moose in a habitat that extends for almost 1.5 miles. Drive slowly and look carefully among the rushes, particularly in early morning or around dusk, for the largest member of the deer family, huge animals that can grow up to 7 feet tall at the shoulder and weigh over 1,500 pounds. The rich feeding area of this 1.5 miles provides some cover for the shy animals, as well as for sandhill cranes and Canada

These mountains beckon to hikers and climbers.

geese. Remember to respect the wildlife; if you spot a moose, do not approach it. Watch from the road, and for traffic and safety reasons, find a pullout for your car. Although moose appear docile, unpredictable bull moose will charge when threatened, and females ardently protect their young.

Continuing the drive, aspen-graced hills begin to appear on the left, as the road opens up beyond the moose flats. Watch for Sawmill Ponds overlook to the right, where the ridge allows a glimpse of the river and spring-fed pools, another good wildlife habitat. Look for beaver dams, which have enlarged the ponds over the years. You are out of the woods here, so to speak, but the road continues to wind through sagebrush-covered hills and valleys for a little over a mile.

Just before reaching the junction with the highway leading to the park's inner loop, as the road curves north, a sign indicates the **Murie Center,** a retreat center on the property of the old **Murie Ranch.** The Muries—Olaus, Mardy, Adolph, and Louise—were early proponents of the importance of maintaining wilderness, and were integral in work that led to the passage of the Wilderness Act in 1964. The work continues at the retreat center, where sponsored talks and workshops promote conservation and ecological management of wild places.

The road emerges near the southern entrance station to **Grand Teton National Park, Moose,** reached by turning left. The Moose post office, almost directly across the road, presents a chance to mail those postcards you've been planning to send. The **Craig Thomas Discovery and Visitor Center,** found by taking a right turn, displays wildlife and geologic information and focuses on themes of people, place, and protection of this area. The center is named for Wyoming Senator Craig Thomas, a member of the natural resources sub-committee, who was a devoted friend of the national parks.

As always, rangers are available to answer questions and give directions. National Park passes, boating, and backcountry hiking permits can be purchased from the backcountry permit desk. The visitor center contains a **Grand Teton (Natural History) Association Bookstore,** offering maps, posters, books, tapes, gifts, and more. You can purchase a membership to the association, which will allow you a 10 percent discount in their gift shops throughout the park, give you reciprocal discounts with other natural history and historical societies nationwide, and enable you to support their important work of education about the Tetons.

In addition, a new 155-seat amphitheater opened here in 2011, enabling the center to hold events such as a summer speaker series, the Conservation Film Festival in the fall, and other productions. This wonderful first stop remains open year-round. Give it a visit before proceeding through the park. When you have exhausted your curiosity at the visitor center, return to the road and drive west a few hundred yards to begin the inner loop drive through Grand Teton National Park from the Moose entrance.

27

Moose, WY, to the Rockefeller Parkway

General description: This 37-mile drive by some of the most spectacular scenery in America runs the length of the park, from the southern entrance at Moose to the northern border at the Rockefeller Parkway. The road, often called the Inner Loop Road, passes the Tetons close to their base. One spectacular view after another unfolds as you drive, prompting frequent stops for both photographers and nature lovers.

Driving time: Close to 1 hour, if you make no stops; but that is not recommended, and is nearly impossible to do. If you stop to enjoy hikes around Menor's Ferry and Jenny Lake, or take in the museum at Colter Bay, this can be an all-day excursion.

Special attractions: Menor's Ferry, Taggart Lake, Jenny Lake, Jackson Lake, Colter Bay Village, and the expanse of the Teton Range.

Location: Northwestern Wyoming.

Drive route names & numbers: Teton Park Road, or the Inner Loop Road.

Travel season: Late May through Oct, depending on weather.

Camping: Official park camping in designated areas at Jenny Lake (49 sites), Signal Mountain (86 sites), Colter Bay Village (350 sites), Lizard Creek (60 sites), all first-come, first-served, except Colter Bay RV Park, which accepts reservations.

Services: Full services at Moose, Signal Mountain Lodge, Colter Bay Village, and Jackson Lake Lodge in the park. Food only at Leeks Marina. Anyone may have lunch at Jenny Lake Lodge. Cell service is intermittent.

Nearby points of interest: Many hidden mountain lakes for eager hikers or rock climbers, Jenny Lake loop road, String Lake, Leigh Lake, the RKO Road, Signal Mountain summit road.

For more information: Grand Teton National Park Headquarters, Moose Visitor Center, Jenny Lake Lodge, Signal Mountain Lodge, Colter Bay Visitor Center, Jenny Lake Visitor Center.

The Route

The tour of the Tetons is referred to by many as a loop, with an inner and an outer road. **Inner Loop Road** (aka the Teton Park Road) skirts the base of the mountains, and **Outer Loop Road** (or US 89) lies to the east across the valley known as Jackson Hole. Begin the tour in **Moose** near park headquarters to drive the inner road, then loop back to Jackson. To drive the entire park from this starting point, a small amount of backtracking is necessary, but not at all undesirable if you have time. If time is short, turn east at Jackson Lake Junction 20 miles away, and return to Jackson on the Outer Loop Road. Note that if you are taking this ride on the bicycle or multi-use path, it ends at the southern end of Jenny Lake. Twelve new miles of the path, from Jackson to Moose Junction, opened in 2012.

Moose, WY, to the Rockefeller Parkway

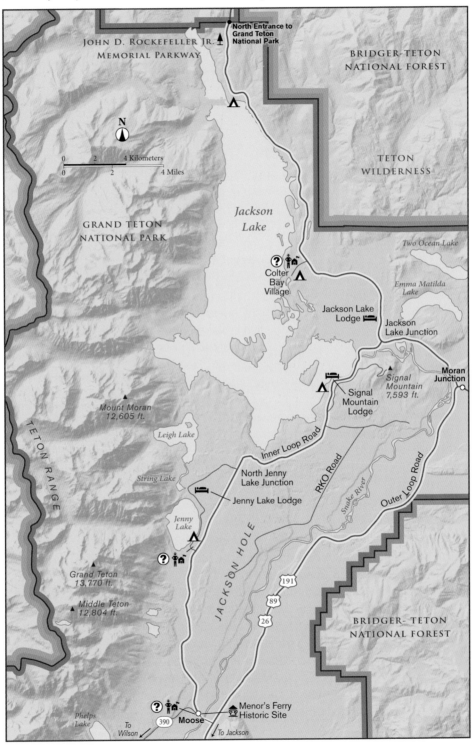

John D. Rockefeller Jr.
Memorial Parkway

North Entrance to
Grand Teton
National Park

BRIDGER-TETON
NATIONAL FOREST

N

0   2   4 Kilometers
0   2   4 Miles

Jackson
Lake

TETON
WILDERNESS

GRAND TETON
NATIONAL PARK

Two Ocean Lake

Colter
Bay
Village

Emma Matilda
Lake

Jackson Lake
Lodge

Jackson
Lake Junction

Moran
Junction

Signal
Mountain
7,593 ft.

Mount Moran
12,605 ft.

Signal
Mountain
Lodge

Leigh Lake

Inner Loop Road

RKO Road

Snake River

Outer Loop Road

String Lake

North Jenny
Lake Junction

Jenny Lake Lodge

Jenny
Lake

JACKSON HOLE

TETON RANGE

Grand Teton
13,770 ft.

Middle Teton
12,804 ft.

191

89

26

BRIDGER-
TETON
NATIONAL FOREST

Phelps
Lake

390

Moose

Menor's Ferry
Historic Site

To
Wilson

To Jackson

Bicycles are acceptable in the park anywhere vehicles are allowed, and many travelers choose this mode of sightseeing and exercise.

Moose lies 12 miles north of Jackson, off US 26/89/191. Turn left at Moose Junction to reach the southern entrance station to the park. You can also reach the starting point by taking Scenic Route 26 from Wilson (page 246). Go north on Teton Park Road through the park entrance, picking up your copy of *Grand Teton Guide*, the official park publication. Emergency numbers, visitor services, wildlife information, self-guided hiking trails, schedules for ranger-led activities, and more are included in the newspaper. Proceed through the gate to make your first stop at Menor's Ferry about 0.2 mile from the entrance.

Menor's Ferry

In 1894 Bill Menor came to Moose to establish the first homestead in the area and exploit his entrepreneurial skills. Along with his cabin he built a blacksmith's shop and a general store. He realized that because of the difficulty of crossing the Snake River, people were hindered from settling the western side of the valley. Before the upstream dam hampered the river, it was wide and the current fast, particularly in spring. Although a toll bridge was located at Moran, about 20 miles north, no other easy crossing existed in the valley. Near Menor's homestead a relatively easy crossing was possible as the river was not braided but flowed in a single stream. Menor built a cable-style ferry, basically a small platform with room for one wagon and a few people, charging 50 cents for a team of horses or a wagon, or 25 cents for a rider on horseback. People on foot were free, he said; if they couldn't afford a horse, they obviously couldn't afford a fare. Menor's ferry changed the face of the valley as settlers spread across its girth.

To stop at **Menor's Ferry,** turn right and drive 0.5 mile to a parking lot. To envision life a century ago, walk around the complex of pioneer cabins and shops. Begin with the **Noble cabin,** the home of Maude Noble, who bought the ferry from Menor in 1918. It was at the Noble cabin in 1925 that Maude Noble, Horace Albright from Yellowstone, and several valley residents met to discuss the possibility of preserving the surrounding area as a national recreation area, or annexing it to Yellowstone National Park to the north. The Teton Range itself was set aside as a national park in 1929, but a battle for the rest of the park's land lasted another 20 years. Remnants of hard feelings and controversy remain in Jackson today.

A free self-guided trail leads you through other buildings at Menor's Ferry, including a general store and Menor's cabin. A restored ferry sits at the riverside, and when conditions allow, it operates across the Snake. A building filled with

Enter the chapel at Menor's Ferry to view the scene behind the altar.

old carriages includes an open coach, a buckboard buggy, a covered wagon, and a coach once used by the old JY Ranch.

Near this complex of early buildings stands the **Chapel of the Transfiguration,** an Episcopal chapel built in 1925 on land donated by Maude Noble. Look inside the chapel, set in a field of wildflowers and backed by the magnificent mountains. Two beautiful stained-glass windows depicting summer and winter adorn the entrance, and the view of the mountains from the window behind the altar is spectacular.

To continue your journey, retrace your path to Inner Loop Road and turn right. As you leave Menor's Ferry, take in the range you are about to approach. Many peaks make up the Teton Range, but some are seen only at particular angles, generally hidden from view by dominant peaks or even shifting daylight. The mountains have been called by many names—Hoary-Headed Fathers, Pilots' Knobs, Teewinot (meaning "many peaks" in Shoshone). At one time it was even suggested that the Grand Teton be named for Ferdinand Hayden, the leader of the federally sponsored surveying expedition of 1871 that did much of the exploration of Yellowstone and its surrounding territory. He modestly rejected the honor.

The Peaks

The peaks south of the park entrance include **Rendezvous Peak,** elevation 10,450 feet, the mountain where the ski area is built. **Mount Hunt** is the first prominent mountain within the borders of the park, rising to a "mere" 10,783 feet and named for Wilson Price Hunt, the guide who led the Astorians through Teton Pass in 1811. At the Moose entrance, you are almost due east of **Static Peak,** 11,303 feet, named for its qualities as a lightning rod, and **Buck Mountain,** 11,938 feet, named for George Buck, recorder for Thomas M. Bannon's mapping party of 1898. **Mount Wister,** at 11,490 feet, rises slightly to the north and behind Buck Mountain; it was named in honor of part-time resident Owen Wister, author of *The Virginian,* a novel that takes place partly in Jackson Hole.

Beyond Mount Wister the peaks become more imposing, rising starkly from the valley floor. The **South Teton,** 12,514 feet, is better viewed from the western side of the range between the towns of Victor and Driggs. On the eastern face it is hidden by **Nez Perce,** 11,901 feet, named for the Native American tribe that once hunted in northern Wyoming. The name means "pierced nose" but is a misnomer for this tribe, attributed to the interpreter for the Lewis and Clark expedition who mistook these Indians for the Chinook tribe that lived closer to the Columbia River. The Nez Perce's own name for themselves, the Niimiipu, translates as the "people who walked out of the forest."

The **Middle Teton,** 12,804 feet, has a vertical black diabase dike, a darkened slab on its eastern face, making it easily identifiable. The dike formed when liquid magma seeped into a crevice of previously cooled, solidified granite, before the underground fault was raised to form mountains. The **Grand Teton,** 13,770 feet, was named by French-Canadian trappers of the Hudson Bay Company. They were the first to apply this name to the mountain range, likening the peaks to three breasts, an interesting concept likely thought of by men who had been too long alone. This name is more obvious when the peaks are viewed from the western side in Idaho. The Grand Teton is the second-largest peak in Wyoming, dominated only by **Granite Peak** in the Wind River Range, at 13,804 feet (the champion by only 34 feet). **Mount Owen,** 12,928 feet, is next, lying slightly behind the Grand Teton and thus not easily seen from the road. It is named for W.O. Owen, who scaled the Grand Teton with Bishop Spalding and other companions in 1889. **Teewinot,** at 12,325 feet, generally obscures Mount Owen. **Mount St. John,** about 11,430 feet, is actually a series of peaks that are almost the same size. This peak is named for Orestes St. John, the geologist with the 1877 Hayden Survey who wrote some of the first monographs, or scholarly brochures, about the northern Wyoming mountains. **Rockchuck Peak,** 11,144 feet, is named for the small marmots that proliferate on the mountain, *rockchuck* being a variation of the term

A summer rainbow falls at the foot of Mount Moran.

woodchuck. Next, **Mount Woodring** stands at 11,590 feet. Samuel Woodring was a packmaster and guide who came to the region in 1920 as a ranger for Yellowstone National Park. He later became the first superintendent of Grand Teton National Park. **Thor Peak,** 12,028 feet, named for the Norse god of thunder, is hidden by **Mount Moran.** This peak, at 12,605 feet, was named for landscape artist Thomas Moran, whose paintings made a compelling argument for creating the national parks of the West. Mount Moran also boasts a black dike of basalt.

As the range diminishes to the north, **Bivouac Peak** rises to 10,825 feet. The mountain was named when locals Fritiof Fryxell and Gustav and Theodore Koven made an ascent of the difficult western summit but descended so late that the Kovens spent the night at the foot of the mountain without food or bedding. Fryxell, who had hightailed it back to Jenny Lake, with tongue in cheek named the peak in his friends' honor. **Eagles Rest,** at 11,258 feet; **Doane Peak,** 11,354 feet, named for a member of the Langford expedition of 1870 that explored Yellowstone; and **Ranger Peak,** 11,355 feet, complete this Rocky Mountain chain. Part of the fascinating mystery of the whole range is the ever-changing nature of the appearance of these magnificent mountains, whether by season, time of day, light, or angle of view.

Near Moose, as you begin northward, you pass rather innocuous-looking hills with sagebrush and occasional pine viewed on the slopes to the west. The open fields to the right are frequently inhabited by pronghorn antelope or elk. Along the way, several pullouts on both sides of the road provide information and occasional picnic spots and restroom facilities.

The Turnouts

The first stop, **Windy Point,** is located to the right about 1 mile north of the entrance station. From here you can view the reddish stripe called the **Gros Ventre Slide** on the **Sleeping Indian Mountain** to the east, evidence of a rock slide in 1925. The opportunity to have a closer view of Sleeping Indian is found in Scenic Route 28, "Jackson Lake Junction to Jackson, WY." The interpretive signs at the pullout explain the desertlike sagebrush plains to the east, the wildlife they support, and the importance of ecological balance inherent here. The plains were created by glaciers, massive flat ice sheets about 3,000 feet thick, that once covered the valley floor, flattening the terrain and depositing glacial debris. This debris is too porous to hold moisture well, making the kind of ground where sagebrush flourishes. Glacial moraines, on the other hand, do retain moisture and are often rich in nutrients, making them perfect spots for growth of lodgepole pine.

Sagebrush, the abundant, fragrant plant that grows in the rocky soil here, supports pronghorn and grouse and provides winter graze for elk, bison, and moose as it protrudes from the snow. Coyotes and badgers inhabit the outwash plains, hunting other small animals the plains support. Wildlife is easiest to spot in early morning or just before dusk, although buffalo stand out at any time of day. Wildflowers—sulfur buckwheat, scarlet gilia, and lupine—grow in profusion here and among the grasses closer to the base of the mountains. Arrowleaf balsamroot is the sunflowerlike plant with long, arrow-shaped leaves that covers the valley floor in June and July. It is disturbing to note that encroaching air pollution now threatens this seemingly pristine wilderness.

At 1.9 miles from the park entrance, park personnel cabins are seen to the left. The mountains beyond show stark evidence of the 1985 fires in Grand Teton National Park, three years before the conflagration in Yellowstone, but new growth will shortly take over these hills. A turnout for **Taggart Lake Trailhead** is found to the left at 2.4 miles. Picnic tables and restrooms are available here. The trail leads toward the foothills, proceeding 1.6 miles to **Taggart Lake** and 1 mile beyond to **Bradley Lake,** a nice afternoon's walk. Taggart Lake is held in by a glacial moraine deposited when a glacier flowed out of Avalanche Canyon 15,000 years ago. It is named for W. Rush Taggart, a member of the 1872 Hayden Survey party who had visited Jackson Hole 12 years before while traveling with Captain W.F. Raynolds and the US Army Corps of Engineers. Maps are available for your use at the trailhead. In winter a popular cross-country ski trail leads from here to Jenny Lake.

The next turnout, a picnic area at **Cottonwood Creek,** is found about 3 miles into the drive. Here you'll find information about the Beaver Creek fire and the renewal process of the forest. The fire was sparked by lightning but smoldered undetected for 4 days before flaring up at the end of August 1985. As in Yellowstone, park policy dictates that when conditions are right, a natural fire be monitored and allowed to burn. Policy-makers believe that natural process is best for the care and regeneration of forests. Firefighters do intervene when human lives or property is at stake or when weather conditions are dangerous. Ecologically, forest fire is essential for the cycle of natural renewal; it helps maintain balance by removing diseased or dead wood and allows new growth to flourish on nutrient-replenished hills. Fire replaces nutrients in the soil much faster than the process of death and decay. As ash covers and permeates the soil, new seeds germinate into healthy young trees. Lavish wildflowers also grow, luring new wildlife in search of a more diverse food source and habitat.

The creek here is open to fishing from the beginning of August through the end of October, and this is a fine place for casting a line or just dangling your feet on a hot summer day. Remember that the park, although usually crowded in the thick of summer, is also wonderful in late spring or early to mid-fall. October is rutting season for elk, and they restlessly wander by the sides of the road here in evening, magnificent with their huge antler racks and bellowing calls.

At about 3.6 miles you approach a road to the **Climbers' Ranch,** where a rustic group of cabins and campsites is clustered. Rock climbers can stay for a nominal fee as they enjoy one of the more challenging endeavors offered by the park. A two-lane road to the left turns into one narrow lane of dust after it leaves the highway. The Climbers' Ranch is supported and maintained by the American Alpine Club, which exists on donations. All climbers are welcome. Several thousand people make the rigorous climb to the summit of the Grand Teton each year. Many more assault the various peaks of the range.

At 3.9 miles the **Teton Glacier** turnout offers an interpretive sign that tells how great glaciers carved the mighty peaks of the mountain range. It points out the still-existing Teton Glacier, which lies to the northeast of the base of the Grand Teton, one of about a dozen remaining glaciers. These glaciers are young in geologic time, only about 5,000 years old, and diminutive compared to those that originally sculpted the peaks.

A glacier is formed when winter snowfall, over the long term, equals or exceeds summer melt. Often in high mountain valleys, snow buildup compresses the snow beneath, turning it into heavier ice. The heaviness of the ice underneath the lighter snow causes the bottom of the glacier to move under the snow above, resulting in a flow. In this way glaciers act as conveyor belts, trapping and moving rock debris caught in the ice down from the height of the mountains. In a glacier, ice moves by gravity's pull. The ice of the Grand Teton glacier currently flows about 30 feet a year. This does not mean that the glacier itself moves to that degree, but that the ice underneath may travel that far.

Other turnouts from which to admire this view appear directly in front of the **Grand Teton,** at about 5 miles. To the right of the Grand Teton is Mount Owen, followed by Teewinot. To the right of the road from this lookout, watch for pronghorn that often graze in the area. The road continues through open fields where the Tetons to the left rise impressively from the valley base. To the right is an abnormal amount of vegetation. An outcropping of trees on a ridge, known as **Timbered Island,** sticks out as an oasis of lodgepole pines, spruce, and fir trees. The sagebrush surrounding the island grows in glacial outwash, porous soil that does not support other vegetation. Timbered Island is made possible because the soil comes from glacial moraine, which holds moisture very well, making it possible for the trees to flourish. Timbered Island often harbors elk.

In summer, at about 6 miles, fields of lavender-blue lupine signify Lupine Meadows, where elk can sometimes be spotted in daytime. Located in front of Teewinot Mountain, **Lupine Meadow** has trails leading to **Surprise and Amphitheater Lakes.** To reach the trails, take the rough gravel road to the left where a one-lane bridge crosses Cottonwood Creek. This left fork leads to a parking area for the trails; the right fork goes to a boat launch for the southern end of Jenny Lake. A restroom is available at the trailheads, but facilities at nearby Jenny Lake are less rustic.

Jenny Lake Loop

The **Jenny Lake** area is one of the two major playgrounds of Grand Teton National Park. The lake is a wonderful spot for hiking or canoeing. Boat rides cross the lake toward the falls every 15 to 20 minutes, leaving from the boat ramp at the southern end of the lake. The cost is $10 round-trip for adults, or $7 one-way; children 6 to 12 pay $5 whether round-trip or one-way, and those younger than 6 ride free. A 6.6-mile hiking trail circumnavigates the lake through beautiful mountain wilderness. The most popular hike in the park leads from the visitor center to **Hidden Falls,** 2.5 relatively easy miles, and beyond to **Inspiration Point,** 0.5 mile and 400 feet above the falls. The wonderful view from Inspiration Point spans Jackson Hole. If hikers continue, the trail proceeds 3.5 miles to the end of **Cascade Canyon** with an unparalleled view of the Grand Teton along the way. Hike another 2.7 miles to reach **Lake Solitude.** This trail, like many in the park, has many offshoots, but the main trail to Inspiration Point remains popular because its easy access to the falls makes it a good family hike, neither too strenuous nor too long. Although this area at the southern end of the lake has a large parking area, you will have the best luck parking if you arrive in the morning. Visitor services here include a ranger station, a visitor center for information, a general store, and restrooms. Boat tickets are available at the boat dock.

As you continue north on Teton Park Road, a turnout on the left allows a view of Cascade Canyon, the "gateway to the alpine region." Cascade was formed by flowing glaciers, which carved out its U-shape. Named for the creek that tumbles toward Jenny Lake, Cascade Canyon has many trails that lead from here into mountain recesses and climb above the timber line. The interpretive sign tells of alpine ecology and vegetation. Hikers should heed the warning to stay on trails to avoid destroying the delicate slow-growing grasses. From this pullout, the view of the Grand Teton, often with its peak encased in clouds, is impressive.

At a little over 9 miles into the drive, at the northern end of Jenny Lake, a one-way, 3-mile scenic loop takes you by three piedmont lakes—lakes created by glacial depressions—Leigh, String, and Jenny Lakes. Don't miss the **Jenny Lake Loop,** which offers exceptional views of the mountains. Turn left at the scenic loop drive sign. The road curves slightly to the north, where you can have a good look at **Mount Moran.** The speed limit is 45 miles an hour, and the road heads south as you almost parallel the mountains on a two-lane road.

Cathedral Group

One of the most impressive views of the mountains is seen from the **Cathedral Group** pullout, the first stop on the Jenny Lake loop. The Cathedral Group consists of Teewinot, the Grand Teton, and Mount Owen, the second-highest peak of the range. The three mountains from this vantage point are called the Cathedral Group because their pointed peaks bring to mind the spires of the great gothic cathedrals. This is one of the most photographed views in the park. The inscription at the interpretive sign quotes the poetic description by Fritiof Fryxell, a Ph.D geologist and the park's first ranger naturalist, who wrote: "More evident here than in many of the great cathedrals of men . . . the gothic note . . . it is seen in the profiles of the countless firs and spruces . . . congregated like worshippers on the lower slopes. It reappears higher in the converging lines of spire rising upon spire . . . it obtains supreme expression in the figures of the peaks themselves . . . that towering above all else, with pointed summits, direct one's vision and thoughts yet higher." Fryxell eloquently recorded impressions and history of the area. An ardent explorer and educator as well, he developed public education programs, and his book, *The Tetons, Interpretations of a Mountain Landscape,* published in 1938, is still an eloquent testimony to the inspiring scenery in the park.

The spires of these peaks give rise to the name "Cathedral Group."

To the right, at the base of **Rockchuck Peak,** a fault scarp, a cliff formed by movement along the fault, allows geologists to measure how much the valley drops and the peaks rise. Caused by earthquakes both felt and unfelt, the movement will undoubtedly continue, as it has for the last 9 million years.

From the Cathedral Group turnout, continue south and slow to 25 miles an hour. The first turn to the right leads to the **String Lake Picnic Area.** From here, a 1-mile trail leads to Leigh Lake directly to the north. Leigh Lake, String Lake, and Jenny Lake are connected by continuous water flow from drainages high in the mountains. **String Lake,** directly south of Leigh, is a perfect place for a family to picnic, canoe, kayak, sunbathe, and wade, no matter how young the family. With an average depth of 6 feet, String Lake remains calm. It connects at its southern end to Jenny Lake through a small cascade. The picnic area connects to trails to both Leigh and Jenny Lakes and hooks up with the hiking trail that circles Jenny Lake.

Leigh Lake, 2 miles long, has an average depth of 250 feet. If you continue on the trail around its perimeter, at a little over a mile you reach a white sand beach where the water is sometimes warm enough to invite a swim in this beautiful, deep, green lake. For hikers and campers, the trail continues on to two small cirque lakes, **Bearpaw Lake** and **Trapper Lake,** about 1.5 miles back. Leigh Lake is named for Beaver Dick Leigh, one of the legendary early trappers and guides who dared to live here year-round. Jenny Lake is named for his wife, a Shoshone woman. Their life together had a desperately sad ending when Jenny and their six children all died of smallpox during Christmas week, 1876. Though ill himself, Beaver Dick cared for them all, but watched as one by one they died of the disease. His writings of early pioneer life are both startling and heartrending.

Beyond String Lake the loop becomes a one-way road that continues south on a scenic route to just north of the South Jenny Lake turnoff. **Jenny Lake** is the second-largest lake in the park, with a 6-mile perimeter. It was formed by a moraine, a place where a glacier deposited sediment carried as the ice flowed, which created a natural dam. Boulders surrounding the lake are erratics, large rocks conveyed to unexpected spots by moving glaciers. With an average depth of 200 feet, Jenny Lake is an excellent place for boating.

Superb **Jenny Lake Lodge** is located here in rustic surroundings. Four-star lodging and dining can be had for a high price, but the cost includes gourmet meals (breakfast and dinner), horseback riding, boating, and lodging. It's a good idea to book reservations well in advance of your planned stay. Jenny Lake campground, the most popular campground in the Tetons, is a National Park Service campground where the 50 sites are spoken for by early morning in summer. Plan early and arrive early if you want a campsite.

The loop road proceeds through Douglas fir and subalpine fir that provide a sense of solitude and serenity, even among the masses visiting the park. Jenny Lake overlook is to the right at a little beyond a mile on the one-way road. Rather hidden by the trees, it allows a look at the lake and Cascade Canyon beyond. The pointed peak of **Teewinot** stretches an abrupt vertical mile above the lake, looming so tall that it is often mistaken for the Grand Teton. Teewinot's summit is so pointed it diminishes to a tip about the circumference of an adult's thumb. This view is especially beautiful in the morning, when the light clearly reflects the height of the mountain in the water.

As the one-way loop road ends, turn left (north) to continue toward Jackson Lake Junction and the northern end of the park. The next turnout along Teton Park Road, immediately north of Jenny Lake Loop Road, looks directly at **Mount Moran,** the square-topped mountain in the range. **Mountain View** turnout, at about 10 miles from the park entrance, has interpretive signs that explain the formation of the range. The noticeable black dike on Mount Moran was formed about 1.5 billion years ago when the earth's underground metamorphic rock cracked and filled with magma. The magma hardened, and later when the mountain lifted up, the dike, being the harder material, remained as surrounding rock eroded away. The dike is 150 feet wide and extends in depth to Idaho, 7 miles to the west.

From here you have a good view of **Hanging or Falling Ice Glacier** on the southeastern face of Mount Moran above Leigh Lake. Gravity pulls blocks of this glacier's ice to the valley below, thus the name. Mount Moran is capped with a thick layer of Cambrian sandstone, which covered the entire Teton Range millions of years ago, before erosion did its work. A companion layer of sandstone lies about 24,000 feet below the earth's surface, pushed down by the sinking block that forms the valley. The **Skillet Glacier** on the northeastern side of Mount Moran, the second large glacier on this formation, is more easily viewed from vantage points to the north. Elk and pronghorn often frequent the meadow above the Mountain View turnout.

Another short side trip to the left at about 11 miles leads to **Spalding Bay** at the southern end of Jackson Lake. The bay is named for Bishop Spalding, who ascended Grand Teton in 1898 with W.O. Owen and others. To get to the boat launch, turn left on the rough dirt road and drive a little less than a mile through terrain entirely different from that of the loop around Jenny Lake. Camping and fires are permitted here in specific sites only, and permits must be obtained at a ranger station. Four-wheel-drive vehicles are recommended for the road, which is not really wide enough for RVs. The road dead-ends at the bay.

Continuing on the Teton Park Road, as you pass the Spalding Bay turnoff, picture the meadow to the right being occupied by grazing buffalo. Only 150 years ago, over 50 million bison roamed free in the West, as untold numbers of herds grazed on the fertile plains. Because of unfettered hunting, or some say a US government program to wipe out the Native Americans' food source, by the turn of the 20th century fewer than 50 of the animals composed the last of the wild herds. Yellowstone National Park came to the rescue with a mission to nurture the remaining animals into a healthy herd. That goal was accomplished, and although the animals are relatively few in number, they have, for the time being, been saved from extinction. Today, Grand Teton National Park gives refuge to a much smaller, but equally stable herd, than the herds found in Yellowstone.

Another view is available of the Falling Ice Glacier toward the south, and Skillet Glacier to the north, at the Mount Moran turnout, next along the road. Mount Moran was named by Dr. Ferdinand V. Hayden for Thomas Moran, his friend and expedition companion. If you have ever seen Moran's early drawings and watercolors of this parcel of the West, it is easy to understand why his paintings had such a convincing effect on Congress during their discussion about preserving these lands as national parks. A few of his drawings and paintings are housed at the Albright Visitor Center in Mammoth, Yellowstone. If you're heading that way, the museum is worth a stop.

Although it is sometimes closed, a spur road to the right, called the **RKO Road,** a little beyond 15.4 miles from the entrance, heads to a rim overlooking the

Snake River. Named for the movie studio that used this location in the early 1950s for movies such as *The Big Sky* and *The Far Horizons,* the road is about 3.5 miles of a tortuous, slow drive as it bumps along through meadows of sagebrush. As you approach a stand of cottonwoods you are closing in on the river. The riverbank is a fine place to picnic or wade, although there are no tables or facilities. One might think it hardly worth the trip, except it is a beautiful drive back to the Teton Park Road as you face the mountains.

At about 2.2 miles along this spur, a dirt road, known as the River Road, heads 16 miles to the south. However, rough winters and erosion have rendered this road unusable, and plans to repair it are on hold. The River Road emerged at the old Bar B C Ranch, which is no longer in operation. Today the RKO Road makes a wonderful biking trail for those with good tires and an effective patch kit. The turnoff to the RKO Road lies to the right as you head toward the river, just before you reach the grove of trees. Many movies have been filmed on location in Jackson Hole, with the most memorable being the incomparable western, *Shane,* filmed in 1953.

Signal Mountain Area

Back on the Inner Loop Road, the route passes quickly into a wooded area. At about 15.7 miles, it reaches **Signal Mountain Road** to the right, about 3.5 miles from the North Jenny Lake turnoff. This side route climbs close to 5 miles of paved road to the summit of **Signal Mountain.** No RVs or trailers are allowed on this narrow winding road, even though it is paved. If you make the drive, a panoramic view of both mountains and valley awaits you at the summit. From this vantage point it is possible to see how the valley tilts down to the west toward the mountains, evidence of the dropping fault that created the area. This is an incredible spot to see either sunrise or sunset.

A favorite hiking trail from the bottom of the mountain covers about 3 miles to get to the top. The trail begins a little to the north of Signal Mountain Road and can be reached by parking at the **Signal Mountain Lodge** complex. The Signal Mountain summit, at 7,593 feet, offers a beautiful vista of the Tetons to the west and the Snake River as it winds its way across the floor of Jackson Hole. Signal Mountain was named when Robert Ray Hamilton, a local and colorful entrepreneur, was lost in Jackson Hole while hunting in August 1890. The search party agreed to light a signal fire on the hill's summit when he was found, signaling to other volunteers that their search was over. He was found, drowned, two weeks after the search began, and the fire was lit.

A mile beyond the summit road, on the left, is the privately owned Signal Mountain Lodge area, where full services are available. Cozy cabins on the shore of Jackson Lake offer a peaceful summer or fall stay. Again, make reservations well in advance of your visit, although it never hurts to check on last-minute cancellations. A popular campground here, run by Signal Mountain Lodge, is filled each season with those wanting access to the water on this beautiful lake. Jackson Lake and the surrounding area of Jackson Hole were named for Davey Jackson, one of the original trappers of the area and eventual part-owner of the Rocky Mountain Fur Company, along with William Sublette and Jedediah Strong Smith.

At 17.4 miles the **Chapel of the Sacred Heart** appears to the left, tucked back in the pines. A Catholic church erected in 1935, this chapel was called Our Lady of the Tetons until 1964, when someone translated the French word and decided the name was unseemly. Services are still held in the small log chapel. At about 18 miles, a private residence near the left side of the road is now owned by the park. Known as the old Brinkerhoff "blue house," it was bought by the government in 1955 for $70,000 and renovated for official park visitors and VIPs. Presidents Jimmy Carter and George H.W. Bush, and newsman Walter Cronkite are among the famous guests who have stayed here.

Two miles from Signal Mountain you come to **Jackson Lake Dam.** The lake, once about 386 feet deep, was originally dammed by a natural moraine, debris left by a retreating glacier. People first tried to enhance the work of nature in 1906, when a log dam was constructed above the original dam, raising the level of the lake by 3 feet. The log dam was washed out by heavy rain and melting snow in 1910 and subsequently was replaced with an earthen dam that again raised the lake's level, this time by 10 feet. Between 1914 and 1916 the earthen structure was replaced by a concrete dam, which raised the lake's level by 39 feet to its current depth of 425 feet. As the dam was moved north, it added 7,200 acres of water capacity. The final rebuilding in 1989 made the structure earthquake proof, and the lake now covers 26,000 acres. Beyond its use as a recreation area, the reservoir provides water to Idaho's farmers downstream on the Snake River. An exhibit near the dam tells of the Waterfall Canyon fire that damaged this area in the summer of 1974.

Beyond the dam is **Jackson Lake Junction,** almost exactly 20 miles from the Moose entrance. To the north, boat launches and fishing access make this a good day-use area for fishing, picnicking, and wildlife viewing. Beyond the dam but before the junction, watch for moose in the fields of willows that flank the road. If you are lucky enough to view one, please watch it from your car. The animals are easily spooked, but they love the area. As the pundits say, you are a guest in the moose's home, not the other way around. Show them respect.

From Jackson Lake Junction you can drive east to reach the outer loop drive at Moran Junction, which intersects US 89/191/287 (see Scenic Route 28). Or

Boating is a popular pastime on beautiful Jackson Lake.

proceed left to head north to drive the remaining 17 miles of the park drive. The left turn leads to the northern entrance and the John D. Rockefeller Jr. Parkway.

Beyond the Lake

If you head north, the willow flats located 0.5 mile from the dam offer a good chance for wildlife viewing. Willow rushes and standing water make a delicious habitat for moose. Because the road rises away from and overlooks the willows, the large animals are easy to spot. The **Willow Flats** overlook to the left (west) of the road is provided for just such a purpose. From here you also have a good view of **Skillet Glacier** on the eastern face of Mount Moran, identifiable by its long skillet "handle." While watching for moose, be alert for anything that is not green in the sagebrush-colored fields or reddish willow flats. A tan or buff color can signify a pronghorn, deer, or elk on the landscape; dark brown or black may reveal a bison, moose, or bear, sometimes mistaken for logs or rocks. Look closely to discern what may be present.

The **Jackson Lake Lodge** complex, 1 mile northwest of the dam, is the second true resort in the park. Riding stables, lodging, good restaurants, and other resort amenities, as well as a medical clinic, are conveniently located here. It is worth a stop to view the lake and mountains exactly as John D. Rockefeller wanted you to see them—from the gigantic picture windows that he personally framed to catch the scene at its most magnificent. Rockefeller, builder of Jackson Lake Lodge, was frequently criticized for profiting from the Jackson area; but this disregards the fact that, if not for his efforts, much of this land would be irretrievably lost to extensive development and exploitation.

Beyond Jackson Lake Lodge the road returns to forests of lodgepole pines. As you leave the resort, look to the right of the road for **Christian Pond,** where a pair of trumpeter swans often makes its home. A road near **Pilgrim Creek,** 2.5 miles above the lodge, provides access to hiking in the Teton Wilderness to the northeast. A turnout to the left gives another view of Jackson Lake and the mountains beyond. Past Pilgrim Creek, the road to the north begins to climb.

Colter Bay Village, on the left 2 miles beyond Pilgrim Creek, has a very good museum of Native American arts. The museum is free and open daily from mid-May through Sept. A visitor center, food, lodging, gas, and camping are also available at Colter Bay. Camping here is especially appealing to many families, as this is where the popular tent cabins are located. Tent cabins have two hard sides and two canvas sides, and come equipped with a woodstove. They are a good alternative for those who do not have their own camping equipment, although you must rent or provide your own bedding and cooking utensils. Although the tent cabins are a bit rustic, they are more affordable than many of the rooms in Jackson or the park. Because of this, reservations should be made early. Cabins can also be rented at Colter Bay. Short, easy trails lead from the camping area to the bay.

Colter Bay was named for John Colter, who most historians believe was the first Caucasian to travel through the Teton area, after he left the Lewis and Clark expedition to explore the West. He traveled by foot through the winter of 1807–08 in search of trapping sites and Native Americans with whom to trade. He was working for Manuel Lisa, a trapper who was establishing a trading outpost northeast of Yellowstone. Colter passed on information about the wonders he discovered to his friends in the East, prompting an enthusiasm for further western exploration. His story is one of the most amazing of the tales of the early explorers.

Beyond Colter Bay, begin to climb very gradually through pines toward Yellowstone. The road remains close to the lakeshore for a couple of miles, and several turnouts and at least three good picnic areas are provided for the first or last views of the northern end of the Teton Range at Sargent's Bay, Arizona Island, and Lakeview. At about 16.2 miles, a road to the left leads to **Leeks Marina,** an access point to Jackson Lake, with a boat ramp and the only pizza restaurant around. US 89/191/287 climbs steadily for the next 10.5 miles through lodgepole forest. A good but primitive camping spot at **Lizard Creek operates on a** first-come, first-served basis. No reservations are necessary, but the campground fills quickly in the summer. Lizard Creek was probably mistakenly named for the salamanders found in the water; lizards actually live on dry ground.

Two more picnic areas, **Arizona Island** and **Sargents Bay,** invite you to stop before you end this drive. Sargents Bay is named for John Sargent, an unorthodox and sinister early settler, who, it is speculated, may have been responsible for the death of his partner, Robert Hamilton, for whom the fire was lit on Signal Mountain. To make his story murkier, Sargent was also charged with second-degree murder after the death of his first wife. His former property now carries his name.

Proceed north a total of 17 miles from Jackson Lake Junction to the park exit and the beginning of Rockefeller Parkway. From here you can either go on to Yellowstone (Scenic Route 21), or turn and retrace your steps to Jackson Lake Junction, where a left turn will take you to Moran Junction to continue on the Outer Loop Road of the park (Scenic Route 28).

28

Jackson Lake Junction to Jackson, WY

General description: A 34-mile drive east of the Tetons on the valley road, surrounded by working ranches, dude ranches, and sagebrush outwash plains, alongside the Snake River. Two side drives, one to Kelly and the Gros Ventre (Groh-VONT) Slide area, and one on Antelope Flats Road, are worth the trip, and of course the ultimate western tourist town, Jackson, awaits at the end of your drive.

Driving time: 35 to 45 minutes, depending on stops, and without the side drive.

Special attractions: Oxbow Bend, several mountain view overlooks, Blacktail Butte, Gros Ventre Slide area, fishing, wildlife viewing, rafting, and a taste of Old West history.

Location: North of Jackson on the eastern side of Grand Teton National Park, northwestern Wyoming.

Drive route names & numbers: US 26/89/191 (the Outer Loop Road, or the continuation of the Rockefeller Parkway).

Travel season: As this road is a US highway, it remains plowed and accessible year-round.

Camping: Gros Ventre Campground at Kelly (361 sites), National Park Service, first-come, first-served; National Forest Service campgrounds at Atherton Creek (20 sites), Red Hills (5 sites), and Crystal Creek (10 sites); several commercial campgrounds in the Jackson area.

Services: Full services in Jackson; gasoline and food at Moose Junction, at Dornans. Good cell service everywhere on this drive but in the Gros Ventre Wilderness.

Nearby points of interest: Two Ocean Lake, Emma Matilda Lake, Bridger-Teton National Forest, Antelope Flats, Mormon Row, Kelly, Kelly Warm Springs, the Gros Ventre Slide drive through red rock country, National Fish Hatchery, National Museum of Wildlife Art, and the National Elk Refuge. In Jackson, excellent food, art galleries, nightly summer rodeos, and the Snow King ski area with an alpine slide in the summertime.

For more information: Jackson Area Chamber of Commerce, the National Park Service at Moose or Moran Junction.

The Route

The first segment of this route, from **Jackson Lake Junction** to Moran Junction, covers about 5 miles of good two-lane road. The road passes through willow thickets, cottonwoods, and wildflower-laden hills along the Snake River. Several old hotels and homesteads used to grace this area, but now only their ghosts remain. Just beyond the first mile you reach the Oxbow Bend in the Snake River. Moose, river otters, swans, pelicans, and other wildlife swim and hunt for food near Oxbow Bend; coupled with the view from here of the mountains, this remains one of the favorite and most recognized photographic spots in the park.

Jackson Lake Junction to Jackson, WY

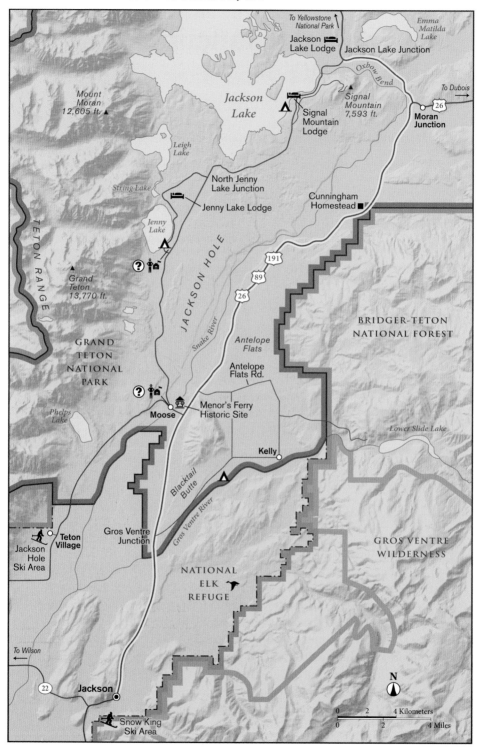

Many people canoe or kayak on this quiet branch of the river, mingling with the wild; others trust a good pair of binoculars and a careful sense of observation to reveal hidden wildlife.

Tales of the Old West

About 2 miles beyond Oxbow Bend, Pacific Creek Road on the left heads into the Teton Wilderness. Supposedly, both Jim Bridger and Osborne Russell, two trappers and mountain men of the Old West, used this route to the north during their explorations. If you follow the markers up Pacific Creek Road about 4.5 miles to a small parking area, you reach secluded but misnamed **Two Ocean Lake,** which drains only into the Pacific. Hiking trails from here lead to its twin, **Emma Matilda Lake,** to the south. Hidden in a beautiful area, surrounded by trees and quiet, Two Ocean Lake is a secret for Jackson residents and park employees. Whispered sounds of birds, frogs, and the breeze create a cloistered retreat from the crowds of Jackson. A good place to cast a line, launch a canoe, or watch for itinerant moose, Two Ocean Lake is isolation at its best.

To continue toward the Outer Loop Road, retrace your drive and continue east on US 89/191/287. Cross Pacific Creek at about 3.2 miles from Jackson Lake Junction and watch for **Pacific Creek Landing** to the right, a good spot for launching rafts and canoes onto the Snake River. Remember, boating permits (available at visitor centers) are required for any boating on lakes or rivers. Beyond the landing, a park exit leads to Moran Junction, and a turnoff to the left leads to the Moran post office. Pass through the Buffalo Fork Station exit and turn right (south) onto US 26/89/191 to head toward Jackson, about 30 miles away. If you turn left (north), you will go over Togwotee Pass to Dubois, WY, 56 miles to the east—Scenic Route 22.

Reset your odometer and head toward Jackson. About 0.2 mile from the turn, cross the Buffalo Fork of the Snake River, a tributary that drains the Teton Wilderness to the northeast. The highway remains within the borders of the park for most of the drive, even though the terrain is very different from that closer to the mountains. The road proceeds along the Snake River, which braids and twists its way through the valley, with the Tetons as its western backdrop. Slopes of cottonwoods edge the flow. In contrast to the high jagged peaks to the west, grassy fields with gentle hills roll to the east of the road, all distinctly Western landscape.

The ranches along the road are both working ranches, which still raise cattle, and dude ranches, where easterners come to play cowboy. Ranching was the earliest experiment for earning a living in Jackson Hole, but as ranchers soon found out, winter was easier on dudes than cattle. Dude ranches sprang up before the

This bull moose pauses for a tasty afternoon treat.

turn of the 20th century, making the scenery the most valuable asset of the valley. Dudes still flock here today.

Elk Ranch Flats turnout, to the right, is the first of many scenic viewing areas. At 5.2 miles, take the side road on the right 0.4 mile to a parking area for the old **Cunningham Homestead,** one of the earliest homesteads in Jackson Hole. The main cabin still stands, a widely photographed vestige of the past. Pick up a brochure for the self-guided trail that, in summer, leads you on a tour of the property. The Cunningham place, once known as the Bar Flying U Ranch, was the site of a legendary shootout between an unofficial posse and two supposed horse rustlers. The rustlers had rented the cabin, thinking Jackson Hole a safe place to winter their horses in preparation for selling them in spring. Cunningham himself wasn't there when the posse hid near the shed in 1893. Barking dogs alerted the two men in the cabin to intruders. When they stepped outside with their guns cocked, the ensuing battle ended their nefarious careers, as well as their lives. A marker notes the probable gravesites of the alleged rustlers. The legitimacy of the posse is still in question; most likely this was vigilante justice, the Old West at its most questionable.

Almost directly across the highway from the Cunningham Homestead, FR 30290 gives access to the Bridger-Teton National Forest, where small lakes and hiking trails spread across the landscape. As you continue on the Outer Loop Road, the **Triangle X Ranch,** less than a mile away on the left, was owned by a family who sold the property to the "Snakes" in 1929, then leased it back to operate it as a ranch. (The story of acquisition of the valley's land for Grand Teton National Park is told in the Introduction to the Tetons. See page 191.) Today the proprietors run a dude ranch, guiding pack trips and raft floats for the paying public. The films *Jubal* and *Spencer's Mountain* used the ranch as a shooting location in the 1960s and 1970s.

The road descends a little, then curves around on flat, beautiful terrain, bordered on three sides by mountains—the Tetons to the west, the Wind River Range to the east, and the Gros Ventre mountains to the south. This is the northern end of **Antelope Flats,** named for the pronghorn that graze here in summer. At 8.7 miles, a steep descending road to the right crosses **Deadman's Bar** and leads to a raft launch on the Snake River for the most scenic float available in the area. Deadman's Bar is named for the three miners' bodies that were found here in 1886. Their partner, charged with the killings, pleaded self-defense and was freed, as only circumstantial evidence had indicated his guilt. Jackson is honest in its portrayal of itself as a town of the Wild West.

A half mile beyond the Deadman's Bar river access, the Snake River overlook on the right side of the road cuts from the roadside for a broad view of the Tetons. This vista, made famous by photographer Ansel Adams, is often considered to be the superlative view of the mountain range and valley. I'm not sure how any one view could be counted better than others. While taking in the scene, notice the braiding of the Snake River, and imagine its spring fury before the dam slowed its waters.

About 1.5 miles down the road from the Snake River overlook is a scene that will be remembered by devotees of the movie *Shane*. To the east of the road, less than 0.25 mile back, was one location for several town scenes. Farther back is the "cemetery hill," and north of that on the slope of "Chip's Lookout" grew three trees in a unique configuration, recognizable by anyone who saw the movie more than once.

Another overlook, **Teton Point,** is to the right of the road, a little over 12 miles from Moran Junction. Here the view aims across the braided river toward the three Tetons. Rafters putting in to the north must know which channels to take to successfully navigate the river. A picnic spot is about 1.2 miles south of Teton Point at **Schwabacher Landing,** one of the easiest accesses on the river. A half mile farther, the last viewpoint of the mountains is **Glacier View** turnout. The view of the mountain range to the north is truly exquisite.

Descend from the Outer Loop Road to the Snake River terraces. At 16.4 miles the **Blacktail Ponds** overlook, a good wildlife viewing area, is on the right at the

Even the suburbs have wonderful views. Location, location, location.

end of a short drive on gravel road. This is another fine wildlife habitat, attracting a variety of animals to the waters of the ponds and rivers. Osprey, eagle, elk, moose, and beaver frequent the ponds, feeding in the still waters or foraging wood for dams.

Just beyond, on the Outer Loop Road, **Antelope Flats Road** lies to the east, marking the area where thousands of pronghorns used to migrate every year from the Green River Valley, until harsh winters early in the 20th century along with unhampered hunting almost brought them to extinction. Strict hunting regulations helped revitalize the herd, which today is large and healthy. This road offers a good side trip. The pronghorn for which it was named are usually grazing somewhere on the flats, although at a distance they blend into the scenery. They are skittish, and if you stop to watch them, they most likely will try to remove themselves from view.

About 1.5 miles, traveling east on Antelope Flats Road, a pink house to the north designates the parking area for **Mormon Row,** a settlement community from the early 1900s. The row is to the south of the road, an unpaved road that really makes a good trail. Remnants of cabins and outbuildings still stand, the most famous being the oft-photographed John Moulton barn. If you like a pleasant walk, rather than a strenuous hike, this makes a great stop. You can continue on the Antelope Flats Road to loop back through Kelly, or venture into the Gros Ventre area, or you can backtrack to the highway to continue on to Jackson. On the highway continuing south, **Blacktail Butte,** named for another resident member of the deer family—the blacktail or mule deer—crops up near the road on the left, a rock climber's challenge. Many climbers practice here before trying to conquer the more treacherous Tetons. Blacktail Butte extends south for about 2.5 miles. The southern end is easier to ascend than the northern end, as several trails lead to the top.

The turnoff for **Moose Junction,** the southern entrance to the park, is less than a mile beyond, to the right. If you need to stock up on almost anything— food, gear, pizza, wine, cheese, gasoline—a great stop is **Dornan's,** a turn to the right shortly after heading for the Junction. The deli and grocery selection here is good, the wine and cheese selection is great, and the gas prices are a little less expensive than they are in Jackson. Dornan's elevated deck makes an excellent spot to watch the sunset over the mountains. If pizza is not your craving, a chuck wagon located here offers a barbeque alternative.

From Dornan's you can turn right to complete the Teton loop by returning to the **Craig Thomas Discovery and Visitor Center,** where exhibits of the people, places, and protection of the Tetons are explored in interactive displays, or you can go back to the highway to proceed to Jackson. If this is your route, a turnout to the left at about 19.5 miles allows a look back at the Tetons, where directly to the west lies **Mount Hunt,** with **Prospectors Mountain** rising behind it. This valley actually lies high among the surrounding mountains, at 7,000 feet, with the Absaroka Range to the north, the Wind River Range to the northeast, and the Gros Ventre Range to the southeast and south. Sheep Mountain to the southeast, the mountain with the reddish slash of the Gros Ventre slide, was named for the bighorns that graze there in summer. The mountain is also known as the Sleeping Indian, an imaginative form seen when the mountain is viewed from Jackson.

Think of the struggle it took early settlers just to arrive in Jackson Hole, much less stay during long and intemperate winters. For a more modern challenge, fly into Jackson and land at the airport to the right, beyond Blacktail Butte and about 4 miles from Moose Junction. The tiny airport has heavy traffic year-round, which tests the skills of many mountain-flying pilots as well as the basic white-knuckled passenger. Beyond the airport turnoff, watch for Gros Ventre Junction at about 24.5 miles. At the junction, a right turn would take you by the Jackson Hole Golf and Tennis Club on Warm Springs Road, through an upscale residential section of Jackson. You could go straight ahead on the highway to quickly arrive in town. But instead of taking either of those options, for one of the best side drives of your trip, turn left at the junction onto Gros Ventre River Road to explore the Gros Ventre wilderness. Several Forest Service campgrounds are located on this drive, so as much as your time and the condition of your car will allow, head toward Kelly and the Gros Ventre Slide area and beyond.

Kelly, Campgrounds & Beyond

To make the side trip, turn left at the junction and head northeast on Gros Ventre Road toward the town of Kelly, about 5 miles away. Gros Ventre is French for "big belly," a name given by French trappers to a group of Blackfeet Indians. The Blackfeet were a warring tribe, and trappers from the rendezvous at Pierre's Hole in 1832 encountered their ire when passing through here on their way to and from the gathering on the other side of the Tetons.

Around 4.5 miles, the **Gros Ventre Campground** is to the right of the road on the banks of the Gros Ventre River. The National Park Service operates the campground, where a $15 fee per day is required, but reservations are not. The river along here forms the boundary of Grand Teton National Park, so park regulations apply. Follow the road northeast to Kelly, a small community with a harrowing history.

At the turn of the 20th century **Kelly** was, if not flourishing, at least populated. With about 30 families it was an early contender for the county seat, but lost out to Jackson. By 1927 Kelly's population had risen to 35 families, making it a substantial community. On June 23, 1925, the largest landslide in North America, known as the Gros Ventre Slide, was loosed upstream a few miles from Kelly. A huge portion of Sheep Mountain broke off and rushed and tumbled across the broad ravine, creating a natural dam about 225 feet high. As water backed up behind the dam, the downstream community watched nervously. As time went on and nothing happened, scientists and engineers proclaimed the dam safe, and residents began to relax their watch on the potential hazard.

During the winter of 1926–27 heavy snow fell, accompanied in spring by intense rains. On May 18, 1927, the top of the dam gave way, flooding the town of Kelly and killing six people, including two elderly sisters who were attempting to flee the great rush of water and debris. Fortunately for the townspeople, forest ranger Charlie Dibble had been upstream and had seen what was coming. He raced back to Kelly, giving about a 15-minute warning that allowed residents time to seek higher ground. Had he not done so, the death toll would have been much higher. Many townspeople watched from the hills as the destructive waters swept through the town. When the flood had passed, only the Episcopal church, the parsonage, and the schoolhouse had not been ravaged; all 35 homes had been demolished.

Drive beyond Kelly about a mile to a junction with Gros Ventre Road. At the junction head right (east) if you want to continue your excursion. This narrow paved road leads eastward, becoming a gravel road when it enters the national forest. The road is not recommended for RVs, although they are not forbidden. This road was once a major path for Native Americans and early explorers. Wilson Price Hunt took this route when he crossed from the east through Union Pass, near Dubois. The route connected with both the Green River and Wind River Valleys to the south and west, making it more passable than most of the surrounding mountain terrain. On a western expedition, President Chester A. Arthur and his entourage of 300 camped here, as well as along the banks of the Snake River near Moran Junction. Within miles the road becomes winding, narrow, and steep, but the scenery is diverse and beautiful.

At about 6.4 miles, **Kelly Warm Springs** is found to the right of the road. This spot is a favorite with locals in the summer, and people swim or practice their kayak rolls in the small temperate pond. The spring also has become a habitat for guppies, as rumor has it that tropical fish are released here at the end of each school year. The spring flows out of a fault at the rate of about 5 million gallons a day, warmed to 85 degrees Fahrenheit by the molten rock below.

Less than a mile beyond the warm springs, a deteriorating cabin to the north was another shooting location for *Shane* in 1951. Where pavement turns to gravel, the road travels beyond the boundary of Grand Teton National Park and enters the Bridger-Teton National Forest. At about 3.5 miles from the junction of Gros Ventre River Road and Gros Ventre Road, an area called the **Devils Elbow Slide** is seen across the river to the south, proof that the geologic features along this drive have been rearranged by nature many times. As you move along, watch for evidence of the many slides that have been triggered through here. Several conditions lead to the slides. The mountains and hills are composed of many sedimentary layers of limestone, sandstone, and shale. When the layers absorb excessive moisture, becoming heavy and cumbersome, and the lower layers of shale become slippery, then land slides. Adding to those conditions, the river has cut through the lower layers, allowing the hills to hang over the banks, top-heavy. The area also has frequent seismic activity, so slides can be activated by small earthquakes.

At almost 5 miles beyond the junction of Gros Ventre River Road and Gros Ventre Road, you approach the **Gros Ventre Slide** area, where an interpretive pullout explains the causes of the 1925 landslide. The story told about the community of Kelly is one of double jeopardy, as 2 years before the flooding, this landslide had devastated a portion of the valley where ranchers had settled. The landslide in 1925 sent 50 million cubic yards of rock across the narrow valley, as a 2,000-foot-wide, over 1-mile-long portion of the wall of Sheep Mountain collapsed. The rock was hurled across the ravine with a force that generated

The Gros Ventre landslide occurred almost a century ago.

200-mile-an-hour winds. The resulting dam across the Gros Ventre River was 225 feet of rock and rubble. Look to the north side of the road about 350 feet up to see where marks were left by debris thrown by the slide. The entire event lasted 3 minutes, but it must have seemed endless. When the dam blocked the river it created a Lower Slide Lake, often called Sudden Lake by the locals. The river downstream was dry for 2 weeks before water found its way through the porous rocks of the natural dam. Amazingly, although so much property was damaged when the huge portion of Sheep Mountain fell, no one was killed.

Beyond the turnout the route winds up and down a narrow slice of road toward three National Forest Service campgrounds: Atherton Creek, Red Hills, and Crystal Creek. The campgrounds are well marked, directly off the road. The nightly fee is $12, and you can reserve sites. Near **Atherton Creek Campground,** a little over 14 miles from the highway, beautiful red rock replaces the brown and sage-colored hills to the west. Signs of rock slides are all around as the natural geologic process of undermining stone with water continues. In winter, bighorn sheep reside on the red cliffs to the northeast. The Gros Ventre River provides good fishing and lovely camping spots. Use your own judgment and knowledge of your car as you proceed beyond the campgrounds. You can continue as far back on this road as your sense of adventure and automobile tires will allow, to about

27 miles from the junction with the highway, but the road continually worsens, and you must decide when to turn around.

If you continue on to the east, at 22 miles, about 6 miles beyond Crystal Creek Campground, you can view **Upper Slide Lake,** the results of a smaller slide in 1911. Kayaks and canoes float on the streams throughout this area. Beyond the ranches and campgrounds, various forks in the road lead to outback trails or small lakes; the road itself becomes little more than a path toward the wilderness. As you turn to retrace your route back to Kelly, the Tetons pass in and out of view, for one of the loveliest drives of your trip.

Back to Jackson

When you return to Gros Ventre Junction and US 26/89/191, turn left toward Jackson. The **National Elk Refuge** is to the left, across the Gros Ventre River 25 miles from Moran Junction. Often in August you can find part of the bison herd here. You leave the boundaries of the park at about 26 miles. If you look directly west you can see **Rendezvous Mountain,** the site of Teton Village ski area. The scenery closes in on the right as you approach East Gros Ventre Butte. At 26.4 miles a marked road to the east will take you to the **National Fish Hatchery,** where you may watch the trout. Here, fingerlings are nurtured before being transplanted into streams in Wyoming and Idaho.

About 28 miles from Moran Junction, a turnoff to the left of the road overlooks the National Elk Refuge where the large animals congregate in winter to be fed. In summer they seek natural grazing lands. About 7,500 elk are harbored on these 23,754 acres in winter. When snow covers the ground and the feeding of the herd begins in November, sleigh rides through the refuge are a popular evening activity for winter visitors. The elk is another animal that has been saved from almost certain extinction here, through the efforts of both valley residents and Congress. In the 1880s the herd size was estimated to be about 25,000 animals. Elk used to be valued for their ivory canine teeth, known as tusks. At the turn of the 20th century the animals were killed without restraint for their teeth. After several harsh winters when thousands of animals starved and the practice of tusking thinned the herd to dangerously low numbers, compassionate ranchers began feeding the elk during the severe winter of 1908–09. In 1909 the ranchers were joined by the state legislature in their effort to save the animals. Legislators passed a bill to contribute money to buy feed. In 1911 Congress appropriated money for feed and to purchase land, and by 1912 it was possible to buy the land for the feeding ground.

Across from the refuge turnoff, at about 28.4 miles, look on the hill to the right for the **National Museum of Wildlife Art.** This beautifully designed stone building artfully blends into the side of the hill. The museum houses a complete art facility with space for art and environmental education programs for Jackson residents, and interactive computer projects on biology, wildlife, and the cultural history of the area. Any who visit may indulge in computer play. The art collection is worth a stop, the first of many interesting gallery stops in the area where many of the country's eminent artists show at local galleries.

Near the border of town another wildlife viewing area is located to the left along Flat Creek. Trumpeter swans and sandhill cranes migrate to the area in summer, along with various other waterfowl. Cross Flat Creek to enter Jackson, elevation 6,209 feet, named for Davey Jackson, the early mountain man who, with William Sublette and Jedediah Strong Smith, owned the Rocky Mountain Fur Company. As you draw near town, a calculated aura of the Old West assaults you. Four elk-antler arches mark the corners of the town square, identifying Jackson on postcards sent all over the world.

Commercial as all get-out, but friendly and fun, **Jackson** builds year by year on its good saloons, food, and lodging. A walk around the town square takes you by excellent art galleries and gift shops ranging from western tacky to truly elegant. The wooden boardwalks lead to saloons that have silver dollars encapsulated in the bar counter, or that use worn saddles as barstools. Range a little farther around the perimeter of town to find all ranges of shops and lodging, live musical theater, one of the best school systems in the country, and an economy based on pleasing visitors.

Besides the obvious pleasures of town, other entertainment abounds. An in-town ski area, **Snow King,** offers skiing in winter and a 2,500-foot alpine slide in summer. In summer, shootouts occur every evening on the town square, and rodeos entertain dudes from all over the world. On almost every corner of town you can arrange a float trip, but shop around for both the best price and location to raft. Jackson is a tangle of motels, shops, western hype, saloons, people, and very good restaurants. Walk through or stay at the old **Wort Hotel** near the center of town, a mainstay of the tourist trade for more than half a century. Prices in Jackson are high, but a bargain can be found if you hunt for it.

The beauty of the Tetons has always lured people, which historically has made Jackson susceptible to rapid growth. In 1909 the town's population was nearly 1,500—a huge town for such a remote location. Development has changed the southwestern end of town, as the road toward Hoback Junction fills with new residences and businesses. Intense growth for the past 30 years has kept the controversies of development alive here, almost the same controversies that swirled when John D. Rockefeller Jr. and the "Snakes" were buying up available land. A vacation spot in such natural splendor cannot avoid the tensions between exploitation and conservation.

Having your photo taken under the elk antler arch is almost a requirement of a visit to Jackson.

Still, Jackson struggles to find its way. One of my favorite signs in town says it all:

FROM JACKSON . . . TETON VILLAGE IS 12 MILES AWAY
WILSON IS 6 MILES AWAY
TETON PASS IS 8 MILES TO THE WEST
THE AIRPORT IS 8 MILES TO THE NORTH
MOOSE VILLAGE IS 12 MILES TO THE NORTH
YELLOWSTONE IS 58 MILES TO THE NORTH
HOBACK JUNCTION IS 11 MILES SOUTH
PARADISE IS ALL AROUND. . . .

APPENDIX A:
FOR MORE INFORMATION

Chambers of Commerce

Bear Lake Convention and Visitor
Bureau
69 N. Paradise Pkwy. Building C
Garden City, UT 84028
(800) 448-2327
www.bearlake.org

Big Sky Chamber of Commerce
Box 160100
Big Sky, MT 59716
(406) 995-3000 or (800) 943-4111
www.bigskychamber.com

Bozeman Area Chamber of Commerce
2000 Commerce Way
Bozeman, MT 59771
(406) 586-5421 or (800) 228-4224
www.bozemanchamber.com

Cody Country Chamber of Commerce
836 Sheridan Ave.
Cody, WY 82414
(307) 587-2777 or (800) 393-2639
www.codychamber.org
www.yellowstonecountry.org

Cooke City Chamber of Commerce
Box 1071
Cooke City, MT 59020
(406) 838-2495
(406) 838-2341 Avalanche advisory
www.cookecitychamber.org

Dubois Chamber of Commerce
PO Box 632, 616 W. Ramshorn
Dubois, WY 82513
(307) 455-2556
www.duboiswyoming.com

Ennis Chamber of Commerce
Box 291
Ennis, MT 59729
(406) 682-4388
www.ennischamber.com

Garden City Utah Chamber/
Bear Lake Rendezvous Chamber of
Commerce
PO Box 55
Garden City, UT 84028
(435) 946-2197 or (800) 448-BEAR
(2327)
www.bearlakechamber.com

Gardiner Chamber of Commerce
Box 81
Gardiner, MT 59030
(406) 848-7971
www.gardinerchamber.com

Island Park Area Chamber of
Commerce
PO Box 83
Island Park, ID 83429
(208) 558-7755
www.islandparkchamber.org

Jackson Hole Chamber of Commerce
PO Box 550, 112 Center St.
Jackson, WY 83001
(307) 733-3316
www.jacksonholechamber.com

Jackson Hole and Greater Yellowstone
Visitor Center
532 N. Cache
Jackson, WY 83001
(307) 733-9212
www.fws.gov/nationalelkrefuge/
JacksonHoleVisitorCenter.htm
www.fed.us/jhgyvc

Jackson Hole Reservation Center
(800) 443-6931 or (888) 838-6606
www.jacksonholewy.com

Livingston Chamber of Commerce
303 E. Park St.
Livingston, MT 59047
(406) 222-0850
www.livingston-chamber.com

Montpelier Chamber of Commerce/
Greater Bear Lake Valley Chamber of
Commerce
PO Box 265, 925 Washington St.
Montpelier, ID 83254
(208) 847-0067
www.bearlakechamber.org

Pinedale Chamber of Commerce/
Sublette County Visitor Center
PO Box 176, 19 E. Pine St.
Pinedale, WY 82941
(307) 367-2242 or (888) 285-7282
www.pinedale.com

Red Lodge Chamber of Commerce
601 N. Broadway
Red Lodge, MT 59068
(406) 446-1718 or (888) 281-0625
(888) 285-4636 Beartooth Highway
information update
www.redlodge.com

Teton Valley Chamber of Commerce
PO Box 250, 255 S. Main St.
Driggs, ID 83422
(206) 354-2500
www.tetonvalleychamber.com

Three Forks Chamber of Commerce
PO Box 1103, 215 Main St.
Three Forks, MT 59752
(406) 285-4753
(406) 285-3011 Visitor center
www.threeforksmontana.com

Virginia City Chamber of Commerce
PO Box 218
Virginia City, MT 59755
(406) 843-5555 or (800) 829-2969
www.virginiacitychamber.com

West Yellowstone Chamber of
Commerce
PO Box 458, 30 Yellowstone Ave.
West Yellowstone, MT 59758
(406) 646-7701
www.westyellowstonechamber.com

Museums

American Computer Museum
2023 Stadium Dr., Unit 1-A
Bozeman, MT 59715
PO Box 771, 59771
(406) 582-1288
www.compustory.com

Buffalo Bill Historical Center
720 Sheridan Ave.
Cody, WY 82414
(307) 587-4771
www.bbhc.org

Carbon County Historical Society
Museum
224 N. Broadway, PO Box 881
Red Lodge, MT 59068
(406) 446-3667
www.carboncountyhistory.com

Colter Bay Indian Arts Museum
Grand Teton National Park
PO Drawer 170
Moose, WY 83012
(307) 739-3594 Summer only

Dubois Museum
PO Box 896, 909 W. Ramshorn
Dubois, WY 82513
(307) 455-2284 Summer only
www.duboismuseum.org

Headwaters Arts and Conference
Center
PO Box 26, 20 Stalnaker St.
Dubois, WY 82513
(307) 455-2687
www.headwaterscenter.org

Museum of the Mountain Man
PO Box 909, 700 E. Hennick St.
Pinedale, WY 82941
(307) 367-4101 or (877) 686-6266
www.MMMuseum.com

Museum of the Rockies
600 W. Kagy Blvd.
Bozeman, MT 59717
(406) 994-2251
(406) 994-3466 Dinoline
www.museumoftherockies.org

National Bighorn Sheep Interpretive
Center
PO Box 1435, 907 W. Ramshorn
Dubois, WY 82513
(307) 455-3429 or (888) 209-2795
www.bighorn.org

National Museum of Wildlife Art
PO Box 6825, 2820 Rungius Rd.
Jackson Hole, WY 83002
(307) 733-5771 or (800) 313-9553
www.wildlifeart.org

National Oregon/California Trail
Center
PO Box 323, 320 N. 4th St.
Montpelier, ID 83254
(208) 847-3800 or (866) 847-3800
www.oregontrailcenter.org

Old Trail Town
PO Box 546, 1831 Demaris Dr.
Cody, WY 82414
(307) 587-5302
www.oldtrailtown.org

The Pioneer Museum
317 W. Main St.
Bozeman, MT 59715
(406) 522-8122
www.pioneermuseum.org

Rails and Trails Museum
PO Box 323, 320 N. 4th St.
Montpelier, ID 83254
(208) 847-3800 or (866) 847-3800
www.railsandtrails.net

Yellowstone Historic Center Museum
PO Box 1299, 104 Yellowstone Ave.
West Yellowstone, MT 59758
(406) 646-1100
www.yellowstonehistoriccenter.org

National Forests

For camping reservations in National
Forest campgrounds, call (877) 444-
6777.

Bridger-Teton National Forest
PO Box 1888, 340 N. Cache
Jackson, WY 83001
(307) 739-5500

For camping reservations at Granite
Creek Hot Springs
(800) 280-CAMP
or
PO Box 220
Pinedale, WY 82941
(307) 367-4326

Caribou-Targhee National Forest
1405 Hollipark Dr.
Idaho Falls, ID 83401
(208) 524-7500
www.fs.fed.us/r4/caribou-targhee

Custer National Forest
1310 Main St.
Billings, MT 59103
(406) 657-6200

Gallatin National Forest
PO Box 130
Bozeman, MT 59771
10 E. Babcock St.
Bozeman, MT 59715
(406) 587-6701

Avalanche advisory (West Yellowstone)
(406) 646-7912

Shoshone National Forest
808 Meadow Ln.
Cody, WY 82414
(307) 527-6241
(307) 578-5194 TDD
www.fs.fed.us/r2/Shoshone

National Parks

Albright Visitor Center
(307) 344-2263

Bridge Bay Marina, Canyon Lodge,
Lake Lodge and Cabins, Lake
Yellowstone Hotel and Cabins,
Mammoth Hot Springs Hotel and
Cabins, Roosevelt Lodge and Cabins,
Xanterra Reservations
(307) 344-7311
(307) 344-7901

Camping at Bridge Bay, Canyon, Grant
Village, Fishing Bridge RV Park, and
Madison, Xanterra Reservations
(307) 344-7311
(307) 344-7901

Camping at Tower Fall, Slough Creek,
Pebble Creek, Norris, Lewis Lake,
Indian Creek, and Mammoth Hot
Springs
(307) 344-7381

Canyon Village Visitor Center
(307) 242-2550

Colter Bay Village and Marina
Reservations
(Grand Teton Lodge Company)
PO Box 250
Moran, WY 83013
(307) 543-3100 or (800) 628-9988
www.gtlc.com

Colter Bay Visitor Center
(307) 739-3594

Craig Thomas Discovery and Visitor
Center
PO Drawer 170
Moose, WY 83012
(307) 739-3399
(307) 739-3400 TDD
Open every day but Christmas

Fishing Bridge Visitor Center
(307) 242-2450

Grand Teton Lodge Company
PO Box 250 or PO Box 240
Moran, WY 83013
(307) 543-3100 Reservations
(307) 543-2811 Non-reservations
(800) 628-9988
www.gtlc.com

Grand Teton National Park
Headquarters
PO Drawer 170
Moose, WY 83012-0170
(307) 739-3300
(307) 739-3400 TDD
(307) 739-3682 Road conditions
(307) 739-3300 Visitor packet
www.nps.gov/grte

Grant Village Visitor Center
(307) 242-2650

Jackson Lake Lodge
(Grand Teton Lodge Company)
(307) 543-2811 or (800) 628-9988

Jenny Lake Lodge
(800) 628-9988
(307) 543-2811 Non-reservation calls

Jenny Lake Visitor Center
(307) 739-3392

Leeks Marina
(307) 543-2546

Madison Junction Visitor Center
(307) 344-2821

Mammoth Hot Springs Visitor Center
(307) 344-2263

Mountain Weather and Avalanche
Activity
(307) 733-2664
www.mountainweather.com

Norris Information Center
(307) 344-2812

Old Faithful Inn
(307) 545-4601 Front desk
(307) 345-4999 Dinner reservations
(307) 344-7311 Xanterra reservations
(307) 344-7901

Old Faithful Lodge, Snow Lodge, and
Cabins
(307) 545-4810 Front desk
(307) 344-7311 Xanterra reservations

Old Faithful Visitor Center
(307) 545-2750

Signal Mountain Lodge
PO Box 50, Inner Park Road
Moran, WY 83013
(307) 543-2831
www.foreverresorts.com
www.signalmtnlodge.com

Yellowstone National Park
Free Trip Planning Kit
(307) 344-2111

Yellowstone National Park
Headquarters
National Park Service
PO Box 168, Attn: Visitor Service
Yellowstone National Park, WY 82190
(307) 344-7311 Reservations
(307) 344-7381 Information
(307) 344-2386 TDD
(307) 344-2117 Road updates
www.nps.gov/yell

Xanterra Reservations
(307) 344-7901
(307) 344-7311

National Wildlife Refuges

Bear Lake National Wildlife Refuge
PO Box 9, 370 Webster St.
Montpelier, ID 83254
(208) 847-1757
www.fws.gov/bearlake/

Harriman State Park and Wildlife
Refuge
3489 Green Canyon Rd.
Island Park, ID 83429
(208) 558-7368
www.parksandrecreation.idaho.gov/
parks/harriman.aspx

National Elk Refuge
PO Box 510, 532 N. Cache
Jackson, WY 83001
(307) 733-9212
(307) 733-0277 Winter sleigh rides
www.fws.gov/nationalelkrefuge

National Fish Hatchery
1500 Fish Hatchery Rd.
Jackson, WY 83001
(307) 733-2510
www.fws.gov/jackson/

Resorts & Inns

Big Sky Ski and Summer Resort
PO Box 160001, 1 Lone Mountain Trail
Big Sky, MT 59716
(406) 995-4211 or (800) 548-4486
(406) 995-5900 or (800) 548-4486 Ski
information
www.bigskyresort.com

Bridger Bowl Ski Area
15795 Bridger Canyon Rd.
Bozeman, MT 59715
(406) 587-2111 or (800) 233-9609
www.bridgerbowl.com

Brooks Lake Lodge
458 Brooks Lake Rd.
Dubois, WY 82513
(307) 455-2121
www.brookslake.com

Chico Hot Springs
PO Box 29, 1 Old Chico Rd.
Pray, MT 59065
(406) 333-4933 or (800) 468-9232
www.chicohotsprings.com

Flagg Ranch
PO Box 187
Moran, WY 83013
(307) 543-2861
(800) 443-2311 Reservations
www.flaggranch.com

Gallatin Gateway Inn
PO Box 376, 76405 Gallatin Rd.
Gallatin Gateway, MT 59730
(406) 763-4672
(800) 676-3522 Reservations
www.gallatingatewayinn.com

Grand Targhee Resort
PO Box SKI, Ski Hill Road
Alta, WY 83414
(307) 353-2300
(800) TARGHEE (827-4433)
www.grandtarghee.com

Irma Hotel
1192 Sheridan Ave.
Cody, WY 82414
(307) 587-4221 or (800) 745-IRMA
(4762)
www.irmahotel.com

Jackson Hole Teton Village Ski Resort
PO Box 290, 3395 W. Village Dr.
Teton Village, WY 83025
(307) 733-2292
(888) DEEPSNO (333-7766) or (307)
733-2291 Ski/snow report
www.jacksonhole.com

Lakeside Lodge Resort and Marina
PO Box 1819
Pinedale, WY 82941
(307) 367-2221 or (877) 755-LAKE
www.lakesidelodge.com

Mack's Inn
4292 Highway 20
Island Park, ID 83429
(208) 558-7272 or (888) 558-7272
www.macksinn.com

Pahaska Tepee Resort
183 N. Fork Hwy.
Cody, WY 82414
(307) 527-7701 or (800) 628-7791
http://pahaska.com

Pollard Hotel
2 N. Broadway
Red Lodge, MT 59068
(406) 446-0001 or (800) 765-5273
www.pollardhotel.com

Red Lodge Mountain Ski Resort
PO Box 750, 305 Ski Run Rd.
Red Lodge, MT 59068
(406) 446-2610 or (800) 444-8977
(406) 255-6973 Snow report
www.redlodgemountain.com

Sacajawea Hotel
PO Box 648, 5 N. Main
Three Forks, MT 59752
(406) 285-6515
www.sacajaweahotel.com

Snow King
PO Box SKI, 400 E. Snow King
Jackson Hole, WY 83001
(307) 733-5200 or (800) 522-5464
(307) 733-7680 Alpine slide
www.snowking.com

Togwotee Mountain Lodge
PO Box 91
Moran, WY 83013
(307) 543-2847 or (866) 278-4245
www.togwoteelodge.com

State Agencies

Idaho Department of Commerce
PO Box 83720, 700 W. State St.
Boise, ID 83720
(208) 334-2470 or (800) 842-5858
(800) 377-3529 TDD
www.commerce.idaho.gov

Idaho Department of Fish and Game
600 S. Walnut St., Box 25
Boise, ID 83707
(208) 334-3700
(800) 377-2529 TDD
www.fishandgame.Idaho.gov

Idaho Department of Parks and
Recreation
PO Box 83720
Boise, ID 83720
(208) 334-4199
(888) 922-6743 Reservations
(800) 377-2529 Idaho Relay Service
www.idahoparks.org

Idaho Tourism Department
(800) 847-4843
(208) 334-2470
(888) 844-3246
www.visitidaho.org

Idaho Winter Road Conditions
511
(888) 432-7623

Montana Department of Fish, Wildlife
and Parks
1420 E. 6th Ave.
Helena, MT 59601
(406) 444-2535 or (406) 994-5700
(406) 444-1200 TDD
www.fwp.mt.gov

Bozeman Region
1400 S. 19th St.
Bozeman, MT 59718
(406) 994-4042

Montana Road Conditions
511
(800) 226-7623
(406) 444-7696 TDD or (800) 335-7592
www.mdt.mt.gov/travinfo

Travel Montana, Department of
Commerce
1424 9th Ave.
Helena, MT 59601
(800) 847-4868
http://visitmt.com

Utah Division of Wildlife Resources
PO Box 146301, 1594 W. North Temple
Salt Lake City, UT 84114
(801) 538-4700
http://wildlife.utah.gov

Utah Tourism Department
www.utah.gov
www.travel.utah.gov

Wyoming Game and Fish Department
5400 Bishop Blvd.
Cheyenne, WY 82006
(307) 777-4600
http://gf.state.wy.us

Wyoming Travel Commission
(800) 225-5996 Planning guide
Road and Travel Information
511 or (888) 996-7623

Wyoming Travel and Tourism
1520 Etchepare Circle
Cheyenne, WY 82007
(307) 777-7777 or (800) 225-5996
www.wyomingtourism.org

State Parks

Bear Lake State Park
PO Box 297
Paris, ID 83261
(208) 945-2565
www.utah.com/stateparks
www.parksandrecreation.idaho.gov

Buffalo Bill State Park
47 Lakeside Rd.
Cody, WY 82414
(307) 587-9227
www.recreation.gov
www.wyomingtourism.org

Harriman State Park
HC 66, Box 500
3489 Green Canyon
Island Park, ID 83429
(208) 558-7368 or (888) 844-3246
www.stateparks.com.harriman.html
www.visitidaho.org
www.parksandrecreation.idaho.gov

Henry's Lake State Park
3917 E. 5100 North
Island Park, ID 83429
(208) 558-7532
www.idahoparks.org

Lewis and Clark Caverns State Park
PO Box 949
Three Forks, MT 59752
(406) 287-3541 or (406) 287-5424
Summer only
http://fwp.mt.gov/parks

Missouri Headwaters State Park
1400 S. 19th St.
Bozeman, MT 59715
(406) 994-4042
www.fwp.mt.gov/parks

USDA Forest Service Offices for Information about Campgrounds

Ashton Ranger District
PO Box 858
Ashton, ID 83420
(208) 652-7442

Beartooth Ranger District
6811 Hwy. 212 South
Red Lodge, MT 59068
(406) 446-2103
(877) 833-6777 TDD

Bozeman Ranger District
Gallatin National Forest
3710 Fallon, Suite C
Bozeman, MT 59718
(406) 522-2520
(406) 587-6981 Avalanche advisory
www.fs.usda.gov/gallatin

Buffalo Ranger District
PO Box 278
Moran, WY 83013
(307) 543-2386

Clarks Fork Ranger District
203 A Yellowstone Hwy.
Cody, WY 82414
(307) 527-6921
www.fs.usda.gov

Gallatin National Forest Office
PO Box 130
Bozeman, MT 59718
(406) 587-6949

Gardiner Ranger District/Gallatin
National Forest
PO Box 5, Highway 89 South
Gardiner, MT 59030
(406) 848-7375
www.fs.fed.us

Grey's River Ranger District
PO Box 339, 671 Washington St.
Afton, WY 83110
(307) 886-5300

Hebgen Lake Ranger District
PO Box 520, Highway 191 North
West Yellowstone, MT 59758
(406) 823-6963
(406) 646-7369 TDD

Island Park Ranger District
3726 Highway 20
Island Park, ID 83429
(208) 558-7301

Jackson Ranger District
PO Box 1689
Jackson, WY 83001
(307) 739-5400

Livingston Ranger District
5242 Highway 89 South
Livingston, MT 59047
(406) 222-1892

Madison Ranger District/Beaverhead
National Forest
5 Forest Service Rd.
Ennis, MT 59729
(406) 682-4253

Montpelier Ranger District
431 Clay St.
Montpelier, ID 83254
(208) 847-0375

Pinedale Ranger District
PO Box 220
29 E. Fremont Lake Rd.
Pinedale, WY 82941
(307) 367-4326

Teton Basin Ranger District
PO Box 777
Driggs, ID 83422
(208) 354-2431

Wapiti Ranger District/Shoshone
National Forest
203 A Yellowstone Ave.
Cody, WY 82414
(307) 527-6921
www.fs.usda.gov

Wind River Ranger District/Shoshone
National Forest
PO Box 186, 1403 Ramshorn
Dubois, WY 82513
(307) 455-2466

Miscellaneous

Buffalo Bill Dam Visitor Center
1002 Sheridan Ave.
Cody, WY 82414
(307) 527-6076
www.bbdvc.org

Dornan's
Moose, WY
(307) 945-2325
www.dornans.com

Grand Teton Association
PO Box 170
Moose, WY 83012
(307) 739-3403
www.grandtetonpark.org

Grand Teton Climber's Ranch
PO Box 57
Moose, WY 83012
(307) 733-7271
www.americanalpineclub.org

Grizzly and Wolf Discovery Center
PO Box 996, 201 S. Canyon St.
West Yellowstone, MT 59758
(406) 646-7001 or (800) 257-2570
www.grizzlydiscoveryctr.org

IMAX Theater of Yellowstone
101 S. Canyon St.
West Yellowstone, MT 59758
(406) 646-4100 or (888) 854-5862
www.yellowstoneimax.com

Jackson Hole Wildlife Foundation
PO Box 8042
Jackson, WY 83002
(307) 739-0968
www.jhwildlife.org

Livingston Depot Center
PO Box 1319, 300 Park
Livingston, MT 59047
(406) 222-2300
(406) 222-2401
www.livingstondepot.org

Minnetonka Cave Information
(208) 847-0375

Quake Lake Visitor Center
Open Memorial Day to Labor Day
(406) 823-6961
www.fs.fed.us/r1/gallatin

Star Valley Information
www.starvalleywy.com

Yellowstone Association
PO Box 117
Yellowstone National Park, WY 82190
(406) 848-2400
www.yellowstoneassociation.org

Yellowstone Association Institute
PO Box 117
Yellowstone National Park, WY 82190
(307) 344-2294 Year-round
(307) 344-2289 Membership
www.yellowstoneassociation.org

Yellowstone Visitor Information
(unofficial)
www.yellowstoneparknet.com

APPENDIX B:
ADDITIONAL READING

Alt, David D. and Donald W. Hendman. *Roadside Geology of the Northern Rockies.* Missoula, Mont.: Mountain Press Publishing, 1978.

Brock, Thomas D. *Life at High Temperatures.* The Yellowstone Association, 1994.

Bryan, T. Scott. *Geysers . . . What They Are and How They Work.* Niwot, Colo: Roberts Rinehart, 2005.

Cahill, Tim. *Lost in My Own Backyard.* New York: Crown Publishers, 2004.

Craighead, Frank C., Jr. *A Naturalist's Guide to Grand Teton and Yellowstone National Parks.* Guilford, Conn.: Globe Pequot, 2006.

De Voto, Bernard, ed. *The Journals of Lewis and Clark.* Boston: Houghton Mifflin, 1953.

Fritz, William J. and Robert C. Thomas, *Roadside Geology of Yellowstone Country.* Missoula, Mont.: Mountain Press Publishing, 2011.

Good, John M. and Kenneth L. Pierce. *Interpreting the Landscape . . . Recent and Ongoing Geology of Grand Teton and Yellowstone National Parks.* Moose, Wyo.: Grand Teton Natural History Association, 1997.

Haines, Aubrey L. *The Yellowstone Story, Volumes I and II.* Niwot, Colo.: University Press of Colorado, 1996.

Hendrix, Marc S. *Geology Underfoot in Yellowstone.* Missoula, Mont.: Mountain Press Publishing, 2011.

Holdsworth, Henry. *Yellowstone and Grand Teton Wildlife.* Helena, Mont.: Farcountry Press, 2003.

Johnson, Jerry, (ed). *Knowing Yellowstone: Science in America's First National Park.* Lanham, Md.: Taylor Trade Publishing, 2010.

Josephy, Alvin M., Jr. *Chief Joseph's People and Their War.* The Yellowstone Association, 1964.

Lageson, David R. and Darwin R. Spearing. *Roadside Geology of Wyoming.* Missoula, Mont.: Mountain Press Publishing, 1988.

Love, J. David, John C. Reed Jr., and Kenneth L. Pierce. *Creation of the Teton Landscape.* Moose, Wyo.: Grand Teton Natural History Association, 2003.

Mattes, Merrill J. *Colter's Hell and Jackson's Hole. The Yellowstone Association, 1962.* Literary Licensing, 2011.

Miller, M. Mark. *Adventures in Yellowstone: Early Travelers Tell Their Tales.* Guilford Conn.: Globe Pequot, 2009.

Moulton, Candy. *Roadside History of Wyoming.* Missoula, Mont.: Mountain Press Publishing, 1995.

Muir, John. *The Yellowstone National Park.* Golden, Colo.: Outbooks, 1986.

Neburn, Kent. *Chief Joseph and the Flight of the Nez Perce: The Untold Story of an American Tragedy.* New York: Harper Collins, 2005.

Rinehart, Dr. John S. *A Guide to Geyser Gazing.* Santa Fe, N.M.: HyperDynamics, 1976.

Russell, Osborne, edited by Aubrey L. Haines. *Journal of a Trapper.* Lincoln: University of Nebraska Press, 2002.

Schneider, Bill. *Best Easy Day Hikes Grand Teton National Park.* Guilford, Conn.: Globe Pequot, 2011.

Schneider, Bill. *Best Easy Day Hikes Yellowstone and Hiking Yellowstone National Park.* Guilford, Conn.: Globe Pequot, 2011.

Shaw, Richard J. and Marion A. Shaw. *Plants of Yellowstone and Grand Teton National Parks.* Salt Lake City: Wheelwright Press, 2008.

Sholly, Dan R. with Steven M. Newman. *Guardians of Yellowstone.* New York: William Morrow, 1991.

Smith, Diane. *Letters from Yellowstone.* New York: Penguin, 2000.

West, Caroll Van. *A Traveler's Companion to Montana History.* Helena, Mont.: Montana Historical Society Press, 1986.

Whittlesey, Lee. *Death in Yellowstone: Accidents and Foolhardiness in the First National Park.* Roberts Rinehart, 1995.

Yellowstone Place Names. Helena, Mont.: Montana Historical Society Press, 1988.

Interactive

Yellowstone Expedition Guide. Bedford, N.H.: TravelBrains, 2005, (888) 458–6475.

APPENDIX C:
GOOD BIKING TRAILS & ROUTES
IN YELLOWSTONE & THE TETONS

Near Mammoth

The abandoned railroad bed paralleling the Yellowstone River between Gardiner and the park boundary at Reese Creek (5 miles).

Golden Gate service road between Golden Gate and Joffee Lake (1.5 miles).

Mammoth service road beginning at the top of the hill on the Old Gardiner Road above Mammoth, running northwest to the telephone microwave station (1.5 miles).

Swan Lake gravel pit road 6 miles south of Mammoth on the Mammoth Norris Road (1 mile).

Superintendent's Campground Road, adjacent to the entrance to the Indian Creek Campground (4 miles).

West Entrance Area

Riverside Trail from the entrance area to Barns Road (1.4 miles).

Old Faithful Area

Lone Star Geyser Road from the Grand Loop Road to the Lone Star Geyser parking lot (2 miles).

The paved trail beginning in front of the Lower Hamilton Store at Old Faithful to Morning Glory Pool (2 miles). Bikes aren't allowed on the unpaved trail continuing beyond Morning Glory Pool to Biscuit Basin.

Fountain Freight Road located 6 miles north of Old Faithful (5 miles).

Daisy Geyser cutoff to Biscuit Basin, an abandoned service road (1.4 miles).

Lake Area

Natural Bridge Road near Bridge Bay (1 mile).

The old roadbed near the lakeshore between Lake Hotel and where the roadbed joins the main road south of Lake Junction (1 mile).

Tower-Lamar Area

The Mount Washburn Service Road, from the Chittenden Road parking area to the summit of Mount Washburn (3 miles). Bicycles are not permitted on the trail between the summit and the Dunraven Pass parking area.

The Old Chittenden service road, between Grand Loop Road and Tower Fall Campground (2 miles).

The Rose Creek service road behind the Lamar Ranger Station (1 mile).

In Grand Teton National Park

On the Inner Loop—the RKO Road to the Snake River. The River Road that goes south from the RKO road to the Bar B C Ranch (about 16 miles) has eroded, and may be closed, even to bicycles.

On the Outer Loop—The area around Antelope Flats Road, to Mormon Row, and on to Kelly.

INDEX